CHILDREN AND YOUTH DURING
THE GILDED AGE AND PROGRESSIVE ERA

CHILDREN AND YOUTH IN AMERICA
General Editor: James Marten

Children in Colonial America
Edited by James Marten

Children and Youth during the Civil War Era
Edited by James Marten

Children and Youth in a New Nation
Edited by James Marten

*Children and Youth during the
Gilded Age and Progressive Era*
Edited by James Marten

Children and Youth during the Gilded Age and Progressive Era

Edited by James Marten

NEW YORK UNIVERSITY PRESS
New York and London

NEW YORK UNIVERSITY PRESS
New York and London
www.nyupress.org

© 2014 by New York University
All rights reserved

References to Internet websites (URLs) were accurate at the time of writing.
Neither the author nor New York University Press is responsible for URLs that
may have expired or changed since the manuscript was prepared.

LIBRARY OF CONGRESS CATALOGING-IN-PUBLICATION DATA
Children and youth during the Gilded Age and Progressive Era / edited by James Marten.
pages cm
Includes bibliographical references and index.
ISBN 978-1-4798-9414-7 (hardback) — ISBN 978-1-4798-4981-9 (pb)
1. Children—United States—History. 2. Youth—United States—History. 3. Progressivism
(United States politics) I. Marten, James Alan.
HQ792.U5C423 2014
305.230973—dc23
20140

New York University Press books are printed on acid-free paper,
and their binding materials are chosen for strength and durability.
We strive to use environmentally responsible suppliers and materials
to the greatest extent possible in publishing our books.

Manufactured in the United States of America

10 9 8 7 6 5 4 3 2 1

Also available as an ebook

CONTENTS

Foreword   vii
   Paula S. Fass

Acknowledgments   xi

Introduction   1
   James Marten

PART I. SHAPING THE FUTURE: INSTITUTIONS AND THE LAW   17

1 Playing Progressively? Race, Reform, and Playful Pedagogies in the Origins of Philadelphia's Starr Garden Recreation Park, 1857–1904   19
   Deborah Valentine

2 Model Schools and Field Days: Colorado Fuel and Iron's Construction of Education and Recreation for Children, 1901–1918   42
   Fawn-Amber Montoya

3 Of Families or Individuals? Southern Child Workers and the Progressive Crusade for Child Labor Regulation, 1899–1920   59
   Gwendoline Alphonso

4 "I Was So Glad to Be in School Here": Religious Organizations and the School on Ellis Island in the Early 1900s   81
   Claire B. Gallagher

5 The Trajectory of Benevolence: Progressivism in the *Little Colonel* Books   102
   Sarah E. Clere

PART II. MANAGING CHANGE: CHILDREN, YOUTH, AND FAMILIES — 121

6 Willful Disobedience: Young People and School Authority in the Nineteenth-Century United States — 125
   James D. Schmidt

7 The Contested Meanings of Child Marriage in the Turn-of-the-Century United States — 145
   Nicholas L. Syrett

8 Sex, Abortion, and Prostitution in the Lives of Gilded Age Chicago Girls — 166
   Mary Linehan

9 Ohio Departures: George as Progressive Youth in Sherwood Anderson's *Winesburg, Ohio* — 187
   John James and Tom Ue

10 Fit Body, Fit Mind: Scandinavian Youth and the Value of Work, Education, and Physical Fitness in Progressive-Era Chicago — 208
   Erika K. Jackson

11 Duty and Destiny: A Progressive Reformer's Coming of Age in the Gilded Age — 230
   Anya Jabour

Documents: Thinking with Their Heads — 253

Questions for Consideration — 282

References — 283

About the Contributors — 289

Index — 293

FOREWORD

PAULA S. FASS

Mandatory schooling, citizenship training, and anti–child labor laws: If we want to sum up what the late nineteenth century brought to childhood, these would form a sturdy pyramid for government action. In the United States, during the period from 1880 to 1920, these concerns came prominently to the fore when a variety of individuals, private groups, political parties, and government agencies turned their attention to improving both child life and the social fabric. Throughout the Western world, the increasing emphasis on child welfare and its relationship to social stability and national prosperity made states turn their attention to these matters.

Once we add play and recreation to the mix of factors, we can neatly summarize the goal of progressive reformers, those women and men who sought through private and public means and through prominent media activity to illuminate the plight of the many who were not fully part of the nation's life. This largely meant immigrants and especially the children of immigrants. Jane Addams, the founder of Chicago's Hull House, is usually viewed as emblematic of this movement to improve the quality of life for immigrants and their children. But progressives ran the spectrum from those most concerned with the state of city politics to those eager to reorganize schools in order to improve instruction. All of them were responding to the industrial transformation that had remade the lives of many Americans starting in the second half of the nineteenth century and that, by the early twentieth century, threatened to undermine social coherence and national identity, as well as the quality of lived experience among American citizens.

In all these matters, children often became the central subjects of attention. What kinds of citizens, workers, and family members would they grow up to become? How could their futures be directed toward social ends as well as stable, productive adulthoods? How could they be kept from criminal activity and, if already involved, effectively served by the justice system? Childhood came into focus at this time for all kinds of reasons: new scientific inquiries into growth and development in both physical and psychological terms; altered requirements for literacy in a maturing industrial economy; concerns about race and ethnicity; worries about health and accidents in a society increasingly centered in cities; and the newly prominent and public activities of women. Above all, children came into view because they were so often employed in unsavory environments like factories and mines from an early age in conditions that threatened them physically and morally. The visibility of working children in the second half of the nineteenth century and early twentieth century cannot be underestimated. They caught the attention of women, photographers, journalists, and many others. No longer sheltered in rural family farm settings, children were now seen as threatened and a threat. These children incurred the moral outrage and caretaking sentiments of middle-class reformers everywhere in the West as anti–child labor became a central rallying cry for reformers on both sides of the Atlantic. School augmented by play, not exploitative work, should be the domain of childhood, in their view. Everything else was to follow from that axiom: a reformed schooling, a renewed focus on citizenship training, protections against disease and early sexual encounters, new juvenile courts, and social work.

As the essays in this collection make clear, these ideas worked themselves out on the ground in different ways in many locales across the nation. This contagious spirit of concern for children, for child protection, and for enhancing the quality of childhood helped to define the times as Americans addressed the worst aspects of the problems associated with industrial and urban change. In the American context, this meant the children of the many nations who had come to fuel that change. Several of the authors focus on the question of how immigrant values fit in the context of these nationalizing (and internationalizing) imperatives, and this question is worth a moment's consideration. As the reformers turned their attention to helping children, they sometimes demonstrated hostility to parents who saw their children in different terms or as necessary to their own well-being. As Americans turned to government to protect the young, they inscribed their own understanding of childhood into state and national policy. It is indeed during this period, the Progressive period, that the profound question of a multicultural society comes most clearly into focus: How can government action meant to serve the public good be genuinely attentive to the complex nature of a society composed of many different groups with their own values and ideas of child and family welfare? This is a question that has not gone away as the world around us shrinks and the world's people are ever more insistently at home in America.

ACKNOWLEDGMENTS

It was a pleasure working with the dozen authors who contributed essays to this fourth volume in the Children and Youth in America series. It was an honor for Paula Fass, an old friend and one of the pillars of the field, to write her thoughtful foreword. The anonymous readers provided helpful comments that strengthened the individual essays as well as the editor's introductions, while copyeditor Emily Wright did a fabulous job. Finally, a number of people at New York University Press helped see the book through from conception through production, including Alexia Traganas, Alicia Kirin Nadkarni, and assistant director and editor-in-chief Eric Zinner.

Introduction

JAMES MARTEN

Two quotations from books published at the turn of the twentieth century have inspired historians of children and youth for many years. Perhaps the most famous is the declaration by the Swedish sociologist Ellen Key that the twentieth century would be "The Century of the Child," a new era in which the lives of the young would be shaped by understanding and compassion, by educational policies and practices that promoted imagination rather than rote learning, by more child-centered parenting methods that would improve the lives of children and help solve long-standing social problems. The optimism and humanity reflected in Key's writings were firmly embraced by American reformers. Yet historians have often used the term ironically, knowing with a century's hindsight that the high hopes and serious purpose displayed by the "child savers" of the last decade or two of the nineteenth and first two decades of the twentieth century fell far short of solving the problems of the world's children. The second quotation appeared a few years later in an academic book by Florence Kelley, a social worker and child welfare advocate who coined a phrase that would provide another motto and goal for advocates of children and youth throughout the century when she asserted that a society must guarantee to its youngest members "a right to childhood."[1]

A third quotation—from a historian rather than an activist, and written more than half a century later—puts Key's and Kelley's words in a larger context. It comes from one of the iconic books on the history of the Gilded Age and Progressive Era, in which Robert Wiebe argued that a defining characteristic of the period was a "search for order" by reformers responding to the social, cultural, and economic chaos spawned by post–Civil War urbanization, industrialization, and immigration. He argued that the Progressive movement that began to percolate through society in the late 1880s and dominated the first two decades of the twentieth century sought to overcome the disorder in modern America by instilling rationality in politics and the economy through the use of scientific methods, professional experts, and well-managed bureaucracies.[2]

Although his argument has been challenged and modified over the years, Wiebe provided the lens through which two generations of historians have viewed the period. The search for order, perhaps inevitably, failed to control fully the torrent of changes that buffeted Americans during this period, just as Key's and Kelley's suggestions that a right to childhood would be secured during the century of the child encountered numerous obstacles. Yet these three phrases together make a useful prism for historians viewing children and youth during the Gilded Age and Progressive Era.

These forty-odd years offer a particularly useful period in which to study the lives of America's young people. Myriad forces—inspiring, troubling, complicated—began exerting pressure on families and children during this period. And the attitudes formed and programs proposed on behalf of children expand our understanding of the era because it was the first time anyone had tried to shape and mold young Americans with quite so modern intentions and methods.

In one way or another, the essays in this book all show children and youth, parents and guardians, policy makers and reformers, judges and employers, all trying to bring order to their own lives and to the world around them. Although this anthology does not pretend to tell the whole history of children and youth during this period, or to summarize the entire campaign to improve the lives of children and youth that emerged during it, each author provides a case study of the ways in which children, women, and men came to grips with the industrializing, increasingly complex world in which they lived. It seemed to be a world rife with possibilities—but those possibilities did not reveal themselves equally to all children, and were perceived differently by adults and children.³

The essays have been divided into two parts and complemented by a third devoted to primary documents. Part 1 shows some of the ways in which reformers, governments, manufacturers, and even writers attempted to shape the ways in which children and youth perceived the world around them and became useful members of that world. Deborah Valentine's essay on the prequel to the twentieth-century playground movement in Philadelphia focuses on age and race as well as on the diverging ways in which children and reformers defined play. Claire Gallagher takes a material-culture approach to the school on Ellis Island, where, despite the difficult conditions in which they worked and the inevitably transient status of their students, educators sought to introduce literacy and citizenship to immigrant children and youth. Fawn-Amber Montoya looks at the way in which a major employer—the Colorado Fuel and Iron Company—used educational and recreational programs to socialize children not only to become reliable workers but also to be "good citizens," while Gwendoline Alphonso uses congressional testimony and debates over child labor to explore not only the rhetoric of reform and opposition to reform but also the "lived experience" of children as revealed in testimony from parents, children, and advocates for both sides of the issue. Sarah E. Clere's essay on the "Little Colonel" books finds the origins of local Progressivism in the life of the series' main character, who despite her small-town, southern environment is drawn in small ways to notions of "social uplift."

Although the points of view of children and youth are glimpsed in a few of the essays in part 1, the book's second section shifts more purposefully to the ways in which children and youth seized—or attempted to seize—control of their own lives and to the ways in which parents and other authority figures attempted to influence those lives. James D. Schmidt finds children and parents alike resisting through courts school teachers' and administrators' efforts to control children through corporal punishment, while Nicholas L. Syrett uses the movement to regulate "child marriage" as a way to explore the changing definitions of childhood in the United States and some of the ways in which some of those "children" resisted raising the marriage age. Mary Linehan argues that Chicago girls, far from seeing their sexuality as a "problem"—Progressives tended to see any sexual expression or diversion from what they believed to be social norms as "problems"—took it as an opportunity express their independence and agency in the modernizing city, while Erika K. Jackson moves beyond the typical studies of immigrant children in this era (which tend to focus on southern and eastern European immigrants) to focus on Scandinavian students' efforts to bring organized recreation and sports into their schools. John James and Tom Ue highlight the ways in which the attitudes displayed and choices made by George Willard, the protagonist in Sherwood Anderson's *Winesburg, Ohio*, reflected the "generation gap" between the Progressive generation and the previous generation implicit in the movement's rejection of old assumptions. Anya Jabour discovers a kind of proto-Progressivism in the Kentucky childhood of one of the women who would later try to reform the lives of Chicago children, Sophonisba Breckenridge.

Finally, part 3 publishes excerpts from legal testimony, a study of boys and girls who passed through the juvenile justice system, a survey of newsboys' interests and ambitions, and school newspapers to provide snapshots of some of the ways in which children and youth perceived their lives and their worlds.

* * * *

The Gilded Age and Progressive Era saw the United States become "modern" in almost every sense of the word. During this time the country became the leading economic power in the world, producing more steel, coal, and other products than the industrial powers of western Europe combined. And although she had always been a nation of immigrants, the forty years before the First World War saw perhaps twenty-four million immigrants come to the United States, mostly from eastern and southern Europe; the percentage of Americans who were immigrants or the children of immigrants was around 45 percent in 1920. Agriculture would, of course, remain a key industry in the United States, but industrialization was also accompanied by urbanization; by

1920 a majority of Americans lived in cities, suburbs, or small towns. Countless books explore this period in American history.[4]

Some of the changes that took place during these forty-odd years are obvious. A child living in 1880 would have gotten around largely with various forms of horsepower—on horseback, in buggies, or in horse-drawn omnibuses—while a child living in 1920, depending on where he or she lived, could have traveled via automobile or even subway. (Of course, most children in both eras would have simply *walked* to any place they were likely to need to go!) Communication in 1880 took the form of letters and telegraphs; by 1920, most people would have had access to a telephone. Children in the 1880s were entertained by traveling shows, lectures, books, and magazines; children in 1920 were drawn almost obsessively to movies and, within a few years, radio. These dramatic shifts were only the tip of the iceberg of social, technological, and cultural changes that buffeted and inspired Americans of all ages as the nineteenth century gave way to the twentieth.

In addition to these broad transformations, the essays in this anthology can be better understood within two contexts: (1) specific developments in the lives of children and their families; and (2) the Progressive movement, which underlay many of the programs and experiences explored in the volume. But an emerging idea that influenced both thinking about children and the reforms related to them streaks through virtually all of the essays in this volume: the so-called discovery of adolescence as a separate phase of life. Articulated by a Clark University psychologist named G. Stanley Hall and inspired by the emerging theories of Sigmund Freud, the idea that there was a stage of life between childhood and adulthood with its own needs and dangers quickly caught on. At one level it made Americans aware of a developing "youth" culture separate from that of "grownups." But it also made adults and policy makers believe that this was a period of sexual tension, high emotions, and striving for independence that had the potential to threaten relationships and social stability. Young men and women needed to be guided through these volatile years and shielded from inappropriate temptations in specialized institutions like high schools and organized activities like sports lest they grow up too fast amid "our urbanized hothouse life" that, Hall wrote, tended "to ripen everything before its time." The growing awareness of youthful sexuality—indeed, all of the changes described in previous and succeeding passages of this introduction—intersected with the redefinition of "girlhood." Progressive reformers' worries about the "boy problem" (a euphemism for juvenile delinquency) did, in fact, find equivalent if not exactly the same sorts of concerns about girls, as Syrett's and Linehan's essays suggest. But "girlhood" came to be thought of as a broader category between childhood and adulthood, as female teenagers came increasingly to be recognized as consumers, as participants in the popular culture that drew them outside their proper places in the home, and, more troubling to many, as sexual creatures.[5]

This still-developing but powerful recognition of adolescence paralleled the many other ways in which the era intersected with the lives of young Americans. Howard Chudacoff offers an elegant catalogue of several:

> As urbanization, industrialization, and immigration overspread the nation in the second half of the nineteenth century, a number of factors set apart and complicated the status of children. These included a general decline in birthrates, the separation of place of work from place of residence, a budding consumer economy, the emergence of a middle-class ideal of longer residence within the family and greater socialization role for mothers, widespread imposition of compulsory school attendance, and heightened age-consciousness and age-grading with resulting formation of peer cultures. Largely prevalent among economically advantaged families, some of these factors nevertheless had an effect on other children as well.[6]

The Gilded Age and Progressive Era occurred in the middle of a remarkable drop in the size of the average American family and in the percentage of the total population they made up. The number of children born to American families decreased markedly during the century after 1820. In 1830, for instance, there were 128 people under age twenty for every 100 people twenty and over (among whites). By 1890, the ratio was seventy-nine to 100 and by 1920 it was only sixty-six. To put it another way, while in 1850 an average American mother gave birth to five children in her life, by 1900 the average number was only three.[7]

The steady decline in family size, which had begun before the Civil War, was accompanied by the rise of a child-centered, nurturing form of childrearing that emphasized emotional intimacy and sought to extend the innocence and dependence of childhood through schooling and through shielding children from economic responsibilities until well into their teens. This version of childhood only applied to a tiny fraction of American children before the Gilded Age, but the economic expansion of the late nineteenth century also expanded the number of middle- and upper-class families and the number of children who could enjoy this modern form of childhood. Its material and psychological effects were many. As the middle class moved into roomy townhouses or bungalows in the suburbs, children and youth were given more room—literally and figuratively—and enjoyed greater privacy and opportunities to develop their own interests. Commercially made toys, books, and magazines published for children and youth filled the nurseries and bedrooms that the luckiest children did not have to share with two or three siblings. (These had, of course, been available for centuries, but the production and consumption of objects made for children exploded during these decades.) Kindly methods of correction had begun to replace sterner forms of discipline. The number of children and youth in school also increased steadily; between 1870 and 1915 the number of youngsters attending school jumped from seven to twenty million, as states increasingly required longer terms and higher compulsory ages. By 1920, three-fourths of all children were in school at any given time and 20 percent of all teenagers attended high school, especially boys and girls from well-off families. High schools gave them a chance to participate in sports, music, and other organized activities unavailable to poor youth.[8]

The new way of thinking about children changed the economics of family life, and few children in this segment of the population worked outside the home. Rather than measuring the value of children by the work they could do or the income they could produce—traditional measures of the "worth" of children, especially in agricultural societies—the urban middle class drew value from the emotional relationships they formed with their children.[9]

The expanding economy offered opportunities to some families and children, but it also demanded more of others. Working-class children were also far more likely to work to help support their families. Although working-class parents also cherished their children, they simply could not afford to keep them out of the work force. Young boys and many girls worked in factories, coal mines, packing plants, iron foundries, and cotton mills, among other industrial sites. In fact, during the last three decades of the nineteenth century, the percentage of children between the ages of ten and fourteen who worked for wages increased from 16 percent to 22 percent. While in 1870 one out of eight children fourteen or under worked, by 1900 it was one out of six. Importantly, those figures failed to include the tens of thousands who worked on family farms, or labored in the "street trades" selling newspapers, apples, flowers, or other cheap items, or worked alongside parents and siblings as tenement-bound "homeworkers" producing clothing, placing snaps and buttons on cards, stringing rosary beads, setting stones in cheap jewelry, packaging shoelaces, and making artificial flowers, for a nickel per hour or less. Many others worked as domestic servants.[10]

Moreover, among many immigrant groups and the working class, large families remained the rule rather than the exception, and their material lives were quite different. The six, eight, or even dozen members of immigrant or working-class families often crowded into two-room tenement apartments without indoor plumbing or adequate ventilation in some of the most crowded neighborhoods in America. The Jewish section on the Lower East Side of New York, for instance, contained half a million people per square mile, one of the highest population densities in history.[11]

The crowding inevitably led to extraordinary health problems for adults and children alike. By early-twenty-first-century standards, the rates of infant and child mortality were extremely high. Over 12 percent of children died before the age of one, while another 5.7 percent died before they reached the age of five. The most common causes of death were premature births and digestive and respiratory illnesses. For children under the age of five, pneumonia and other respiratory ailments were responsible for a third of all deaths, while measles, scarlet fever, and diphtheria—none of which could be prevented by vaccinations—also killed many young children. Epidemics of diphtheria and flu could flash through whole communities in a matter of days. Although all classes suffered from these childhood maladies, the urban poor suffered more. Just before the First World War, researchers found that the infant mortality rate was 22 percent in families where the main bread-winner earned less than fifty dollars per family member, while it was "only" 6 percent in families whose income was at least four hundred dollars per family member.[12]

In many ways, the Progressive movement—a collection of nonpartisan efforts that sought to find systemic, comprehensive solutions to the problems caused by industrialization, urbanization, immigration, and other conditions of modernization—was a product of these social and economic differences. The middle class promoted the reforms, while the working poor and immigrant classes were the primary objects of their campaigns. There were other issues, of course, and Progressive reforms at the national level ranged from regulating trusts to lowering tariffs on imports; from women's suffrage to the prohibition of alcohol; from regulating the packaging of food and the sale of drugs to preserving the environment. At the state level, Progressives established processes for holding referendums to consider legislation and for recalling elected officials. At the local level, reformers in many cities reduced the size of city councils and hired city managers to break the power of corrupt political bosses and made public utilities out of urban transportation, power, and sewer systems. Progressives and their predecessors came from a number of different political and reform traditions with widely varying solutions and approaches. But most could agree that one of the nation's top priorities should be its children and youth, who, they believed, suffered more from the disorder plaguing the rapidly growing nation than any other group.[13]

Children had not been ignored before this period, of course; nineteenth-century reformers had founded numerous local Children's Aid Societies, chapters of the Society for the Prevention of Cruelty to Children, and orphanages, refuges, and other private institutions that cared for "dependent" children during the years after the Civil War. By 1910, there were 1,151 institutions for dependent children in the United States. Perhaps the most famous child welfare effort was the "orphan trains," sponsored by Charles Loring Brace's New York–based Children's Aid Society (as well as other organizations), which between the 1850s and 1920s carried as many as 150,000 urban children to live with rural families. The settlement houses established in immigrant slums in the 1880s and 1890s—Jane Addams's Hull House, on Chicago's West Side, was only the most famous—offered training for mothers, English-language classes, and citizenship training, but also kindergartens, day care, and camps for children.[14]

But these efforts to help children were local, limited, and reliant on private charity and individual commitment. Progressives sought bigger solutions to the growing need sparked by the alarming changes in the United States. Some of the most popular reforms among Progressive activists had to do with children: juvenile justice, playgrounds, pensions for widowed mothers, health care, housing, even child labor laws received almost unanimous support from the various branches of the Progressive movement. According to Steven Mintz, "Progressive child-savers greatly expanded public responsibility and professional administration of child welfare programs." But the two Progressive-era reforms that relate most directly to the following essays—and that were, in some ways, the flagship efforts of late-nineteenth- and early-twentieth-century "child-savers"—were the creation by many cities and states of separate juvenile justice systems and the anti–child labor movement.[15]

Ever since the modern conception of childhood began to emerge before the Civil War, American reformers had advocated the notion that young lawbreakers should be treated differently than adults. Reformers' interest in delinquency transcended the issue of how to punish delinquents; they wanted to prevent delinquency in the first place and to rehabilitate young people who did run afoul of the law. They responded with growing alarm over girls' sexuality by raising the age of consent for sexual intercourse in most states from ten or twelve years to sixteen or eighteen.[16]

The campaign to establish juvenile courts was accompanied by a campaign to offer alternatives to the aimless and demoralizing pastimes of poor children, which ranged from card playing and gambling to smoking, watching endless hours of silent movies, and hanging around street corners and candy stores. Reformers believed that providing wholesome, orderly pastimes would discourage behavior that would lead to delinquency. For instance, the playground movement, which began in the 1880s and 1890s, created local associations that hired supervisors for school playgrounds during the summer months, published guides to group games and activities, formed baseball teams, created ice skating rinks and sand piles, and lobbied schools and cities to include recreational facilities in their budgets. Other efforts to occupy the time and to shape the morals of youngsters were the Boy and Girl Scouts and Boys Clubs established in many cities during the early part of the century.[17]

But reformers understood that not all delinquency could be prevented, and they also pushed for the creation of a criminal justice system that would rehabilitate boys and girls who failed to resist the temptations of petty thievery, gambling, loitering, and other minor crimes. Some efforts to ease the treatment of young criminals had appeared in the 1880s and 1890s, when some states began holding separate court hearings for children, putting some young offenders on probation rather than in jail, and establishing schools for incarcerated youngsters.

Juvenile court advocates emphasized protecting children from further corruption and the necessity of removing youth from the grim and harsh realities of the criminal courts and prisons, where, they believed, youngsters would simply learn new vices rather than repent their past offenses. Women's club members, settlement house workers, and social workers took the lead in the movement and were eventually successful. The first court devoted solely to youngsters was created in Chicago in 1899 and by 1920 virtually every state in the union had passed laws establishing special courts, probation systems, and detention homes for juvenile offenders where they would be housed separately from adult criminals. The differences between juvenile courts and their adult equivalents were both substantial and subtle. As Mintz writes,

> [U]nlike [in] the adult courts, cases were begun by petition, not indictment, and judges presided over hearings, rather than trials, and made findings rather than rendering verdicts. The accused were called respondents, not defendants, and were described as offenders rather than criminals. . . . Court records were kept private, and when a youth reached adulthood, the criminal record disappeared, so that a youth was not stigmatized for life. Instead of being incarcerated, most youthful offenders were handled by a probation system.

These reforms were accompanied by a loose definition of "criminal" activity—sometimes parents or educators simply turned troubled youth over to the courts—and certain elements of due process were also sacrificed.[18]

A second major priority for Progressive-Era child-savers—and one that appears in one way or another in several essays—was the campaign against child labor. The idea of limiting child labor was not new; throughout the nineteenth century, trade unions had advocated restrictions on child labor, arguing that work deprived children of equal access to education—the typical working-class child left school at the age of twelve or thirteen to take a job—and that the low wages paid children depressed the wages of working adults. Later, many other humanitarian and philanthropic organizations, including church groups, women's clubs, settlement house workers, and members of social service organizations, joined the fight. By the turn of the century, child labor committees had been formed in New York, Alabama, and several other states, and by 1900 significant child labor legislation had been passed in twenty-eight states. Most of the laws limited the number of hours or weeks a child could work or set minimum ages (often as young as twelve).[19]

The Progressive Era saw leaders of the movement decide to agitate for a national approach to child labor. In 1904 they formed the National Child Labor Committee (NCLC), which worked to gain publicity for child labor and to mobilize the public, labor unions, and politicians against it. Its many publications highlighted the injuries and disease caused by child labor, which they often called the "slaughter of the innocents." The model law promoted by the NCLC was fairly minimal by twenty-first-century standards: a minimum age of fourteen for working in factories and of sixteen for working in mines; an eight-hour day for fourteen- and fifteen-year-old industrial workers; and no night work for youth under the age of sixteen. Although the NCLC successfully lobbied Congress to pass the Keating-Owen Act of 1916, the law was limited in scope and was declared unconstitutional by the U.S. Supreme Court only nine months after its passage. It would be more than twenty years before the federal government would effectively regulate child labor.[20]

Child labor and juvenile justice reform were just two of many ways in which Americans tried to ensure a "right to childhood" for every infant born in the United States at the beginning of the twentieth century.

Many of those reform efforts do not appear in this volume, which is less a history of Progressive programs for children than it is an effort to capture glimpses of the experiences of children and youth in a number of places and contexts during the half-century when modern notions of childhood and youth emerged and developed throughout the United States. Nevertheless, the children and youth who appear in this volume tend to be the ones who had the most interaction with the adults who wanted to change them—in many ways, those interactions produced the documents on which historians have always based their research. As a result, urban children are a bit overrepresented and rural children are a bit underrepresented. African American children—or at least attitudes about them among whites—appear in a few essays, but during this nadir of race relations in the United States, their race and their location in the rural South rendered them more or less invisible to many reformers. Native Americans appear only briefly in the essays and in just one of the primary documents; again, their race and their location in remote parts of the West made their interaction with reformers unlikely.

But many children are included, as are many of the efforts to shape them, for good or ill, during this dynamic period in history. It is worth noting that in 1924 the League of Nations adopted the World Child Welfare Charter (often called the "Declaration of the Rights of the Child"), which said,

> The child must be given the means requisite for its normal development, both materially and spiritually.
>
> The child that is hungry must be fed, the child that is sick must be nursed, the child that is backward must be helped, the delinquent child must be reclaimed, and the orphan and the waif must be sheltered and succored.
>
> The child must be the first to receive relief in times of distress.
>
> The child must be put in a position to earn a livelihood, and must be protected against every form of exploitation.
>
> The child must be brought up in the consciousness that its talents must be devoted to the service of its fellow men.

These "rights" were not enforceable, of course, and there is a very good chance that most Americans had never heard of them (the United

States was not, of course, a member of the League of Nations). But the sentiments they express, and the goals they lay out, reflected a growing interest in the welfare of children and an emerging sense during this era—in the United States and around the world—that something should be done to protect them.[21]

NOTES

1. Ellen Key, *The Century of the Child* (New York: Putnam, 1909); Florence Kelley, *Some Ethnical Gains through Legislation* (New York: Macmillan, 1905), 99.
2. Wiebe, *The Search for Order, 1877–1920*.
3. For general accounts of children and youth during these decades, see Macleod, *The Age of the Child*, and Clement, *Growing Pains*.
4. For overviews of the period, see Diner, *A Very Different Age*, and Gould, *America in the Progressive Era, 1890–1914*. For politics, see Calhoun, *From Bloody Shirt to Full Dinner Pail*; for industrialization, J. Beatty, *Age of Betrayal*; for culture and society, see Edwards, *New Spirits*; for urbanization, see Mohl, *The New City*.
5. Mintz, *Huck's Raft*, 187–88. For girlhood, see, for instance, Schrum, *Some Wore Bobby Sox*, and De Luzio, *Female Adolescence in American Scientific Thought*.
6. Chudacoff, *Children at Play*, 69.
7. Macleod, *Age of the Child*, 3; Chudacoff, *Children at Play*, 70.
8. Illick, *American Childhoods*, 90; Mintz, *Huck's Raft*, 174–75. Grant's *Raising Baby by the Book* explores the ways in which ideas about childrearing changed during the nineteenth and twentieth centuries.
9. Zelizer, *Pricing the Priceless Child*. See also Reese, *The Origins of the American High School*.
10. Illick, *American Childhoods*, 91; Hindman, *Child Labor*, 31; United States Children's Bureau, *Industrial Home Work of Children* (Washington, DC: U.S. Government Printing Office, 1922).
11. Macleod, *Age of the Child*, 5; Mohl, *The New City*, 51. The classic book on immigrant children is Berrol, *Growing Up American*.
12. Macleod, *Age of the Child*, 34–41.
13. McGerr, *A Fierce Discontent*. For a biographical approach to the leading reform efforts, see Piott, *American Reformers, 1870–1920*.
14. A readable account of Brace and other child welfare workers like him is Holt, *The Orphan Trains*.
15. Macleod, *Age of the Child*, 168–69; Mintz, *Huck's Raft*, 156. For specific reforms related to children, see, among many others, Davis, *Spearheads for Reform*; Holoran, *Boston's Wayward Children*; and Lindenmeyer, *A Right to Childhood*.
16. See, for instance, Odem, *Delinquent Daughters*.
17. "The Playgrounds of 185 Cities," *Charities and the Commons* 21 (October 3, 1908): 4–5; Cavallo, *Muscles and Morals*.

18. Mintz, *Huck's Raft*, 177. Among the many books on juvenile justice during this era are Clapp, *Mothers of All Children*; Mennel, *Thorns and Thistles*; and Willrich, *City of Courts*.
19. Illick, *American Childhoods*, 93.
20. Illick, *American Childhoods*, 91; Hindman, *Child Labor*, 44–89. The standard account of the NCLC is Trattner, *Crusade for the Children*. A more recent exploration of the complex community and family issues related to child labor is Schmidt's *Industrial Violence and the Legal Origins of Child Labor*.
21. "Geneva Declaration of the Rights of the Child," United Nations Documents, http://www.un-documents.net/gdrc1924.htm (accessed August 11, 2012).

PART I

Shaping the Future

Institutions and the Law

The Children's Bureau made history when it was founded in 1912. The United States became the first national government in the world to create an agency dedicated to the welfare of children, and its founding director (or "Chief," as she was called) was Julia Lathrop, the first woman to head a U.S. agency. The legislation establishing the bureau ordered it to "investigate and report . . . upon all matters pertaining to the welfare of children and child life among all classes of our people . . . especially . . . the questions of infant mortality, the birth-rate, orphanages, juvenile courts, desertion, dangerous occupations, accidents and diseases of children, employment, legislation affecting children in the several states and territories."[1]

Lathrop and her successors focused on research and advocacy, particularly on the issues of infant and child mortality and child labor. They commissioned and distributed their findings, held conferences, and published books and pamphlets on infant care, recreational needs of children, and good posture, among other things. The bureau also sponsored annual Baby Weeks, during which local organizers would hold fairs and workshops on feeding and clothing infants and children,

"The Health of the Child Is the Power of the Nation." (Library of Congress Prints and Photographs Collection)

safe and educational toys would be distributed, and proud mothers would enter their children in healthy baby contests.

"The health of the child is the power of the nation" promoted not only child health but also the bureau's contributions to the war effort during the First World War. The idealized, healthy, happy, productive children featured in the poster could contribute now to the present and the future welfare of the United States. The poster epitomized the optimism expressed by Ellen Key when she declared that the twentieth century would be the "Century of the Child," as well as the commitment to justice for all Americans, even the youngest, reflected in Florence Kelley's assertion that everyone deserved a "Right to Childhood."

None of the essays in this section addresses the Children's Bureau directly, yet each shows how nonprofit organizations (as we would call them), corporations, the government, and even writers for young adults attempted to mold the values and promote the well-being—variously defined—of young people in ways that Lathrop and her colleagues at the bureau would have understood.

NOTE

1. Quoted in Dorothy E. Bradbury, *Four Decades of Action for Children: A Short History of the Children's Bureau* (Washington, DC: U.S. Department of Health, Education, and Welfare, 1956), 3. The bureau is now a part of the Department of Health and Human Services.

1

Playing Progressively?

Race, Reform, and Playful Pedagogies in the Origins of Philadelphia's Starr Garden Recreation Park, 1857–1904

DEBORAH VALENTINE

In the summer of 1904, leaders of a small philanthropic organization called the Starr Centre Association announced that they had opened "the first real playground in Philadelphia." Spanning an entire city block in an otherwise densely populated region, it was equipped with "a varied sort of apparatus, consisting of parallel bars, flying rings, travelling rings, trapeze, striking bag, hand-ball court, basket-ball ground, quoit space, sand piles, swings, seesaws and several small games." African American children and a variety of "white" immigrants were present and welcomed at "Starr Garden Playground."[1]

Children across Philadelphia had played regularly in outdoor spaces prior to the establishment of this playground, including some with swings or other play equipment installed. The city could even boast of a six-acre state-of-the-art Children's Playground, located in sprawling Fairmount Park. According to definitions of the nascent American playground movement, however, these were not "real" playgrounds because they lacked trained leaders who would facilitate children's play activities to ensure that play became a vehicle for the children's moral and social transformation, as well as for their pleasure and physical

African American children were regular participants at Starr Garden Park and Playground prior to 1913, when it came under municipal control. (Courtesy Starr Centre Association of Philadelphia)

health. Although play movement leaders certainly did not mind providing children with the pleasure of play, it was play's potentially transformative powers that provided the movement's driving force.[2]

This chapter tells the story of the complex origins of the American Playground Movement using Philadelphia's Starr Garden as a case study, exploring, in particular, the inclusion and exclusion of African Americans in the processes and organizations that led to the creation of Philadelphia's first model playground. The chapter describes the efforts of the playground's namesake, Theodore Starr (white), to support kindergarten advocate Anna Hallowell (white) and African American pastor Reverend Henry Phillips in their child-saving efforts by establishing Starr Garden Park, the seed of the future Starr Garden Playground. It then shows how Starr built on the efforts of a mid-nineteenth-century businessman, George Stuart (white), and his Colored Mission Sabbath School. Finally, the chapter follows the stubborn commitment of Susan Wharton (white) to African American children and families in the neighborhood through her work as a founder of the Starr Centre Association and its predecessors, the St. Mary Street Library and the Philadelphia College Settlement, the latter of which was primarily responsible for Starr Garden Park's expansion, but whose leaders were more interested in working with European immigrants than black young people. These key players in the development of Starr Garden both as a space and as a program were in turn influenced in varying degrees by their interactions with African American children whose participation in, or avoidance of, these programs and organizations helped to shape the playground as well.

Hidden Actors in the American Play Movement

The dominant, national strand of the play movement was institutionalized in 1906 in the form of the Playgrounds Association of America (PAA). In the first decades of the twentieth century, PAA leaders were key actors in a very successful campaign to make the provision of play and recreation for American citizens of all ages a public responsibility. Leaders of the PAA kept extensive records and published a monthly journal and multiple books. These sources have provided historians with a rich record of dominant trends, goals, and actors in the mainstream play movement. It is a necessarily limited view, however, one in which the men who controlled the PAA were the dominant actors and adolescent boys and recent immigrants were the primary targets of their efforts. African Americans are virtually invisible in these sources, leading Jeffrey Pilz to conclude that they were excluded until World War I, when a "colored branch" of the PAA was established.[3]

By contrast, historians who focused primarily on locally produced documents have found traces of African Americans and other nondominant actors that challenge conventionally held notions of play movement history. This scholarship demonstrates that working-class adults played an active role advocating for space for play as they defined it, highlights the importance of women's leadership in the movement's origins, and includes some perspectives and actions of the children who used, or avoided, reform-focused play spaces. However, although several of these studies briefly mention African American presence, none provides any significant detail regarding black participation. Similarly, studies that examine the reform efforts of black women during the Progressive Era demonstrate that African American playground advocacy was common, but provide minimal detail and virtually no mention of the experiences of black children.[4]

This chapter demonstrates that African American children and adults were present and contributed to the development of Starr Garden Playground and that their initial inclusion was intentional. Thus, it indicates that their broad exclusion (explicit and implicit) under the auspices of the College Settlement in the 1890s and in national and regional play movement efforts after 1906 was not accidental.

To see how the story begins, we must travel back to 1882, twenty-two years prior to the opening of Starr Garden Playground in 1904, when a white philanthropist named Theodore Starr spearheaded the transformation of a small, awkwardly shaped plot used as a trash heap into a playground/park complete with swings, an area for playing ball, a fountain, and a garden space. Starr Garden Park, as it was initially called, would be progressively expanded to create the playground described in the opening paragraph.[5]

The Creation of Starr Garden Park/Playground: African American Influences

Starr Garden in its original form was an inverted L-shaped space bound on one very narrow end by an unpaved back alley known as St. Mary Street. The inner two sides of the lot bordered the right side and back of a church property that also opened onto St. Mary Street. Only two blocks long, it ran parallel to Lombard from Sixth Street to Eighth Street, leaving one block in Philadelphia's Fifth Ward and one in the Seventh. The block that housed Starr Park was located within the Fifth at the center of a block crowded with tenement buildings and backing up to a soap factory. Newspapers referred to the neighborhood that would house Starr Garden as "the slums."[6]

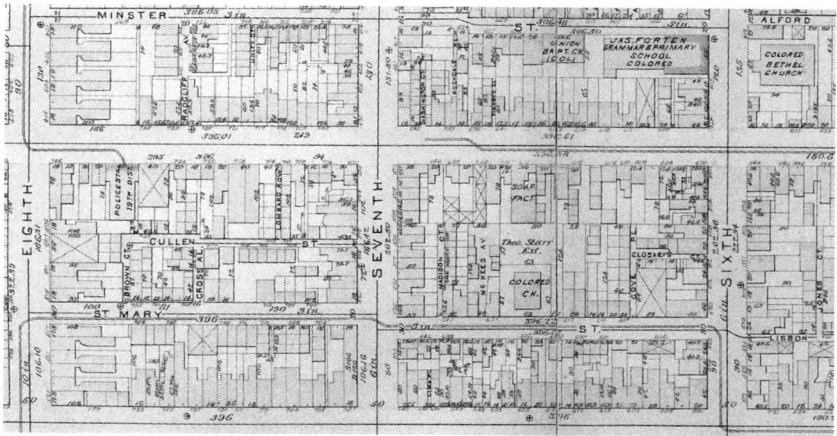

The original Starr Garden was a small, oddly shaped plot of land centrally located in a crowded, interracial tenement neighborhood. (George W. and Walter S. Bromley, *Atlas of the City of Philadelphia*. Philadelphia: Bromley, 1885. Plate H. Courtesy Historical Society of Pennsylvania)

In 1882, the Fifth Ward was literally Old Philadelphia. The entire ward had been within the boundaries of the city in 1770 during a time when Philadelphia had been primarily a walking city with middle-class, elite, and working-class residents traveling by foot to work, shops, places of worship, and social gatherings in and around the central business district. Often referred to as the "city of homes" due to the lack of large tenement buildings, which were common in larger cities like New York and Chicago, Philadelphia's poor were simply better hidden than they were in many big cities. Back-alley streets were created by Philadelphia's somewhat unique method of housing the poor, in comparison to that of other northern industrial cities. Because Philadelphia's residential lots were originally designed with long back yards intended to preserve green space in the city, housing for poor people developed behind the nice large houses that were situated on the front of the lots. Often two houses were built behind the original house, leaving the poorest residents living in dark, poorly ventilated back alleys like St. Mary Street, usually with shared outhouses and surface drainage, which led to very high rates of disease.[7]

Despite these challenges, however, St. Mary Street also had some significant strengths due to the neighborhood's historical importance to African American life in Philadelphia. Since 1787 the neighborhood had been home to a landmark black-led organization, Mother Bethel African Methodist Church. The presence of a variety of other churches and black-owned businesses ensured that the neighborhood retained a level of significance to the social, political, economic, and intellectual life of black Philadelphia. Despite the fact that more financially successful black families were beginning to move west of Twelfth Street as new waves of European immigrants added to the diversity, poverty, and tension of an already-struggling interracial community, children who lived in and around St. Mary Street in the 1880s would have had regular opportunities to encounter, at least from a distance, some of the city's and the nation's most well-known black leaders. Among these leaders was the esteemed pastor Rev. Henry Phillips, who encouraged Starr to invest in the region.[8]

Phillips and Starr met through their shared membership in the Episcopal Church. In the late nineteenth century Philadelphia was home to two black Episcopal congregations of significant size. Starr, though white and not a member, was elected to the governing body (the vestry) of one of them, the Church of the Crucifixion. Established in 1847, the church was located several blocks southwest of St. Mary Street on Ninth Street, just above Bainbridge.[9]

According to historian Roger Lane, it was Phillips who managed to encourage his racially mixed vestry, led by Theodore Starr, "to get involved in the local [black] community in a number of unprecedented ways." Starr participated directly in establishing the church's first charitable organization, the Progressive Workingmen's Club, a social club for black men. Founded in 1878 with Henry Phillips as its president and Starr as treasurer, the club was Starr's first attempt to directly address the needs of black Philadelphians. Because Starr died young, leaving no written record regarding his interest in the concerns of the African American community, further detail regarding his actions and goals is accessible primarily from the perspective of Phillips.[10]

In 1887 Rev. Phillips gave a memorial speech at the unveiling of a stained glass window erected at the Church of the Crucifixion in Starr's honor and funded primarily through donations from the "poor for whom he [Starr] thought and labored." In the speech Phillips praised Starr for his investment in the African American community generally and in the St. Mary Street neighborhood specifically, a choice that involved a shift in Starr's original plans to renovate a neighborhood somewhere north of Market Street. Phillips indicated that it was Starr's experience working with black community members that brought about this change in direction. Another Workingmen's Club founder, N. Du Bois Miller, believed that it was Starr's interaction with the children of Workingmen's Club members that caused him to conclude that "the real field of labor lay amongst the younger generation," thus shifting the focus of his charitable work specifically in the direction of African American *children*. Although undoubtedly Starr was also influenced by broader trends in medicine, education, and psychology that were then designating childhood as a crucial time for social intervention, his focus on child-centered reforms was very likely a result of the experiences Phillips mentioned as well.[11]

No previous scholarship has credited Henry Phillips with having any role in the creation of Starr Park; neither did his white contemporaries when they chronicled the development of the park in a Starr Centre pamphlet titled *History of a Street,* published in 1901. However, the evidence presented here suggests that Phillips did play a significant, though indirect, role, as did an unnamed "colored boy" whom George H. Stuart encountered decades earlier when Starr was still a child himself.[12]

In addition to building on the vision of Rev. Phillips, Starr's work was established on the foundation laid by white founders of two programs housed in the church building adjacent to the future playground: a children's Sunday school founded by George H. Stuart and a free kindergarten/industrial school founded by Anna Hallowell. The Colored Mission Sabbath School, founded by Stuart in 1857, provided services to African American children exclusively. According to an account published in *History of a Street,* Stuart was inspired to start the program by a chance encounter with a young "colored" boy on the street. While visiting the sick on a Sunday, Stuart saw the boy and asked him why he was not attending Sunday school. These were programs designed to provide children who had to work during school hours with both religious instruction and the opportunity to learn to read. The boy replied, "All the schools within my reach are for *white* children," an answer that inspired Stuart to start a Sunday school this boy could attend.[13]

There is no historical record that reveals what the boy's intentions were in crafting his answer, nor is there evidence to confirm whether he was one actual child or a symbolic child designed to fit Stuart's transformation narrative. Assuming that the story of the encounter is at least approximately accurate, it is possible that this boy had no interest in spending what was probably his only day off work in a Sunday school. Virtually all black churches ran Sunday schools, so it is likely that he would have had access to at least one. Although many children were very interested in taking advantage of these programs, one can imagine that some preferred more active pursuits. Certainly, the boy's response provided this wealthy, white stranger with an excuse that would be hard to refute given that segregation was the norm in Sunday schools as elsewhere in Philadelphia. Alternatively, perhaps he knew that white-led programs were generally better resourced than the African American ones and hoped to inspire the stranger to send some of those resources in his direction. In any case, like Phillips, this unnamed boy (or, perhaps, the many boys he represented to Stuart) played a role in the development of Starr Garden Park.[14]

Even more influential were the black children who regularly attended the Mission School, voting in favor of the program with their feet. Without their continued attendance, the Stuart mission would not have remained open for four decades, inspiring the heirs of George Stuart to continue investing in the preservation of this particular physical space, the Stuart Church. Had the building not remained in use, it very likely would have fallen into disrepair or been demolished. Instead, it became the cornerstone for decades of programming used by thousands of children and adults. Without this building and these programs, Starr Garden would not have come to be, at least not in this neighborhood.

Prioritizing Play and Play Spaces: The Influence of Early Childhood Educators

In 1881 Stuart expanded his investment in the community by allowing free use of the Sunday school room by a Quaker philanthropist named Anna Hallowell in support of her desire to start a free kindergarten. Kindergartens were based on the model created by German educator Frederich Froebel, whose theories, first published in 1826 (in German) in his book *Education of Man*, emphasized *early* childhood as a key time of life when moral values and beneficial habits should be taught through play and through contact with the natural world. Kindergarten programs were, thus, defined by their play-focused pedagogy and the need for specifically designed spaces for play. Essential components of a kindergarten included a special play area, preferably grassy, and a garden, outdoors if possible. Thus, though the outdoor garden of the kindergarten was not equivalent to the playground that would become ubiquitous in the twentieth century, it was the kindergarten movement that first provided persuasive rationales regarding the importance of promoting particular kinds of children's play by creating a specific type of outdoor space.[15]

Although the play-focused pedagogy of the kindergarten was understood to be valuable for young children of all classes, *free* kindergartens for "destitute and neglected" children, like those who lived in the "slums" of St. Mary Street, were expected to serve additional purposes, namely, the prevention of crime and "pauperism." According to nineteenth-century social theory, the poor suffered through no fault of their own, but pauperism was the result of "willful error, of shameful indolence, of vicious habits. . . . " Late-nineteenth-century volunteer philanthropists believed that poor children, given the right environment, could avoid the latter. The kindergarten could provide this environment by removing children "from the streets" and their "dismal homes" and bringing them into "wholesome places, good air, play, occupation, friendly sympathy and care."[16]

In addition to emphasizing the importance of these protected, play-centered educational spaces, free-kindergarten advocates claimed that *the way children played* provided evidence that an inner transformation of character had occurred, foreshadowing claims made by future playground advocates. For example, Constance Mackenzie-Durham, a teacher in Philadelphia's first free kindergarten and later director of kindergartens for the Philadelphia Board of Education, described the success of free kindergartens in Philadelphia by relating a story of how children from her class not only refused to "participate in the coarser street romps with the non-kindergarteners" but also brought "many a child into the kindergarten who had been wont to stand at the door, hoot and run." These claims reveal the hope that the purity of the kindergarten could, perhaps, be transferred to the body of the preschool child and from there to the home and "the street."[17]

In 1881, with hopes like these and the offer of space in Stuart Church, Anna Hallowell chose to establish a kindergarten program, a year prior to the creation of Starr Garden Park. By January 1882 Hallowell's kindergarten program was fully enrolled, with two teachers serving fifty children, including a "fair sprinkling of blacks." By March, sixteen of the students were African Americans.[18]

Hallowell, an elite Philadelphia Quaker, had shown an interest in African American education at the age of fifteen, when she began teaching "the little colored children of the neighborhood . . . reading, writing and arithmetic" in her yard on Sunday afternoons. When, in her early forties, Hallowell began to focus her efforts on the establishment of free kindergartens, African American children were among those included in the earliest programs.[19]

In fact, although racial segregation was still common practice, black children had access to six of the ten free kindergartens operating in the city in 1882, three years after the first free kindergarten was opened in Philadelphia in 1879. Two exemplary programs founded by leading black educators served only "colored" children and were housed in buildings largely under the control of Rev. Phillips and Theodore Starr, one in the Workingmen's Club and the other in the Church of the Crucifixion. Four programs were racially mixed, including two St. Mary Street kindergartens: the St. Mary Street Day Nursery Kindergarten and the Stuart Mission Church Kindergarten.[20]

Before discussing how Starr Garden came into being in connection with the kindergarten founded by Hallowell, it is worth noting that the St. Mary Street Day Nursery and Kindergarten was Theodore Starr's first child-focused venture. Founded in 1880, the program was soon moved from its original location to the 700 block of St. Mary Street. What is most significant in relation to the origin of Starr Garden is that almost immediately after the move was completed, Starr purchased an adjoining building and had it demolished in order to "give the ground to the Nursery for a playground, having trees and shrubs planted, and swings erected for the amusement and admiration of the children." This was the first playground Starr created.[21]

Starr's collaboration with Hallowell was a natural next step in his child-saving work. Surrounded by a vacant lot that was being used as a trash heap, Hallowell's kindergarten lacked the outdoor play space needed to fully support kindergarten goals and methods. The school's managers, Hallowell later recalled, wanted to use the lot "as a garden for the children to work in, to have grass and trees and a bit of sweet mother nature to do her part in redeeming the sordid lives that had grown up in the presence of squalor where there should have been beauty." Once the park was complete Hallowell reported that it was used to "carry out the German kindergarten idea." Thus, the establishment of kindergartens and playgrounds was virtually simultaneous on St. Mary Street. In a further demonstration of the important connection between the playground and the kindergarten, Starr left the park to Hallowell when he died on June 1, 1884, at the age of forty. That same year, several new, idealistic young reformers founded yet another charitable organization targeting the needs of children, the St. Mary Street Library.[22]

Ambivalent Advocates: White Quakers, Black Children, and Play at the St. Mary Street Library

Despite its physical proximity to Starr Garden, the story of the St. Mary Street Library does not center on children's play or on play space. However, it is important for two reasons. First, because it operated in Stuart Church, the library supported ongoing investment in the building and the neighborhood. Second, it played a significant role in maintaining and expanding services for African American children in and around Starr Garden.

Many nineteenth-century reformers believed that their concerns regarding the detrimental impact of industrialization, immigration, and urbanization on the health of the nation could be addressed by protecting the vulnerable from the "corrupting, tempting, and distracting influences of the world long enough for a kind but firm regimen to transform their behavior and order their personalities." For its founders, the St. Mary Street Library constituted a logical first step in reforming the character and habits of the community's youth. In response to concerns that "a low class of literature" was being circulated in the neighborhood, they decided to replace such books with others that would influence children in a more positive direction. Starting a few months after Starr's death, the library was a program offered to the children of the Stuart Mission Kindergarten and (newly added) Industrial

School. At the time, the school served African American students primarily; therefore, the nascent circulating library program also served as a resource for African American children especially.[23]

Interestingly, although in 1904 the Starr Centre's leadership would assert play's transformative powers, in 1884 playful activities were used primarily as a lure to attract children to enter a space in which they might come under the uplifting influence of the volunteers. Library managers made their understanding of play's relative unimportance clear in the organization's seventh annual report, published in 1891: "We have had recourse to our usual minor devices for drawing or holding the children's interests in the ways of playing games and making scrapbooks, but *these entertainments are not essential* [author's emphasis] and we do not often have enough workers to carry them on without making them more of a burden than is desirable."[24]

That play was not viewed as essential to library activities despite the managers' close connections to advocates of kindergarten's play-focused pedagogy can be best understood within the context of philosophies of "scientific charity," which were growing in popularity at the time. According to these theories, indiscriminate charity and lack of contact between the privileged and the poor had exacerbated rather than relieved the problems of the poor, who, having lost their self-respect and ambition through dependence on charity, were now defined by their "idleness" and "unthriftiness." The eradication of these two character flaws remained the library's central goal for many years. Concerns regarding idleness, in particular, made play-focused activities somewhat suspect.[25]

Children's playfulness was not entirely discouraged, however. The library's managers did not object to the provision of some forms of entertainment. The reader can almost see a twinkle in the writer's eye as a manager described a young boy, "colored, about 10 years of age" who "carried books from one part of the room to another by going down on all-fours and putting the books on his back." Through their actions, children to some extent redefined the purposes of the library's space and programs. For example, it is likely that children's preferences for more active endeavors than reading, such as "turning [cart]wheels rapidly over the floor of the library," led to the expansion of the library's services, which soon included music lessons two afternoons a week and Saturday morning "games and recreation." In addition, the library began providing "entertainments" such as concerts, magicians, and magic lantern exhibitions. Still, the provision of playful fun remained secondary, not central, to their approach.[26]

The provision of outdoor space for play was even less a priority. Library activities, even when they expanded beyond the provision of books to more active play, took place inside. As a result, no mention of Starr Garden appeared in any of the St. Mary Street annual reports until 1891, a year before the library was temporarily transformed into the Philadelphia College Settlement. "The garden, being on two sides of the building, is a great advantage in many ways, and with music every week during two months of the summer, has been a wholesome attraction in the neighborhood," the report stated. Like play-focused activities, the park was described as useful primarily because of its ability to attract people to engage with positive influences. Still, because the mission kindergarten's tenancy on site was short lived, it was the library's presence that encouraged ongoing investment in the building and region, giving it an important role in the development of the playground. More importantly, it was Susan Wharton, the library's most influential manager, who was primarily responsible for preserving and strengthening programmatic commitments to African American children in the neighborhood, commitments that to some extent also protected their access to the park and, later, playground.[27]

Soon after it began, the library program had moved its activities from a weekday to Saturdays, which changed the racial composition of the library clientele, a foreshadowing of later changes. By 1889, only five years after opening, the library no longer served African American children primarily. That year, for the first time, most members were described by library managers as white, Jewish immigrants, primarily from Russia and other parts of Europe. In an annual report published in 1890, library managers attributed some of the changes they observed to the changing demographic of the neighborhood as more African American families were "pushed" north and west by "foreigners." Still, they were reportedly "baffled" by the extent of the change. The trend continued the following year with more black children leaving or failing to renew their memberships while an increased number of applications were submitted by white children.[28]

Highlighting the intersectivity of race and gender, a closer look at membership statistics for 1889 indicates that there may actually have been little decrease in the participation of black *girls*. Though the overall number of African American members in 1889 was smaller than that of white children, the report showed that African American girls were still well represented. With fifty-three black girls claiming membership, they comprised about one-fourth of the total and slightly exceeded the forty-seven white girls; this fact seemed to be deemed of little importance.[29]

Managers did notice, however, that the perceived change in racial demographics accompanied an increase in new members of higher social-class standing ("from decent homes"), which "raise[ed] the atmosphere" of the library and made it "less of an effort to preserve order." Still, Wharton and her associates did not view the decrease in African American participation as a positive development, nor did they accept the change as inevitable.[30]

In 1890, on the basis of their observations and concerns, library leaders took three steps to increase African American memberships. First, they stopped admitting new white members. Second, they went to visit the homes of former black members and invited them to return. Third, they started two classes to address what they viewed as the needs and interests of African American children: a carpentry class for black boys and a cooking class for black girls. They also added an advisory board, including on it a highly regarded African American educator, Fanny Jackson Coppin, director of the widely respected private high school, the Institute for Colored Youth. Their efforts led to a significant increase in membership for black boys (from thirty-six in 1889 to sixty in 1890) and a small increase in membership for black girls (from fifty-three to sixty-six). No numbers were provided for 1891, but the report for that year again stated that white children were "discouraged" from joining.[31]

None of the children who moved in and out of the St. Mary Street library left a record of their reasons for either staying away or returning, but the seventh annual report (1889), in which decreased African American participation was noted, provides evidence regarding one reason why the participation of black boys declined: namely, they received more attention than they wanted and were often in trouble. The report included excerpts from Wharton's daily notes in which "colored" boys, although they made up only thirty-six of 213 members, less than 17 percent, dominate the notes, usually in connection with a description of some type of disruptive behavior. On February 2, for example, Wharton described a boy who

> came to the Library and making some confusion was put out. He returned several times and so is suspended for a month. He is small and very black, and slips into the room without being noticed. He is a member of what is known as the "Black-fat Gang," and was arrested for theft a few months since. An interesting little fellow.

Although the boy's "blackness" was described by Wharton as a factor that enabled him to go unnoticed, it seems that it was actually what made him more noticeable to her. The following year, the pattern in her notes was the same. Though not entirely negative even in describing what Wharton viewed as misbehavior, these notes suggest that the behavior of black boys was highly scrutinized and that their actions were often deemed unacceptable, issues that may have been factors in their decision to stay away.[32]

Though less racist than the majority of their contemporaries and willing to acknowledge class differences within the African American community, library managers remained ambivalent about the very children they sought to reach. In 1890, for example, they described black girls as "an idle class apparently devoid of almost all wholesome interests." In 1891 they reminded readers that "[n]o work done in St. Mary Street can justly be compared with that carried on among white children only, or with the respectable colored; it is only by comparing one year's results with another's that we can see what is gained." Building on these assumptions regarding race-based inferiority, library managers attributed diminished black participation primarily to the ways in which white children's presence served to highlight the inherent and obvious inferiority of black children. The white children "crowd out the colored," a report explained. "The colored soon feel their inferiority and stay away."[33]

Certainly some black children may have internalized others' views and considered themselves inferior to whites; however, it seems much more likely that invasive scrutiny of their actions, overt race-based mistreatment, and the ongoing challenges of poverty (perhaps at times connected to some embarrassment about clothes or shoes in comparison to children who were more well off) accounted for more of the missing children than a sense of their own race-based inferiority. The fact that so many rejoined when they were specifically told that they were still welcome further supports this view.

Still, although the managers of the library did not believe that poor black children had the same potential as white children (or as the "respectable colored"), neither did they think they were beyond all hope. Susan Wharton and her colleagues acknowledged the existence and needs of African American youth during a time when their needs were largely ignored by the resourced and powerful in Philadelphia. As a result, from 1884 to 1892, she and her colleagues protected black children's access to services they would not otherwise have had. Though the final years of the nineteenth century had a primarily negative impact on black children's access to educational and recreational resources, Wharton would ensure that some of it was at least temporarily regained.

Gaining Play Space and Losing Ground

The year 1892 brought, at the invitation of the library's managers, the establishment of the Philadelphia College Settlement. From 1892 until their departure for a "better" neighborhood in 1899, settlement workers temporarily supervised the work that had been started by the library in addition to adding a wide variety of new programs, mostly clubs and social events, that closely followed patterns established by other social settlements, including Jane Addams's Hull House in Chicago.[34]

Philadelphia College Settlement workers' ideas and efforts reflected the national settlement movement's focus on "Americanizing" new white immigrants rather than developing black youth. This focus on Americanization stood in sharp contrast to the goals of the library's managers, led by Wharton, who had actively sought to address the challenges black communities faced. The change in focus had a direct impact on black access to and participation in previously established and newly developed programs. By 1899, for example, the settlement kindergarten program served only white children, and when white boys requested access to carpentry classes previously attended only by African American boys, the settlement canceled two sessions of classes for black children rather than racially integrating the programs or adding additional classes. Throughout the 1890s, as the settlement grew in size and scope, black children's centrality to its goals and efforts continually shrank.[35]

Most important to this story are the efforts of settlement workers who actively campaigned for the expansion of Starr Park in the 1890s, a process that included the demolition of their own buildings (providing a convenient reason to leave the neighborhood) as well as an entire block of buildings considered to be "nuisances." Some of these were houses of prostitution or gambling establishments, but many were tenements that housed both adults and children. Having already experienced increased exclusion by settlement workers, African Americans (including many children whose level of participation at the library dropped significantly after the demolition) were disproportionately represented among those who lost their homes. Given a high level of housing discrimination in Philadelphia, few African American families were likely to have landed in homes that provided equivalent access to fresh air, kindergarten education, or outdoor play space.[36]

Dr. Beverly Tatum, author of *Why Are All the Black Kids Sitting Together in the Cafeteria?*, has argued that racism's forces are so intertwined with the cultural practices and social institutions of the United States that to do nothing to directly address racist practices and trends is to extend racism's reach and influence. She likens nonintervention to the act of standing still on a moving walkway or an escalator. You may arrive more slowly at the destination than if you walked with the force of motion, but unless you walk against it you follow its direction. This image seems well suited to the story of the Philadelphia College Settlement's virtual abandonment of African American children in the last decade of the nineteenth century. To avoid following late-nineteenth-century trends that encouraged increased exclusion of black youth required conscious action against the tide of racism. Instead, leaders of the Philadelphia Settlement chose to ride along. The comparative lack of intentionality on the part of Philadelphia College Settlement workers and leaders meant that the settlement increasingly moved away from addressing the additional challenges faced by the neighborhood's black residents and led to the erasure of African Americans from these reformers' visions of an improved future.[37]

So how was it that black children were present and welcomed at Starr Garden Playground in 1904? In large part the inclusion of those black youth who remained geographically close enough to make use of the space was the result of Wharton's dogged determination to continue to direct resources toward addressing the unique challenges faced by African Americans in Philadelphia. Though she may have supported settlement efforts to expand Starr Garden, unlike new leaders of the settlement she helped to found, Susan Wharton retained her commitment to African Americans during this decade. She regularly consulted with leading African Americans like Rev. Phillips regarding the problems facing black Philadelphians. In 1895, she convinced Philadelphia Settlement leaders and faculty at the University of Pennsylvania to invite sociologist W. E. B. Du Bois to conduct a study of "the negro problem" in Philadelphia. As a result, almost in spite of itself, the Philadelphia College Settlement was in some sense responsible for one of the most groundbreaking sociological studies of black life ever conducted, *The Philadelphia Negro*.[38]

When settlement leaders chose to relocate to a neighborhood with fewer African Americans in 1899, Wharton was clearly and publicly critical of their choice, tying it directly to a lack of willingness to work with and for African Americans. "At Seventh and Lombard Streets the presence of the negro element has been dwelt upon at great length as a deteriorating, impossible one to cope with," Wharton wrote. "We wish to enter a strong protest against this view of the situation." Unsuccessful in her protest, Wharton disconnected her pet programs from settlement control where she could, and founded the Starr Centre Association in 1901 to continue the work started by the St. Mary Street Library. Under the auspices of the Starr Centre, she started a new kindergarten, established a new library (the one she originally started having been transferred to the city, leading to its relocation as well) and founded a new settlement house. Thus, Wharton, because she was consistent in her dedication to meeting the needs of the black community in Philadelphia, had a significant impact on the access that Philadelphia's African American children had to Starr Garden despite the fact that she was only tangentially interested in promoting play.[39]

Conclusion

In Starr Garden's development, African American children were not simply ignored or unnoticed by playground advocates; rather, they were displaced and erased. In the 1890s, primarily as a result of the decisions made by settlement leaders and their partners, black children lost access to Starr Garden as it expanded. In addition, they were increasingly excluded from connected programs that were originally established primarily for their benefit, programs that, despite their paternalistic foundations, were genuinely helpful to many poor families. Susan Wharton's role in Starr Garden's development resulted in temporarily increased access for black youth, demonstrating that resistance to national trends existed on a local level. However, by 1911, when Starr Garden was transformed once again to create Philadelphia's first model recreation center and placed under municipal control (a pattern repeated in cities across the nation as the play movement grew in organization, power, and influence), black children were largely excluded.[40]

However, the story of Starr Garden's development is one of interracial cooperation and participation as much as it is one of racial segregation and exclusion. White philanthropists Theodore Starr, Anna Hallowell, and Susan Wharton worked alongside, or at least parallel to, African American leaders like Henry Phillips. These relationships led to the construction of a variety of play-focused spaces and programs in the vicinity of St. Mary Street, spaces and programs in which racial segregation was the exception rather than the rule. Perhaps most importantly, African American children were participants in the development of Philadelphia's "first real playground." Though largely hidden from view in national records, these children inspired and shaped the programs that preceded Starr Garden's creation and were in attendance on its opening day, indicating that they too were participants in the American play movement long before World War I.

NOTES
1. Starr Centre Association, *The First Real Playground in Philadelphia* (Philadelphia, [1904?]), Starr Centre Association of Philadelphia Records, MC9, Box 6, Barbara Bates Center for the Study of the History of Nursing, School of Nursing, University of Pennsylvania (hereafter cited as BC).
2. "Children's New Playground in the Park," *Philadelphia Inquirer*, November 12, 1898, 7; *Playground*, April 1907, back cover; "Playgrounds Association of Philadelphia 1909," Annual Reports Collection, Box 76, Urban Archives, Temple University, Philadelphia, PA (hereafter cited as UA). See also Boyer, *Urban Masses and Moral Order in America, 1820–1920*, 233–51; Cavallo, *Muscles and*

Morals; Crantz, *The Politics of Park Design*; Clarence Elmer Rainwater, *The Play Movement in the United States* (Chicago: University of Chicago Press, 1923); Paul C. Violas, "The Play Movement," in *The Training of the Urban Working Class: A History of Twentieth-Century American Education* (Chicago: Rand McNally College, 1978).

3. Boyer, *Urban Masses and Moral Order*; Cavallo, *Muscles and Morals*; Chudacoff, *Children at Play*, 111–13; Rainwater, *The Play Movement*; Violas, "The Play Movement"; Jeffrey J. Pilz, "The Beginnings of Organized Play for Black America: E.T. Atwell and the PRAA," *Journal of Negro History* 70 (Summer–Autumn 1985): 59–72.

4. Rosenzweig, *Eight Hours for What We Will*; Sarah Jo Peterson, "Voting for Play: The Democratic Potential of Progressive-Era Playgrounds," *Journal of the Gilded Age and Progressive Era* (April 2004): 145–75; Hardy, *How Boston Played*; Baldwin, *Domesticating the Street*; Mark A. Kadzielski, "'As a Flower Needs Sunshine': The Origins of Organized Children's Recreation in Philadelphia, 1886–1911," *Journal of Sport History* 4.2 (Summer 1977): 169–88; Suzanne Spencer-Wood, "Turn-of-the-Century Women's Organizations, Urban Design, and the Origin of the American Playground Movement," *Landscape Journal* 13.2 (Fall 1994): 125–37; Jerry G. Dickason, "The Origin of the Playground: The Role of the Boston Women's Clubs, 1885–1890," *Leisure Sciences: An Interdisciplinary Journal* 6.1 (1983): 83–98; Adrienne Lash Jones, "Struggle among Saints: African American Women and the YWCA, 1870–1920," in *Men and Women Adrift: The YMCA and the YWCA in the City* (New York: New York University Press, 1997), 160–87; Lasch-Quinn, *Black Neighbors*; Cary S. Goodman, "Settlements, Schools, and Playgrounds" and "The Playground Association in America," in *Choosing Sides* (New York: Schocken, 1979), 33–82; Elizabeth Gagen, "Too Good to Be True: Representing Children's Agency in the Archives of Playground Reform," *Historical Geography* 29 (2001): 53–64.

5. Starr Centre Association, *History of a Street* (Philadelphia: Sign of the Ivy Leaf, January 1901), Starr Centre Association of Philadelphia Records, MC9, Box 7, BC.

6. Bromley's Atlas of Philadelphia (call #0728, vol. 1), plate H (DAMS 8971), Historical Society of Pennsylvania, Philadelphia, PA (hereafter cited as HSP); Michael B. Katz and Thomas J. Sugrue, eds., *W. E. B. Du Bois, Race, and the City: "The Philadelphia Negro" and Its Legacy* (Philadelphia: University of Pennsylvania Press, 1998); "In the Slums: The Board of Health Cleaning Out St. Mary Street Dens," *North American* (Philadelphia, PA), November 20, 1880; "Death in the Slums: A Tramp Tinker's Body Found in a St. Mary Street Function Shop," *North American* (Philadelphia, PA), December 16, 1886.

7. Sam Bass Warner, Jr., *The Private City: Philadelphia in Three Periods of Its Growth* (Philadelphia: University of Pennsylvania Press, 1968); John F. Sutherland. "Housing the Poor in the City of Homes: Philadelphia at the Turn of the Century," *The Peoples of Philadelphia: A History of Ethnic Groups and Lower-Class*

Life, 1790–1940, eds. Allen F. Davis and Mark H. Haller (Philadelphia: Temple University Press, 1973), 175–200.
8. Roger Lane, *William Dorsey's Philadelphia and Ours: On the Past and Future of the Black City in America* (New York: Oxford University Press, 1991); Katz and Sugrue, *W. E. B. Dubois, Race, and the City*.
9. Rev. Henry L. Phillips, *An Address at the Unveiling of a Memorial Window Erected to the Memory of Mr. Theodore Starr* (Philadelphia: published by request, 1887): 6, HSP.
10. Lane, *William Dorsey's Philadelphia*, 249; Starr Centre Association, *History of a Street*, 21–22.
11. Phillips, *An Address*, 10, 4; Starr Centre Association, *History of a Street*, 26; Starr Centre Association, *The Second Annual Report of the Starr Centre: A Continuation of the St. Mary Street Educational and Social Work* (Philadelphia, November 1901), Annual Reports Collection, Box 84, UA (also available in Starr Centre Association of Philadelphia Records, MC 9, Box 4, BC); "A Good Movement Started," *North American* (Philadelphia, PA), July 12, 1898.
12. Starr Centre Association, *History of a Street*, 47–49.
13. Ibid.,11; *Second Annual Report of the Starr Centre* (Philadelphia, November 1901), 5–6.
14. Lane, *William Dorsey's Philadelphia*.
15. Starr Centre Association, *History of a Street*, 46; B. Beatty, *Preschool Education in America*.
16. A.H., "Free Kindergartens: Movement on Behalf of Neglected Children under School Age, and for the Prevention of Crime and Pauperism," *Friends' Intelligencer*, March 4, 1882 (a complete run of the *Friends' Intelligencer* is available in the Quaker Collection, Haverford College, Haverford, PA); Katz, *In the Shadow of the Poorhouse*, 19.
17. Constance Mackenzie-Durham, *Free and Public Kindergartens in Philadelphia: Prepared for the Sub-Primary School Society* (Philadelphia[?]: Sub-Primary School Society[?], 1897), 8, Van Pelt Library, University of Pennsylvania.
18. "Free Kindergartens," *Friends' Intelligencer*, January 7, 1882, 47; "Free Kindergartens," *Friends' Intelligencer*, March 4, 1882, 39, 3.
19. "Anna Hallowell," *Dictionary of Quaker Biography*, the Quaker Collection, Haverford College, Haverford, PA; "Free Kindergarten," *Friends' Intelligencer*, March 4, 1882, 39, 3, 46; "Anna Hallowell," *Friends' Intelligencer*, June 3, 1905, 62, 22.
20. "Free Kindergartens," *Friends' Intelligencer*, January 7, 1882, 47; "Local News," *The Christian Recorder*, July 28, 1881, Accessible Archives, African American Newspapers Collection, http://accessible.com; "Free Kindergartens," *Friends' Intelligencer*, March 4, 1882, 39, 3.
21. Starr Centre Association, *History of a Street*, 41.
22. Ibid., 47–48; "Mr. Starr's St. Mary Street Lot," *North American* (Philadelphia, PA), June 3, 1885.

23. Katz, *In the Shadow of the Poorhouse*, 68–71; Starr Centre Association, *The Growth of the Starr Library, 1884–1903* (Philadelphia, n.d.), 8, Starr Association of Philadelphia Records, MC 9, Box 14, BC.
24. St. Mary Street Library, *St. Mary Street Library* (Philadelphia, 1891), Settlements Collection, Box 6, Sophia Smith Collection, Smith College, Northampton, MA (hereafter cited as SSC). See also St. Mary Street Library, *St. Mary Street Library* (Philadelphia, 1888), Settlements Collection, Box 6, SSC; also available in Pamphlets Collection, Octavia Hill Association, UA.
25. Katz, *In the Shadow of the Poorhouse*, 66–84; St. Mary Street Library, *St. Mary Street Library* (Philadelphia, 1886), 1–2, Box 6, Settlements Collection, Box 6, SSC; St. Mary Street Library, *St. Mary Street Library* (Philadelphia, 1890), 9, Settlements Collection, Box 6, SSC.
26. St. Mary Street Library, *St. Mary Street Library* (Philadelphia, 1890), 10, 15; Starr Centre Association, *Growth of Starr Library*, 9; St. Mary Street Library, *St. Mary Street Library* (Philadelphia, 1888), 6; St. Mary Street Library, *St. Mary Street Library* (Philadelphia, 1889), 5, Settlements Collection, Box 6, SSC.
27. St. Mary Street Library, *St. Mary Street Library* (Philadelphia, 1891), 4; see also St. Mary Street Library, *St. Mary Street Library* (Philadelphia, 1888), 5; St. Mary Street Library, *St. Mary Street Library* (Philadelphia, 1889), 13.
28. St. Mary Street Library, *St. Mary Street Library* (Philadelphia, 1886), 3; St. Mary Street Library, *St. Mary Street Library* (Philadelphia, 1889), 27; St. Mary Street Library, *St. Mary Street Library* (Philadelphia, 1890), 4–5.
29. St. Mary Street Library, *St. Mary Street Library* (Philadelphia, 1890), 4; St. Mary Street Library, *St. Mary Street Library* (Philadelphia, 1889), 27.
30. St. Mary Street Library, *St. Mary Street Library* (Philadelphia, 1889), 4.
31. St. Mary Street Library, *St. Mary Street Library* (Philadelphia, 1890), 4–7; St. Mary Street Library, *St. Mary Street Library* (Philadelphia, 1891), 2.
32. St. Mary Street Library, *St. Mary Street Library* (Philadelphia, 1889), 14.
33. St. Mary Street Library, *St. Mary Street Library* (Philadelphia, 1890); St. Mary Street Library, *St. Mary Street Library* (Philadelphia, 1891).
34. St. Mary Street College Settlement, *An Account of the St. Mary Street College Settlement of Philadelphia from April 1 to September 15, 1892 together with the Eighth Annual Report of the St. Mary Street Library from November 1, 1891, to April 1, 1892* (Philadelphia, 1892), 8, Annual Reports Collection, Box 11, UA; Starr Centre Association, *The Annual Report of the Starr Centre* (Philadelphia, January 1900), Annual Reports Collection, Box 84, UA (also available in Starr Centre Association of Philadelphia Records, MC 9, Box 4, BC); see also St. Mary Street College Settlement of Philadelphia, *The Second Annual Report of the St. Mary Street College Settlement of Philadelphia: Continuing the Work of the St. Mary Street Library* (Philadelphia, 1893), Settlements Collection, Box 6, SSC; St. Mary Street College Settlement of Philadelphia, *The Third Annual Report of the St. Mary Street College Settlement of Philadelphia: Continuing the Work of the St. Mary Street Library* (Philadelphia, 1894), 13, Van Pelt Library, University of

Pennsylvania (also available in Settlements Collection, Box 6, SSC); St. Mary Street College Settlement of Philadelphia, *The Fourth Annual Report of the St. Mary Street College Settlement of Philadelphia: Continuing the Work of the St. Mary Street Library* (Philadelphia, 1895), 34–35, Starr Centre Association of Philadelphia Records, MC9, Box 8, BC (also available in Settlements Collection, Box 6, SSC); St. Mary Street College Settlement of Philadelphia, *The Fifth Annual Report of the St. Mary Street College Settlement of Philadelphia: Continuing the Work of the St. Mary Street Library* (Philadelphia, 1896), Settlements Collection, Box 6, SSC; St. Mary Street College Settlement of Philadelphia, *The Sixth Annual Report of the St. Mary Street College Settlement of Philadelphia: Continuing the Work of the St. Mary Street Library* (Philadelphia, 1897), Settlements Collection, Box 6, SSC; Lasch-Quinn, *Black Neighbors*.
35. College Settlements Association, *Fifth Annual Report of the College Settlements Association: From September 1, 1892 to September 1, 1893* (Philadelphia: Dunlap, 1894), Van Pelt Library, University of Pennsylvania; Starr Centre Association, Star Kitchen Pamphlet (Philadelphia, October 1899), page titled "Penny Lunch Children at the Ramsey School," Starr Centre Association of Philadelphia Records, MC 9, Box 14, BC.
36. St. Mary Street College Settlement of Philadelphia, *The Fifth Annual Report of the St. Mary Street College Settlement of Philadelphia: Continuing the Work of the St. Mary Street Library* (Philadelphia, 1896), 4; Starr Centre Association, *Growth of Starr Library*, 13.
37. Tatum, *Why Are all the Black Kids Sitting Together in the Cafeteria?*
38. Letter from Dr. Charles F. Judson to Albert J. Kennedy, July 20, 1945, SW0144, Albert J. Kennedy Papers, Box 6, fldr. 55, Social Welfare History Archives, University of Minnesota; W. E. B. Du Bois, *The Philadelphia Negro: A Social Study with a New Introduction by Elijah Anderson* (Philadelphia: University of Pennsylvania Press, 1996 [1899]).
39. Starr Centre Association, *The Annual Report of the Starr Centre* (Philadelphia, January 1900), 13.
40. Board of Recreation of Philadelphia, *Philadelphia Playgrounds: Report of the Board of Recreation of Philadelphia* (Philadelphia: Board of Recreation, January 1, 1913), 4, Free Library of Philadelphia Pamphlets Collection, Box 50, UA.

2

Model Schools and Field Days

Colorado Fuel and Iron's Construction of Education and Recreation for Children, 1901–1918

FAWN-AMBER MONTOYA

Joseph and Carmela Sacco moved their family from southern Italy at the turn of the twentieth century to southern Colorado to work in the coal mines. The Saccos moved into housing in Berwind, Colorado, owned by the Colorado Fuel and Iron Company, Joseph's employer, and bought groceries on credit from the company store. Carmela earned extra money by making food for single miners and supplemented the family diet with chickens, turkeys, and pigeons that she raised. The Saccos were like many immigrants coming into the area of southern Colorado during the Progressive Era. They attended Catholic mass with Mexicans and other Italians. They had a limited understanding of the English language and raised children who would have little understanding of their parents' lives in Italy.

Eugenia "Gene" Sacco, the third child and the first to be born in the United States, grew up loving baseball. She learned baseball at school and carried the love of this most American sport throughout her adult life. While Sacco's parents were both Italian immigrants who only spoke enough English to get by, Sacco recalled growing up with memories that are typically American. Despite her parents' immigrant roots and

European beginnings, Sacco came to identify as an American, not as an Italian. Sacco's experiences and memories of growing up in a southern Colorado coal camp illustrate the process of Americanization promoted by the Colorado Fuel and Iron Company through the company's construction of educational curriculum and leisure time for miners' children.[1]

Early in the twentieth century the Colorado Fuel and Iron Company (CF&I) employed almost sixteen thousand people. With over a third born in the United States, the rest included a variety of nationalities, including Irish, English, Hungarians, Welsh, Germans, Mexicans, and Greeks. The largest immigrant group came from Italy. The company reportedly employed over thirty different nationalities. This large immigrant population was not unique to Colorado or the West, but reflected a large nationwide rise of immigration as the United States expanded its industrial economy. In order to fill a demand for labor, U.S.-based corporations looked outside of the United States to fill their labor pool.[2]

The dramatic growth of immigrant populations in the industrializing United States encouraged Progressives and especially Progressive women to become engaged in the process of "uplifting" these new Americans. They believed that the best methods of uplift focused on "Americanization" programs that would educate women about health, food preparation, and parenting. Progressive women who may not have had a voice in the political dialogue before this historic moment found an opportunity to share their maternal ideals and their methods of structuring an "American" home.[3]

The emphasis on Americanizing immigrants grew during the Gilded Age and became part of the Progressive reformers' interest in racial uplift. They emphasized learning the English language, becoming aware of American history and culture, and literally "cleaning up" through better hygiene and health. In southern Colorado, the CF&I embraced this Americanization process for its many foreign-born employees, hoping that it would make them more productive and that they would substitute American ideals for the political and social notions of their home countries. From 1901 to 1918, CF&I's process of Americanizing immigrant children included the creation of educational curriculum, the establishment of kindergartens and gardening programs, and the sponsorship of field days and sporting events. CF&I's Sociological

Department and the YMCA developed the schools and spaces of leisure designed to Americanize the children of CF&I employees, while the children and their families acculturated to American ideas through education and sporting events.

Colorado Fuel and Iron Company

Coal mining in southern Colorado began with the introduction of the Colorado Coal and Iron Company in 1879. General William Jackson Palmer, owner of the Denver and Rio Grande Railroad and a geologist, observed the large amounts of coal in the region and built a steel mill in Pueblo, Colorado. In the 1880s, the region grew very slowly, but by 1892, with an increase in demand for coal and steel, a number of coal mining companies in the region merged into the Colorado Fuel and Iron Company. In 1903, when the owner of CF&I, John Osgood, found himself on the verge of bankruptcy, he sold a majority interest in the company to John D. Rockefeller and John D. Rockefeller Jr.[4]

At about this time, southern Colorado experienced an economic boom with the growth of the coal and steel industry in the region and the increasing demand for coal throughout the United States. In order to fill a growing need for employees, CF&I, the largest employer in the region, began to employ and recruit laborers from throughout the world. Once employees and their families arrived in southern Colorado, they found themselves entrenched in a CF&I–controlled community accentuated by the limited water in the region. CF&I's vast ownership of mining fields in southern Colorado, the distance between camps, and the new immigrants' unfamiliarity with the region allowed CF&I to construct a life for its workforce by establishing company towns with housing, company stores, and churches. The immigrants working in the coal mines knew very little about Colorado and the United States beyond what CF&I told them.

The Sociological Department

In order to deal with its new immigrant workforce, in 1901 CF&I formed the Sociological Department, which focused not only on improving the lives of the miners and the miners' families but also on shaping their political and economic ideas. The Sociological Department began night schools for the miners to learn the English language and taught sanitation and hygiene for the employees and their families. In addition to improving the lives of individual workers, the Sociological Department set the standards for the education of the miners' and steel workers' children by regulating educational curriculum and encouraging the children to participate in company-sponsored activities. The goals of these programs centered on teaching children what CF&I envisioned as the ideal life for employees and the employees' families. The children who participated in these programs became Americanized through the curriculum and the leisure spaces that the company created, as well as through the necessity of adapting to life in a company town—a reality for many children in mill and mining towns throughout the United States.

At about the same time, the Sociological Department began publishing the *Camp and Plant*, which reflected the ideals of the company and those of the director of the department, Dr. Richard Corwin. Corwin's plans for the Sociological Department centered on Progressive-Era ideals of using education to train and shape immigrants and their children. The publication desired to represent the voices of the miners through stories of the mining camps and the "anecdotes written by the men and members of their families."[5]

Kindergartens

In order to deal with a diverse immigrant and migrant workforce in the coal mines and steel mills, Corwin incorporated an educational structure for the education of children of CF&I employees. Beginning in 1901, he started to promote the idea that kindergartens were the best place to begin the process of Americanizing immigrant children. Corwin saw kindergartens as filling a void where immigrant parents could not or would not educate their young children. Through a series of *Camp and Plant* articles, the Sociological Department promoted the idea of developing curriculum that focused on the "manual training of children."[6] According to the department, children should participate in curriculum that provided ideals of citizenship and industrial training.

CF&I envisioned industrial labor as a component of an educational program that extended beyond an academic perspective. This process separated young children from their immigrant family members, so they could be taught the English language and the importance of industrial labor. The inclusion of gardening in the educational curriculum offers the strongest example of this vision of industrial labor. Gardening taught children how to measure rows, how to plant seeds, and when to water the plants. This new curriculum emphasized that students' work occurred inside and outside the classroom. The Sociological Department in 1899 encouraged the Pueblo School District to have a continuous session from April to December with the garden work being a method of occupying the time of the children. Rather than having children present in the school at only certain times of the year, CF&I wanted children to be engaged throughout the year.[7]

A 1902 article titled "CF&I Kindergartens and Their Work" reported on the activities of the kindergartens in coal mining camps, including the growth in enrollment and implementation of the kindergarten program, which emphasized industrial labor and productivity. To "the incentives of emulation and financial profit," the article predicted, "will probably be added the stimulative effect of displaying representative pieces of these manufactures at our State fairs as well as at other exhibitions."[8] The industrial work that the children produced differed from camp to camp and included basketry, pyrography (burnt wood and leather work), wood carving, and rug weaving. At Camp Engle, "Industrial work has created considerable enthusiasm."[9] The Sociological Department, while providing academic curriculum for its student population, also felt that students needed to be well versed in industrial labor that could reap a financial profit. At least according to the CF&I, the students excitedly participated in industrial labor.

The same article also addressed "The Kindergarten and Citizenship." Employees' children had "the opportunity" to "practice . . . citizenship before real civic duties present themselves. It is a sort of natural training for citizenship."[10] The article reflected Corwin's vision of the kindergarten as a training ground for the immigrant population and as a component of social betterment. Children's interactions with each other would

A *Camp and Plant* photo featuring the Pueblo school district superintendent and teacher with kindergarteners working in the garden. (Courtesy Bessemer Historical Society–CF&I Archives)

help them to be better citizens and to better relate to one another by learning the principles of citizenship and civic duty. Yet, Corwin's ideas did not appear to focus only on American ideals.

While the kindergarten curriculum focused on the belief that the classroom could help assist students in learning to become better citizens, it is interesting to note that the industrial-training component followed European models. Corwin saw gardening as a means of teaching children multiple facets of life, with the outcome being more important than the model. Corwin saw the difference between his model and the European model as being based on the methods of implementation. He felt that in the United States, curriculum would be implemented on the basis of local needs and local demands, while in Europe, schools implemented curriculum, such as the school gardens, in all schools and in all regions with the same approach. Corwin believed that the American approach had a democratic idea of distribution, with the European model being based on socialism or authoritarian rule.[11]

The *Camp and Plant* reported that mothers became more involved in the lives of their children, attending meetings and visiting schools frequently. Parents were often unclear about the purposes and content of the curriculum; teachers explained to the parents that they "directed their efforts at this school along patriotic lines, and have spent a great deal of time in the inculcation of a spirit of love of country. The children have shown surprising interest in the history of America and in the great deeds of the great men."[12] Because workers and families often moved from one camp to another, Corwin dictated a standard curriculum, so when miners moved camps their children would be taught the same curriculum regardless of where they attended school. Corwin failed to notice the contradiction that he made with his critique of European models of education and the implementation of his "democratic" learning process.[13]

Effects of Policies on Children

Many children of CF&I laborers failed to attend school on a regular basis or to complete their education beyond the eighth grade. Yet for some, like Sinfrosa Vigil, the child of a New Mexican mother and an Italian father, school became a central component of their lives. Born late in the 1890s, Vigil attended CF&I kindergartens, but like other children of her generation left school early due to her large family size. Vigil's family expected her to assist her mother in the domestic responsibilities in the home, including food preparation, cleaning, and child rearing. As an adult Vigil spoke more Spanish than English or Italian, and although she attended school from the ages of six to sixteen, she did not complete her education past the fourth grade.[14] Aladino Lopez, another child growing up in CF&I camps, also attended school sporadically. Despite his lack of consistent attendance at school, Lopez saw himself as an American. He did not define himself as a hyphenated American but as one who spoke fluent English. Lopez, whose parents were from New Mexico, traced his heritage in the region to the time when New Mexico was being colonized, but he saw himself not as a New Mexican or as a Mexican but as an American.[15] The process of Americanization depended heavily on how the children in CF&I–run schools viewed themselves and responded to the curriculum.

Corwin believed that the kindergarten and gardening curricula created a space for the children of CF&I employees to come to understand the value of hard work and industrial training. The company and the closely linked public schools allowed immigrant children to interact, learn English, and come to understand the importance of manual labor all under the guise of education and citizenship. CF&I's Americanizing of immigrant children rested on a multifaceted approach, based on kindergartens that focused on children's language, ideologies, and labor.

During the Progressive Era, Americanization programs existed throughout the United States. Programs targeted the home as the best space to begin the process of Americanization. Educational programs targeted women, emphasizing domestic duties, such as sanitation and cooking, as a means of Americanizing the family. These programs also focused on ideas of racial uplift and taught individuals that an American style of life was healthier, cleaner, and more productive than that of other ethnicities. In CF&I camps, the kindergarten teachers came to represent the ideal American woman and the American home. Many of these ideas of female gender both for women and for children were part of a larger effort, encouraged on the national level at the turn of the twentieth century, to define gender for men, women, boys, and girls. This defining of gender reflected the supposed crisis of masculinity, especially among Anglo men, and the discovery that many of the men conscripted during World War I were unfit for military service.[16]

Field Days

While the Sociological Department dictated the educational curriculum of children in the classroom in the 1900s, employees, in the 1910s, organized outdoor athletic competitions to participate in during the summer, referred to as "field days." Field day activities included sporting events for the adults and first aid competitions. These athletic competitions incorporated children in performances that placed children within the context of American history through the stories of westward expansion, industrialization, and immigration.

Children participated in the events through performances organized by their schools. At a 1911 field day held in Trinidad, Colorado, the Sopris school organized a parade with children portraying scenes from the history of the region, including "Pike's Expedition," "The Cliff Dwellers," "Coronado Expedition," "Trials of Gold Seekers," "The Spaniards," "Kit Carson–Santa Fe Trail," "The Coal Miners," and "Other Industries." The children dressed as historical characters representing the history of the region, and in the final piece of the performance, titled "Other Industries," children dressed in work garb and posed in front of an American flag.[17] Children acted out the history of the region and may have come to an understanding of their own ethnic heritage and immigrant story. Their placement with the U.S. flag illustrated to them and the audience that they were part of the American story. The images of the flag also reflect ideas of Americanization that CF&I saw as commonplace in the 1910s.

Field day events offered a separate space created by company employees for children to engage in a dialogue about citizenship and Americanization. While an employee controlled the space, the educational curriculum designed by the Sociological Department organized children for the performance. For the mining camps, the educational structure remained present in their lives, even in the summer time, and in a space that employees controlled. Yet the children's participation in the field day clearly illustrates the curriculum that CF&I schools taught, how they visualized the history of the region, and where they saw themselves placed within its context.

Before 1914, the Sociological Department's and Corwin's ideas dominated the curriculum in kindergartens and public schools throughout CF&I–owned mining camps. The true test of endurance of the Americanization curriculum was what programs or ideas endured or were reinstituted by the company after the Ludlow Massacre in the spring of 1914, when Colorado National Guard troops and striking miners engaged in a skirmish that killed as many as two dozen people, including eleven children and two women who suffocated when the tent colony at Ludlow burned. The victims and their families had created the colony in September of 1913 at the beginning of the Great Coalfield War, after the miners announced a strike, and CF&I evicted the striking miners from company-owned housing. Following the massacre, a Senate committee and media reports questioned CF&I's majority stock owners John D. Rockefeller's and John D. Rockefeller Jr.'s involvement in and knowledge of the massacre. In order to deal with the negative

Children posed as workers in "Other Industries" for the 1911 Sopris Field Day. (Courtesy Bessemer Historical Society–CF&I Archives)

congressional attention and the turmoil in southern Colorado, John D. Rockefeller Jr. toured CF&I–owned properties in 1915 and established an Industrial Representation Plan, a company union that focused on the CF&I Company and its employees. The goals of the plan included establishing employee representation throughout CF&I and considering changes in the coal mining camps that would bring about social and industrial betterment.[18]

The CF&I dealt with the backlash from the Ludlow Massacre and continued to encourage the Americanization of its immigrant labor force by partnering with the Young Men's Christian Association (YMCA). The YMCA established bath houses for the men and attempted to curtail the drunkenness of the miners. It also held "better home" contests in the mining camps, rewarding those who created an ideal American home. With the CF&I, the YMCA brought the physical health and abilities of employees and their families to the forefront of the company, through the publication of *The Industrial Bulletin*, field days, and other YMCA-sponsored events.

The *Industrial Bulletin* revealed a close relationship between CF&I management and the YMCA. Numerous articles described YMCA programs and encouraged employees to join. The magazine established the YMCA as a pivotal player in communicating ideas about citizenship. With YMCA support, the company held athletic competitions that set a standard of the "ideal" body, part of a broader movement to raise the fitness levels of all Americans (especially important as the nation debated its role in the Great War raging in Europe). The inclusion of YMCA activities in company publications and the presence of CF&I management at YMCA functions showed that coal camp residents participated in YMCA-planned activities. The association became an integral part of social life in southern Colorado.[19]

While the pageantry of the field days in 1911 included the participation of children, after 1915, the inclusion of children in company events expanded to athletic events organized by the company. Although employees had organized annual field days since 1911, starting in 1915, they became company-sponsored events that dominated the pages of summer issues of the *Industrial Bulletin*. These CF&I–inaugurated field days were an attempt to improve social relations with employees. They included parades and athletic competitions and catered to all members of the family, regardless of age or gender. At these field days, most of the events focused on competition among children, including basketball games and races of all varieties, including 50- and 100-yard dashes and sack races.[20]

After 1915, the CF&I's educational programs focused not only on the teaching of the English language and American history, but also on Anglo-Saxon institutions. The *Industrial Bulletin* argued that "[t]he public school is the nursery of American ideals." CF&I felt that all schools reflected democratic principles that would help educate future leaders. The schools were where the future leaders learned their ideas. But in the mining camps, the schools were essential because "the school master is burdened with the responsibility of making useful American citizens of children whose parents came from every nation of the Old World. It is in the public school that most of these children acquire their first knowledge of free government and Anglo-Saxon institutions."[21] CF&I schools strove to make good American citizens based on a middle-class, "white" point of view. This "white" point of view reflected the broader U.S. culture, which attempted to assimilate immigrants throughout the United States during the Progressive Era. The "white" point of view emphasized that Anglo-Saxon and Protestant ideals remained superior to southern and eastern European immigrants' lifestyles and Catholic and Jewish religious practices. The CF&I continued to embrace the idea of citizenship and education linked to industrial labor. The policy after the Ludlow Massacre concerning the Americanization of immigrant children mirrored what Corwin developed in correlation with the Sociological Department, with curricula and programs focused on democracy and whiteness. While the Ludlow Massacre changed the way CF&I viewed its employees in regard to company unions, it maintained a policy of Americanization. This was further encouraged by U.S. entrance into World War I.

Americanization did not end in the classroom; CF&I educators expected students to extend the learning process into their homes. CF&I implemented a model referred to as the "Sopris Plan," which envisioned Americanization entering the homes through the students. Mary Bradford, Colorado state superintendent of public instruction, described this model in an article published in the *Industrial Bulletin* titled "Educational Progress in Southern Colorado." She argued that the Sopris Plan would assist the larger immigrant population to learn citizenship ideals by encouraging students to share what they had learned with their parents. Students received extra credit in their classes for teaching their mothers and fathers "reading and writing in English and a rudimentary course in history, civics, and citizenship."[22] During the school year, the principal visited the homes of the children to test the knowledge of the parents and to check on sanitation in their homes. When children shared the Americanization process at home and successfully implemented the ideals that they learned in the classroom, the principal and teachers rewarded the children at school. The children became the conduit through which Americanization spread from the coal camps to their homes. CF&I believed schools could teach manual training to boys, domestic labor to girls, and English to both genders. This marked a subtle shift in the curricula at company schools. While in the 1910s teaching revolved around ideals of civics and citizenship based on "whiteness," after the Ludlow Massacre teaching centered on a more expansive rhetoric about Anglo-Saxon dominance, representing the Progressive-Era ideals of Social Darwinism and racial uplift.[23]

CF&I did not limit its vision of Americanization to the classroom or the home; even sports could instill American values. "Civics and the essentials of American government are carefully instilled by the teachers," declared an article in the *Industrial Bulletin*, "while the pupils eagerly learn American games and sports. Baseball is the universal diversion being drawn from every race of Europe."[24] Baseball offered a successful method to teach citizenship because immigrant populations enjoyed playing baseball. With the learning of American sporting events, curriculum expanded beyond the homes and schools and into the leisure time of the students.

Impact of Americanization on Children

The oral history provided by one coal camp child, Eugenie "Gene" Sacco, puts a human face on CF&I's Sociological Department's Industrial Representation Plan, although it suggests that formal schooling was less important than recreational activities. Sacco's 1983 account of growing up in a CF&I mining camp near the Colorado/New Mexico border included her relationship with her Italian immigrant parents and family, with less of an emphasis being placed on education. Sacco recalled attending an accredited high school but admitted that she went to school because there was nothing else for children to do.[25] Sacco remembered little about the curriculum, yet she enjoyed the socialization schooling provided.

Sacco's Italian heritage emerged from her family's traditions and holidays. She recalled the importance of traditional meals and the family's way of life through holiday gatherings such as Christmas and Easter, and the food—especially the Italian desserts—made for these events. Sacco spoke about her parents' Italian lineage, with both parents having been born in Italy and family members still residing there. Sacco related moments when as a child her family engaged in Italian traditions and spoke of Italy. However, Sacco claimed that her parents rarely shared stories about the old country. They spoke about Italy "among themselves, but never around us kids. . . . We were playing. We weren't that interested."[26] While Sacco did not recall the educational curriculum of

Americanization, the process of Americanization for Sacco was accelerated by her parents limiting what they shared about their lives in Italy and was evident by her ability to speak English.

Despite her apparently unmemorable classroom experiences, the influence of Americanization was nevertheless in Sacco's life, especially in the way she spent her leisure time while a child. One of her favorite activities was hiking. Although she did not mention the circumstance of her hiking trips, she may have been part of another Americanization program in the mining camps, where in the 1910s, both the Boy Scouts and the Campfire Girls took the children of CF&I employees into the Colorado mountains close to the mining camps. Reports of the camping expeditions highlighted the open air, hiking, and getting into physical shape for the beginning of school in the fall. CF&I established outdoor programs for children that focused on their time being "divided between recreation and work. Instructions of various kinds will be given, and Red Cross and other patriotic work will be done."[27]

Eugenia Sacco's Americanization was most evident in the images of her childhood that she most fondly remembered. She grew up in a home where Italian was the first language, and her parents knew only enough English to get by. Sacco's leisure time with her family connected her to Italian foods and gatherings, but the recreational activities that she enjoyed the most illustrate the success—at least for Sacco—of the Americanization process of immigrant children in the schools and the impact of the United States on the bodies of immigrant children. Her favorite sport in her childhood, and even as an older woman, was baseball. She recalled playing baseball at school and in her leisure time; indeed, Saturdays and Sundays were reserved for coeducational baseball at the school grounds. Baseball became one of her favorite pastimes, one that she engaged in as often as she could and one that possibly took her away from the household where her parents discussed life in Italy. "We use[d] to play up there a lot.... And then, when we were older, we lived just a few feet from the high school. And on like Saturday and Sunday, we'd go there and play on the high school grounds."[28] Sacco's love of baseball began with a school team and extended into her leisure time outside of the classroom. Sacco's love of baseball continued for over seventy years. She did not see baseball as an attempt to Americanize her, and she may not have seen baseball as a masculine sport (she also recalled playing coed baseball). For her, playing baseball was simply a pastime that gave her the ability to control her space. Her participation in this pastime illustrated that the Americanization process extended beyond academics and the school day into the children's neighborhoods on the weekend.

CF&I dictated an educational curriculum that focused on American citizenship: at home children taught their parents what they had learned, thereby completing the process of Americanizing the household. Children like Sacco often did not learn Italian history and traditions (other than a few holiday meals) because they busily engaged in an American leisure activity or because their parents chose not to speak about the past. While the schools taught children curriculum to Americanize them, the children participated in this process by choosing a sporting event over family conversations, and compliant parents held discussions about their home countries and ethnic heritage when their children were absent.

During the Progressive Era, the process of Americanization happened in the schools, but American ideals were also brought home by immigrant children, where they flourished in the absence of discussions promoting the culture and history of the non-American past. From 1901 to 1918, the process of Americanization at the Colorado Fuel and Iron Company structured an educational curriculum in which the children of miners, many of them immigrants from Europe and Mexico or migrants from New Mexico, lived in a constructed landscape where CF&I composed their daily lives and created the educational curriculum and leisure time of the coal camps as spaces in which CF&I could implement Americanization.

NOTES

1. Donna Graham, "Knock on Wood: Growing Up among the Italian People: An Oral History Project," Oral History of Berwind, Colorado, 1983, Scamehorn Collection, folder #10, 8–19, Colorado Fuel and Iron Company Archives and Bessemer Historical Society (CFI/BHS), Pueblo, Colorado.
2. H. Lee Scamehorn, *Mill & Mine: The CF&I in the Twentieth Century* (Lincoln: University of Nebraska Press, 1992); Gunther Peck, *Reinventing Free Labor: Padrones and Immigrant Workers in the North American West, 1880–1930* (Cambridge: Cambridge University Press, 2000).
3. Maria Montoya, "Creating an American Home: Contest and Accommodation in Rockefeller's Company Towns," in Vicki L. Ruiz and John R. Chavez, eds.,

Memories and Migrations: Mapping Boricua and Chicana Histories (Chicago: University of Illinois Press, 2008), 31; Sarah Deutsch, *No Separate Refuge: Culture, Class, and Gender on an Anglo-Hispanic Frontier, 1880–1940* (New York: Oxford University Press, 1987); George Sanchez, *Becoming Mexican American: Ethnicity, Culture, and Identity in Chicano Los Angeles, 1900–1945* (New York: Oxford University Press, 1995); Sandra Schackel, *Social Housekeepers: Women Shaping Public Policy in New Mexico, 1920–1940* (Albuquerque: University of New Mexico Press, 1992); Frank Van Nuys, *Americanizing the West: Race, Immigrants, and Citizenship, 1890–1930* (Lawrence: University Press of Kansas, 2002).
4. Rick Clyne, *Coal People: Life in Southern Colorado's Company Towns, 1890–1930* (Denver: Colorado Historical Society, 1999), 1–14; Colorado Fuel and Iron Company, *First Annual Report of the Colorado Fuel and Iron Company, November 1, 1892–June 30, 1893* (Denver, 1893), 15–68; Colorado Fuel and Iron Company, *Second Annual Report of the Colorado Fuel and Iron Co. for the Year Ending June 30, 1894* (Denver, 1894); *Industrial Bulletin,* August 23, 1916; Thomas Andrews, *Killing for Coal: America's Deadliest Labor War* (Cambridge, MA: Harvard University Press, 2008).
5. *Camp and Plant,* December 14, 1901.
6. Clyne, *Coal People,* 91.
7. *Camp and Plant,* September 20, 1902.
8. *Camp and Plant,* September 20 and 22, 1902.
9. *Camp and Plant,* November 22, 1902.
10. Ibid.
11. *Camp and Plant,* March 1, 1902.
12. Ibid.
13. Clyne, *Coal People,* 91.
14. Sinfrosa Vigil Oral Interview, May 1, 1971, Colorado Coal Mining Project, OH 550, pp. 1–3, Center for Oral and Public History, California State University at Fullerton (CSUF).
15. Aladino Lopez Oral Interview, May 22, 1971, Colorado Coal Mining Project, OH 582, pp. 6, 10, 28, Center for Oral and Public History, CSUF.
16. Deutsch, *No Separate Refuge*; Montoya, "Creating an American Home"; Sanchez, *Becoming Mexican American*; and Schackel, *Social Housekeepers*. Nina Mjagki and Margarett Spratt, eds., *Men and Women Adrift* (New York: New York University Press, 1997).
17. "Pictures of pupils of public school, Sopris camp of the Colorado Fuel and Iron Company," Welborn Scrapbook 1915, CFI/BHS. Fawn-Amber Montoya, "From Mexicans to Citizens: Colorado Fuel and Iron's Representation of Nuevo Mexicans, 1901–1919," in *Journal of the West* (Santa Barbara, CA: ABC-CLIO, Fall 2006).
18. Jonathan Rees, *Representation and Rebellion: The Rockefeller Plan at the Colorado Fuel and Iron Company, 1914–1942* (Boulder: University Press of Colorado, 2010).

19. Fawn-Amber Montoya, "Mines, Massacres, and Memories: Colorado Fuel and Iron's Creation of a Community in Southern Colorado, 1880–1919" (PhD Dissertation, University of Arizona, 2007); *Industrial Bulletin,* April 26, 1916, and December 22, 1915; Marc Horger, "Basketball and Athletic Control at Oberlin College, 1896–1915," *Journal of Sport History* 23 (Fall 1996): 256–83; Nina Mjagki, and Margarett Spratt, eds., *Men and Women Adrift*; Peggy Pascoe, *Relations of Rescue* (New York: Oxford University Press, 1990); Debra Shattock, "Bats, Balls, and Books: Baseball and Higher Education for Women at Three Eastern Women's Colleges, 1866–1891," *Journal of Sport History* 19 (Summer 1992): 91–109; Patricia Vertinjski, "Sexual Equality and the Legacy of Catherine Beecher," *Journal of Sport History* 6 (Spring 1979): 38–49.
20. *Industrial Bulletin,* May 27, 1916.
21. *Industrial Bulletin,* August 23, 1916.
22. Ibid.
23. Matthew Frye Jacobsen, *Whiteness of a Different Color: European Immigrants and the Alchemy of Race* (Cambridge, MA: Harvard University Press, 1998); Elizabeth Grace Hale, *Making Whiteness: The Culture of Segregation in the South, 1890–1940* (New York: Pantheon, 1998).
24. *Industrial Bulletin,* August 23, 1916.
25. Graham, "Knock on Wood."
26. Ibid.
27. *Industrial Bulletin,* October 31, 1916, and July 31, 1917.
28. Graham, "Knock on Wood."

3

Of Families or Individuals?

Southern Child Workers and the Progressive Crusade for Child Labor Regulation, 1899–1920

GWENDOLINE ALPHONSO

In 1893 ten-year-old Flossie Moore's life changed irrevocably. On the brink of insolvency, her family had been farming on rented land in the Piedmont countryside when her father died at the age of forty-three. Suddenly her mother found herself in dire circumstances and responsible for eight children whose ages ranged from infancy to nineteen. After harvesting that year's crops and seeking the advice of kin, Mrs. Moore moved her family to the textile mill in Bynum, North Carolina; as Flossie remembered,

> [T]here were several of the men that come out and met first, trying to decide what to do. . . . They knew about Bynum, and it was a good little place to live. . . . And of course the cotton mill was running here then. And the ones that was old enough. . . . Well, I went to work at ten years old.

So began the Moores' new life as wage laborers in the mills, living in a company house in the mill village, younger children earning along with their mother and older siblings.[1]

Children, Families, and the Industrialization of the Southern Countryside

The Moore family experience was similar to that faced by thousands of families across the South in the Progressive era (1890s to 1920s). It illustrates the turbulent dynamic of industrialization occurring then in that region, as well as the upheavals in family life that followed in its wake, often culminating in the entry of children into wage labor.[2]

The following essay focuses on this transformative period at the turn of the twentieth century and investigates the ways in which child workers in the South began to occupy the national spotlight and became the objects of intense policy debate. It demonstrates the competing ways in which children, particularly their family relationships, were conceptualized by three key policy actors at the time: progressive reformers who crusaded for child labor regulation, southern industrialists and their supporters who opposed it, and members of Congress who interrogated them. Building on the nineteenth-century legacy of variation in northern and southern legal codes and in the labor practices of the two regions, this essay argues that northern proponents and southern opponents of child labor legislation used different understandings of children and families when debating policy in Congress in the Progressive era, illustrating two sectional ways in which children were conceptualized in that period.

By analyzing witness testimony recorded in the transcripts of congressional committee hearings and the content of congressional bills, papers, and reports, I assemble two sets of conceptual frameworks of children and their families. One set of conceptions, used by southern opponents of child labor legislation, was based on agrarian, southern family experiences, which I term as "relational" child ideals, and emphasized the organic nature of families, stressing the interdependence between the child and the family and viewing young people in relation to their parents, as inseparable parts of the family unit. The family was front and center in this framework, and children, including child workers, were imagined wholly within the context of their families, indivisible from the family whole. Notwithstanding the emphasis on mutuality and family interdependence, relational child ideals entailed an abiding expectation that parents (especially fathers) exercised authority over their children.

In the South, the family labor system used in mills and other industries was deliberately constructed to build on and reify this ideal of familial, relational systems of labor, recruiting and employing whole packages of family labor and not individual child or teenage labor. When farms failed, southern migrant families deliberately sought work in industries where they could continue to live together as intact families. Martin E. Lowe, for example, needing to augment the meager income of the family's failing farm in the mountains of North Carolina, had previously cooked for a railroad camp fifteen miles away from his home. This arrangement had permitted him only intermittent, often infrequent, visits with his family. Martin describes moving his family to Poe Mill in Greenville, South Carolina: "If I have to go to public works, why not move to them where it would be in my family?" Mill owners also provided housing on a family basis, depending on the total combined number of working members. Martin Lowe's family, with three adults and six children, all of whom worked in the mill, was eligible for a single-floor, four-room house; as Martin recounted, "if they [all] hadn't [worked], we couldn't have got no four-room house. . . . Just a man and his wife working couldn't get but two rooms." Family, children, and work were thus intertwined in the emerging wage world of southern industry, and this interdependence was defended in Congress by southern industrialists and their supporters.[3]

Despite the widespread prevalence of the family-based relational framework of the child, industrialization in the region also opened the door to new, more child-centered ideals, which this essay terms as "individual" child ideals. This second set of ideals, more northern in character, drew sharp lines between children and adult and highlighted not the organic family relation between child and adult members, but the uniqueness and significance of children as a separate class of persons. The onset of industrialization having occurred much earlier in the North, individual child ideals were well entrenched there by the Progressive era. Throughout the nineteenth century reformers of the child-saving movement in the urban North had been emphasizing child welfare in their campaigns, calling attention to children and to the problems and issues specific to them.[4]

In progressive reformers' national crusade to protect and "save" children as a uniquely vulnerable class, regulation of child labor became the primary focus in this era. In the North, the kinds of child labor to which the reformers were most opposed (in factories and on streets) were rapidly declining by the Progressive era as a result of compulsory education laws, massive inflows of inexpensive immigrant labor, and technological innovations such as the widespread use of telephones instead of messenger boys. However, the later timing of southern industrialization meant that an increasing proportion of child workers was now laboring in southern textile mills and manufacturing industries. Thus during this period, when the debate over child labor regulation became nationalized, southern child workers became the primary objects of such policy attention.[5]

The triumph of the progressive crusaders and the realization of national child labor legislation marked the victory of the individual framework over the relational one, the success of reformers' northern ideals of the child over a more agrarian and southern one, a policy victory that did not reflect or resonate in the ideals and practices of the children themselves or those of their families or neighbors in the South.[6]

Histories of childhood and child labor in the Progressive era have long highlighted the ideational divide between elite reformers and working-class families. Reformers are shown to have espoused a middle-class ideal of the sheltered or nurtured child while working-class families, particularly those of new immigrants, are presented as clinging to an ideal of a useful, prepared child, one who shared family responsibility. However, this essay presents an alternative conceptual lens through which to interpret the history of child labor contestations at the turn of the twentieth century. It argues that the battle over child labor in the Progressive era was not merely a battle of substantively different ideals of childhood pitting "useful" against "sheltered." Instead, it was also a contestation more fundamentally between alternative understandings of children and their relation (or lack of it) to their families. In this way, the paper supports and develops a prevailing interpretation found in scholarship on southern mill and factory children that places family more centrally to the experiences of child workers in the South.[7]

While the conceptual framework assembled in this essay does not exclude other classifications of childhood and/or children during the Progressive era, there are advantages to the conceptualization offered here. First, the "relational v. individual" categorization connects the history of children to the history of other legal and social institutions, opening the door for future comparative scholarship. For instance, the triumph of the individual understanding of children over a more relational emphasis on families bears resemblance to legal and conceptual transformations in the meaning of marriage, as in the transformation from the understanding of gender relations as male and female familial roles (wife and husband) to a more modern understanding of gender relations between individuals (man and woman). Secondly, "relational v. individual" is arguably wider than other prevailing categorizations and more attentive to regional differences in ideation and experiences of child work.[8]

The first section in this essay systematically analyzes legislative bills, legal codes, and policy developments related to child welfare and child labor policy in Congress in the Progressive era, highlighting the competing notions of children and families in the North and South. Thereafter, the second section describes and assembles the two frameworks and their associated ideals of children, parents, and work. This section is more qualitative, using the testimony of reformers, industrialists, as well as bureaucratic investigators, all of which was presented before Congress from its 56th session (1900–1902) to its 66th (1918–1920); the objective is to analyze the various ideals of children and their families discussed in child labor policy debates in the Progressive period.

Progressive Politics, Child Welfare Policy, and the Southern Practice of Child Labor

The Progressive era was characterized by a political climate rife with the fervor of reform. Reformist groups decried the excesses and vagaries of the patronage-based political and laissez-faire economic systems and advocated instead widespread civil and social reform. In so doing, interest groups (radicals, agrarians, socialists, progressives, etc., as well as single-issue civic and religious groups) were active directly in society as well as in politics and attempted to press their agenda on the public, Congress, and state legislatures. In a style of politics familiar today, cultural and moral issues infused a variety of social movements, such as temperance and women's suffrage.[9]

The 1900 census had revealed that two million children were working in mills, mines, fields, factories, stores, and on city streets across the United States; this sparked a national debate over child labor led by progressive reformers of the child-saving movement. The so-called child savers had been actively engaging with issues specific to children since the early nineteenth century, focusing on child poverty, juvenile delinquency, and child abuse. However, the 1890s ushered in a new phase. Child savers now invoked and grafted new progressive principles such as professionalization, scientific expertise, and rational administration onto the prevailing "moral outrage" over child exploitation, calling for an expanded role of the state and of trained experts in addressing problems related to children.[10]

As the child-saving movement gathered national momentum through the Progressive period, it gained many allies among members of Congress. Diverse bills relating to the protection and welfare of children were debated and introduced in Congress. These bills called for unprecedented intervention by the federal government in several ways, including the appointment of a commission to investigate child poverty, the public protection of maternal and infant health, mandates for the support of dependent children by fathers, provisions for the institutional care of "feeble-minded" and other dependent children, and the establishment of a Federal Children's Bureau. The northern, urban character of the child-saving movement and of social progressivism in general was also reflected in Congress. Bill sponsorship in Congress demonstrates this regional bias: members from the more urban regions of the Northeast and Midwest, as opposed to those from the agrarian South and West, cumulatively sponsored over 80 percent of all child-welfare bills introduced in Congress from 1899 to 1921.[11]

The legislative campaign to protect children had at least two central objects. On the one hand, reformers sought to expand government responsibility for children's welfare through mothers' pensions, expanded institutional resources, etc. On the other hand, progressive groups and members of Congress also turned to policy to regulate working-class parents by seeking, among other things, mandates for parental support, criminalization of those who "abandoned" minor children, and also institutionalization of middle-class standards of health, nutrition, and hygiene in infant and child care. Thus, among the child-related bills introduced in Congress, a sizeable 33 percent addressed issues of parental regulation. The concern with regulating parents was once again more prominent among members of Congress from the more urban northern and midwestern states, almost half of whose child welfare bills pertained to parental regulation. In contrast, of the many fewer bills relating to child welfare introduced by members from the South and the West, only approximately two out of ten such bills contained provisions directed at parents and their regulation. For northern progressives, the welfare and protection of children thus often implied limiting parental rights and authority over their children, a position less palatable to the more family-oriented, tradition-bound members of the South.[12]

Of all the child welfare campaigns during the Progressive period, none was as potent as the progressive crusade against child labor. Progressives regarded child workers as an exploited class similar to erstwhile slaves, viewing their campaign "as the twentieth-century equivalent of the abolitionist campaign to end slavery." The campaign initially focused on state and local legislatures. However, by the 1910s, lax enforcement and the nonuniformity of laws across the states persuaded reformers of the necessity of federal legislation. The first national bill to prohibit child labor was introduced in Congress by Senator Albert J. Beveridge (R-IN) in December 1906 but did not garner sufficient support to be enacted. Thereafter the Beveridge bill, or its equivalent, the Kenyon bill, introduced by another midwestern senator, William S. Kenyon (R-IA), was introduced in every Congress from 1906 to 1914. In the sixty-third Congress (1914), two further bills by progressive-minded representatives were introduced. The first, the Copley-Poindexter bill, was named after Ira Copley (R-IL) and Miles Poindexter (Prog-WA), and the other, the Palmer-Owen bill, was introduced jointly by Mitchell Palmer (D-PA) and Senator Robert Owen (D-OK). The latter was passed in the House on February 15, 1915, but killed in the Senate on the last day of its session. In 1916, both the Democratic and Republican national party platforms finally called for the immediate enactment of a federal law prohibiting all child labor; this culminated in the passage and signing of the Keating-Owen bill by President Wilson on September 1, 1916. The law was soon challenged, and in 1918 in *Hammer v. Dagenhart*, the U.S. Supreme Court declared the law unconstitutional, ruling that the federal government had no power to regulate manufacturing in individual states.[13]

Whereas national child labor regulation was spearheaded by northern-based, urban progressive reformers and their supporters in Congress, their targets were primarily southern child workers. Not only was the incidence of child work rising in the South rather than the North, but southern states also had much lower standards of child labor regulation, making the southern child textile worker the primary focus of reformers. As Florence Kelley, general secretary of the National Consumers League, proclaimed before Congress, "[W]e cannot go on having favored children in the Northwest" who "shall not work . . . [and] are kept in school, throughout the eighth grade" and "oppressed, helot children in the Southeast."[14]

Both proponents and opponents of child labor regulation acknowledged that the rapid increase in national child labor rates was the result of recent southern industrialization, particularly in the emerging cotton mills of the South. Speaking before the House Committee on Labor, southern manufacturers in 1914 described the "conditions which confront . . . the South," namely, "the growth of cotton manufacturing . . . [which] has been very great within the last 20 years," with the number of spindles in operation in southern mills quadrupling since 1890. Thus, they claimed, "necessarily there have had to be certain conditions which were novel to us . . . and there necessarily had to be readjustments, and the child-labor question was one of those." Florence Kelley acknowledged in the same hearing that "one State after another changes from an agricultural State to a manufacturing State. . . . [T]here are more children under 16 years old working to-day . . . because our manufacturing industries [have] increased stupendously."[15]

Southern industrialists and their promoters, however, used the newness of industrialization in the South to defend the practice of child work, arguing that the very success of the South depended on its availability. A preeminent industrialist from South Carolina, Mr. Lewis Parker, made just such a case to members of Congress: "It [is] very essential . . . that there be an opportunity for the child to work if there is to be a migration from the soil to the industrial centers." South Carolina, he stated, "cannot possibly gravitate from a condition of agriculturalism [sic] to a condition of industrialism without the employment of minors."[16]

Reformers challenged the notion that child workers were indispensable to southern industrialization, instead viewing the phenomenon of child employment as the result of deliberate choice, mostly by avaricious manufacturers interested in increasing their profit margins. For example, the southern secretary of the National Child Labor Committee, A. J. McKelway, a frequent witness before Congress, wrote an influential pamphlet in 1913 on "Child Labor in the Cotton Mills," calling it a system of "modern feudalism." In the pamphlet McKelway described southern cotton manufacturers as "feudal lords" who used "excessive profits" to grow more powerful as employees became more helpless, claiming, "[T]here is no reason under heaven, save that of unenlightened greed, why the same industry in the South should not be put upon a better basis than anywhere else in the world, so that it shall become one of which we may all be proud, rather than one whose profits smell of blood."[17]

Despite the intense contention over federal child labor regulation in the 1910s, a vast majority of states, including southern ones, had had some form of restriction on the employment of children since the 1800s. In an annual report to Congress in 1903, the commissioner of education reported that about thirty states had laws on their books regulating child labor in certain select occupations, such as in mines, manufacturing industries, and mercantile establishments, all described as occupations "dangerous to the life, limb, morals, or health of children."[18]

Crucial substantive differences, however, existed between southern laws and those in the rest of the country, illustrating not only the different levels of commitment to restricting child labor but also a qualitatively different approach to child workers themselves. For one, the age at which children's employment was permitted in the South was comparatively lower than that in most northern states. On average, southern laws regulated labor only of children under twelve (some only applied to children under ten, such as in South Carolina), thus permitting the employment of all children over that age. Most northern states, however, restricted employment even for older children, permitting only those over fourteen years to be employed.[19]

Moreover, most southern legal codes contained a family provision that was unlike any found in northern child labor laws. A majority of southern codes made exceptions for children from poor families, families whose economic survival depended on a child's wages. For example, Alabama prohibited the employment of children (twelve years and younger) in factories "unless orphans, or children of the widowed or disabled," and Maryland prohibited such employment "unless self, widowed mother, or invalid father [was] solely dependent on [child's] employment." Other southern states had broader family provisions, exempting all children from child labor regulations provided they had the "written consent of parent and county judge"; in some, such as Mississippi, the regulation of any child work was limited only to the requirement of parental consent, in such cases permitting for any and all employment "away from home."[20]

Thus much more than others, southern child labor laws evidenced a relational conception of a child as someone embedded within a family and within the purview of a parent's moral and legal authority. Child work was considered a family affair, a result of collective conditions facing the family, rather than an oppressive condition unique to a class of vulnerable persons. This organic model of family and child, found within the relational approach, was endemic to the hierarchical, agrarian, southern social order and has been shown by legal historians to have also pervaded various other laws of the nineteenth-century South, including miscegenation, rape, incest, and child custody laws. This southern ideal was in contrast to a contractual model of domestic-relations laws more evident instead in nineteenth-century northern legal codes, which were centered on individuals rather than on interdependent domestic relations.[21]

The legacy of region-specific legal models of children and families can also be found in the testimony of witnesses appearing before Congress. Using the relational framework, southern opponents to child labor regulation emphasized an organic model of family in which parent-child self-regulation trumped government intervention—a view that was directly challenged by reformers who viewed the protection of individual children as paramount, instead requiring state regulation and superseding all parental authority or family relation.

Relational versus Individual Child Frameworks

In their testimony before Congress, proponents and opponents of child labor regulation differed sharply in their views regarding (a) children, what it meant to be a child and to have a childhood, (b) parents, as helping or harming the welfare of children, and (c) work, whether it conflicted with or complemented childhood and citizenship development.

Progressive reformers viewed children in a very particular way: as a unique class of fragile and vulnerable persons. They imagined child workers as helpless "little sufferers" whose physical and moral growth was eroded by the rigors of work. Several such depictions are found, for instance, in the testimony of Elizabeth Watson, who was employed in 1914 by the New York City–based International Child Welfare League to investigate child labor conditions in the canneries and cotton mills of the South. In her testimony she recounts the case of a boy who "had been worked too hard in one of the canneries" in Mississippi since the age of six and who at thirteen developed "seven abscesses one after the other" on his knee, needing the "bone to be scraped" and leading the doctor to conclude that the boy "would probably be lame (for) the rest of his life." Similarly, Watson remembered "a little girl in an Alabama mill" who "was so small . . . she looked about ten years old" and "not more than 4 feet high . . . [with] a little, old face." The girl was sitting on the stairs outside the room where she worked, with "her feet all wrapped up in some old rags" and on being asked what that was for, "she said she was so tired that she felt like her backbone would go up into her head"; other children were described as "lying on the floor" from exhaustion because "no seats were provided to them," with "no opportunity to go outside . . . all [of] the time [working] in that close, humid atmosphere, amid the noise that prevails at all times in the cotton mills." Watson noted the poignant example of another "little girl" named Margaret C., from Biloxi, Mississippi, whose hands were a "mass of little festering sores" from shrimp picking in the canneries. When Watson asked her about the tin can she was carrying, the girl reportedly replied, "Oh, that is the alum for my hands. I picked shrimp, and they are very sore."[22]

In addition to physical injury caused by hazardous working conditions, progressive witnesses also pointed to cramped, proximate living arrangements in southern mill villages as harming children's moral development. In a report submitted to Congress, Eunice Sinclair, a field agent for the National Child Labor Committee, described the living conditions in the village of Richmond Mill, Laurel Hill, North Carolina, thus: "[T]he homes are absolutely wretched, with roofs leaking, floors falling in and steps broken down . . . [T]he immorality among the people is unspeakably gross. Illegitimacy is prevalent in almost every family . . . [T]here is no Sunday school and church services are only once a month." "It seems incredible," Sinclair reported, "that such conditions can prevail anywhere."[23]

For their part, witnesses for southern industry painted a much rosier picture of child workers, attempting to counter the image of them as a class of exploited "little sufferers." Instead, many would use examples of children from so-called show mills to emphasize the effect of "good mill" management on the overall well-being of children. Mr. J. M. Davis, superintendent of Newberry Cotton Mills, offered as exhibits pictures of healthy-looking children "showing the[ir] character," describing the "sanitary conditions" of their homes and the several opportunities for character building and recreation afforded to them at his mill, such as Boy Scouts, Sunday school, "playgrounds, recreation grounds, and a bathhouse." He recounted the case of a "remarkably smart" boy who worked at the mill from a young age but was also very successful in school, who "won every medal in high school and the Newberry College, and is now going to be an Episcopal minister; that is, he will finish college this year."[24]

Those in favor of child work attributed greater agency to children, particularly to teenage boys, than did progressive reformers, arguing in favor of their prerogative to work, especially amidst family poverty. Congressman Milton Romjue (D-MO) recalled his own example, of being a "young, strong fellow" who "stayed out of school to help my people," stating that "if temporary poverty should overtake my parents, I would much prefer to work for a few months than to have my parents rely on charity." In contrast, reformers did not credit children with sufficient maturity to make weighty decisions, such as whether or not to work; for them even family poverty was not a legitimate reason. Mrs. E. K. Bushee, the executive secretary of the Juvenile Protection Association, responded to Congressman Romjue by arguing that "a child of 14 or 15 would probably feel that he wanted to go out and help his family himself, but . . . that child ought to be protected against his own immature judgment."[25]

Southern textile workers, when recounting the circumstances of how they first began working in the mill as children, often described a combination of events, from voluntarily "helping" their parents and older siblings, out of a sense of family loyalty or personal curiosity, to being introduced to work or "put in" to work by their parents. Unlike the optimistic picture presented by manufacturers, most manufacturing work in the Progressive era was hard, and conditions were indeed harsh for workers, including children. Nevertheless, there is evidence that child workers exercised far greater agency than the reformers' depiction of helpless, compliant "little sufferers," often going against the wishes of their employers and parents. For example, in a 1910 report, federal investigators note cases in which children refused to comply with overseers who tried to hide them during inspections: "one boy was locked in the supply room, but beat the door with a piece or iron until the overseer had to let him out"; "others of the children refused to hide, and the overseer . . . was angry and cursed and scolded them. He sent several home, and one little boy 10 years old who refused to go was locked in the broom closet."[26]

There is evidence that children also independently alleviated the drudgery of their work by spontaneous play; this too was often to the chagrin of their employers and parents. In their recollections, textile workers describe the spinning room in mills of their youth, "generally known as the children's department," in which supervisors were often beside themselves trying to manage their young workers, who found much merriment in "hanging onto the shafting belts as the machinery slowly started and riding towards the twenty-foot ceiling," engaging in "a game of catch, with a ball improvised from yarn . . . while waiting for the machines to fill," and "just plain scuffling" or participating in childish pranks such as "spitting tobacco juice out of the mill windows onto the heads of unwary boss men below."[27]

In differentiating childhood as a sheltered stage of life, separate from adulthood and centered instead on schooling and leisure rather than on work, reformers were unable to appreciate the natural ingenuity of child workers to combine play and work. Instead, progressives insisted that "wholesome" children's play occupy a wholly separate sphere, segregated in form and place from adult/work life. For instance, Dr. Luther Halsey Gulick, president of the Playground Association of America (founded in 1906), in support of a bill sponsored by the National Child Labor Committee to establish a Children's Bureau, emphatically stated,

"Children need sand piles, seesaws, swings, places where they can play ball, and the like. Children also need wholesome play traditions." The crusade to abolish child work was thus also a crusade "to safeguard the leisure of childhood," to carve out and separate a sphere for childish play; other forms of play, especially those in which children combined work and play, were imagined instead as inappropriate, impeding child workers from growing up "wholesome."[28]

In sum, through play, in decisions of where and how to work, or in refusing to comply with the rules of overseers or parents, child workers often navigated their own lives far more than reformers liked or imagined. In their individualist worldview, reformers differentiated children from adults and instead advocated that children be "protected from their own immature judgments," especially the decision to work. In contrast, the testimony of southern industrialists reveals that they imbued children with more capacity to combine work and school or to take an active role in alleviating family poverty.

Secondly, reformers and manufacturers also sharply varied in their conceptions of parents. For reformers, parents were responsible for their children and not the other way around. In their framework the fragility and vulnerability of children meant that, as Charlotte Perkins Gilman claimed in 1906, "the family has no claim on the child comparable to the child's claim on the family." Progressives viewed working-class parents, especially those who put their children to work, in one of two ways. Some, such as A. J. McKelway, offered a more charitable, albeit paternalistic, view and presented southern parents as "ignorant, indifferent or poverty-stricken," being either fresh from the farm or themselves having been "condemned for life" and "enslaved" since a young age in textile work; he described the parents of child mill workers as themselves helpless to resist the temptation of relatively high child wages offered by greedy cotton manufacturers.[29]

Other reformers had a more disparaging view, placing the blame of child work more squarely on parents. They argued that if children worked, it simply meant that "the parent or parents or other members of the family were not doing all they should and could do." For them, parents put self-interest and often indolence before their own responsibility to their children. In the 1906 bill to incorporate the National Child Labor Committee as a national organization, one of the organization's central purposes was thus listed as "rais[ing] the standard of parental responsibility with respect to the employment of children."[30]

In congressional testimony progressive witnesses such as Florence Kelley and Mrs. E. K. Bushee repeatedly alluded to irresponsible fathers who lived off the labor of their children. Commonly known as "tin-bucket-toters" or "cotton mill drones," idle southern fathers were decried by witnesses as a "very shiftless set": "[W]henever there is any work," testified one, "they send their children into the factory, and the children work, at any age and unlimited hours," while the fathers "mostly just sit there." Members of Congress too were concerned about this phenomenon and often questioned witnesses about fatherly indolence. Industrialists responded by presenting these cases as exceptions that did not deserve national regulation. For example, in his response to Representative Edward Keating's (D-CO) question as to the existence of such "pathetic cases" of idle mill fathers, William Kitchin, ex-governor of North Carolina, replied that although "there grew up a habit of some of the men moving to the mills and working their children in the mills while they were loafing," in Roxboro, North Carolina, they "indicted some of the loafers . . . and broke up that condition." This was confirmed by federal investigators in 1910. In the "Report on Condition of Woman and Child Wage-Earners in the United States," investigators in the office of the commissioner of labor found virtually no voluntary cases of southern fatherly idleness in textile mills despite the fact that "much has been written of the idle father—that able-bodied, able-to-work ne'er-do-well who in the South has been stigmatized 'the cotton mill drone.'"[31]

For crusaders against child labor, however, southern fathers were much to blame, being also domineering patriarchs who clung to premodern ideals of family honor and parental authority. Wrote Elbert Hubbard, a prominent thinker and writer on the issue of child labor, "[F]or the cracker father . . . it is a question of 'rights, sah,' and he is the head of the family and you must not meddle—his honor is at stake." Whether lazy, domineering, ignorant, or constrained by poverty, southern parents could not be trusted to ensure the welfare of their own children; instead, reformers imagined the state and trained experts to be more appropriate.[32]

On their part, manufacturers and mill supervisors in their testimony challenged the progressive depiction of southern parents as neglectful or self-interested. Instead, they argued that these parents were just like all others in that they too considered their children's best interests. "We say a great deal has been written about the oppression of the child in the southern mills," declared the superintendent of Newberry Mills in Newberry, South Carolina, to Congress; "[W]hy, do you not know that the southern father and mother love their children as well as any other father and mother?" Dr. T. W. Long, a doctor practicing among the mill villages of Roanoke Rapids, North Carolina, similarly testified about the families there:

> Children whose families can support them do not work in the mills. They send them to school until they have finished their course; that is, those families who can afford to do that . . . but there are innumerable instances where it is absolutely necessary for the children to work in the mills . . . [to] take car[e] of the rest of the family, those who are not big enough to work.[33]

These witnesses thus contended that parents of child workers put their children to work out of economic necessity. Mr. S. F. Patterson, general manager of the Roanoke Mills in Roanoke, North Carolina, attested that child work existed "because it is a necessity, not from a matter of choice . . . [J]ust as rapidly as these people get in comfortable condition, so that they can send their children to school, they are sending them." There is indeed evidence to support the position that mill workers and other southern parents were indeed interested in schooling their children, many of whom supported and, in some cases, called for compulsory education. However, what Mr. Patterson and other industry witnesses neglected to mention was that in almost every instance, due to the combined actions of mill managers, children who were not keen to attend school, and parents, "the mill came first always, the school after."[34]

Further, in contrast to the more paternalistic depiction of mill parents as themselves passive victims of manufacturers' greed, witnesses for southern industry exonerated themselves by attributing a more active role to parents. For example, H. R. Fitzgerald, secretary and treasurer of the Riverside and Dan River cotton mills in Danville, Virginia, in his testimony to Congress, unequivocally stated that he was "not an advocate of child labor" and he did "not think there was any profit to any mill employing children from 10, 11, or 12 years of age." He claimed, however, that mills employed children "not because the mill sought and wanted child help. It was because the family sought and wanted an outlet for the only thing they have as a means of support."[35]

Much like the reformers, albeit arguing for self—not state—regulation, witnesses for southern mills, such as Mr. S. F. Patterson, also made references to the inherent "pride" and "independence" of southern mill parents; "[T]hose people down there are proud. . . . They are native-born American people and just as proud as anybody else, and they do not want their boys to beg or steal or starve." Mr. W. E. Beattie, president-treasurer of the Piedmont Manufacturing Company in Greenville, South Carolina, spoke of the independent organization of mill families, who so strongly opposed increasing the permitted age limit for child work that they "without any suggestion on our part . . . sent delegates to the [state] legislature in Columbia [and] paid the expenses of the delegates themselves." The families were described as having succeeded in convincing the state legislature that the proposal was "emphatically contrary to the wishes of the people" and that they "would rather not be interfered with."[36]

Apart from hardship and necessity, however, southern parents also put their children to work because they believed in the intrinsic value of work, as historian James Schmidt has demonstrated. Southern industrial workers, he writes, held "producer values" that they brought from the countryside into industrial life, which "placed a premium on the physical production of the world's goods and asserted that those who made them comprised the true citizenry of a republic." Within this agrarian-based worldview, "work" built character and kept children from idleness and laziness.[37]

In their testimony before Congress, opponents of child labor regulation made numerous such references to "work" as complementing childhood and school. Mill managers, particularly those who themselves had been "mill boys," pointed to the long-term usefulness of having acquired the habit of work in their childhood. Mr. Lewis Parker, a wealthy industrialist, recalled that his father put every one of this children to work in the mill because "he believed as sincerely as I believe that the best way for a child to do is to work . . . because we believe work is education. . . . He wished to impress upon us the fact that work was necessary and that we could not exist and go through life without working." Members of Congress, such as John I. Nolan (R-CA), also recounted their own childhood experiences as illustrating the value of work on a child's character: "I had to go to work when I was 5 or 6 years old, and I had to work all the time, and the boys who grew up around in my country, more of them went to the bad from not working than those who had to work."[38]

On the other hand, progressive reformers invoked an ideal of a more educated citizenship in contrast to producer citizenship. In support of a bill to fund a federal investigation into woman and child labor, the House Committee on Labor in 1906 acknowledged that the "education of children" follows the "theory that future citizens should be intelligent." President Theodore Roosevelt similarly urged a federal investigation into child labor because "the children of to-day are those who to-morrow will shape the destiny of our land, and we can not afford to neglect them." To progressives, the lack of prohibition against child work amounted to a profound neglect of the nation's most important resource: children. Lillian Wald, founder of the Henry Street Settlement in New York City, thus wrote, whereas "corn, pigs, and other commodities of commerce are wisely watched over with parental care," the "child crop" was being neglected; instead she urged the national government to take a "parental lead" in "the protective care and bringing up of our children, and the building up of the best citizenship possible." In the sheltered-individual-child worldview of reformers, education, not work, was the pathway to successful citizenship.[39]

Conclusion

An analysis of congressional evidence demonstrates the emergence of a bifurcated, regional understanding of children within national policy debates in the Progressive era. Proponents and opponents of child labor regulation offered distinct ideational frameworks, individual versus relational, each containing its own set of ideals regarding children, parents, work, and childhood. Progressive reformers offered an individual framework in which they presented children, notably child workers, as individuals in need of national state protection; in so doing they depicted the parents and families of child workers as limited in their capacity to independently provide for the welfare of their children. On the other hand, southern manufacturers and other opponents of child labor regulation offered a relational framework in which children's welfare was indistinguishable from that of their families. In this framework, children, including child workers, did not require state policy intervention since the families were instead more appropriate, natural guardians. Whereas both sides were sharply divided in their description of southern child workers as "little sufferers" or "responsible family members," the reality of their lives was somewhere in between, their own experiences of work and childhood being a combination of the two in which they were both individual wage workers and also family members, both vulnerable and active agents—a messiness that could not be described or fully imagined by policy actors.

The case of southern child workers and child labor regulation in the Progressive era has implications for the study of children's policy and political history. Firstly, it suggests that contemporary so-called family-values policy battles over children have distinct ideational roots in the Progressive era. The question of whether children are individuals in need of state protection or inseparable parts of families endures in numerous current policy battles—for instance, in debates over the health and welfare of minors seeking abortions or needing contraception, over sex education of adolescents versus parents' prerogatives to know and determine their child's behavior, and over accommodating parents' personal choice of schools for their children through tax vouchers versus the importance of uniform standards of public secular education for minors. Secondly, the Progressive-era debates over southern child workers also highlight the existence of sectional differences in the understanding of children. These conceptual differences are likely to remain and arguably to become even more prominent, given our current state of polarized, "red state–blue state" politics in which southern (red state) relational understandings of family are likely to continue to be pitted against northern (blue state) individual ideals.

NOTES

1. Interview with Flossie Moore Durham by Mary Frederickson, September 2, 1976, interview H-0066, in the *Southern Oral History Program Collection #4007*, Southern Historical Collection, Wilson Library, University of North Carolina at Chapel Hill, 2.
2. Wright, *Old South, New South*, 115–46.
3. Ibid., 138–46; interview with Martin E. Lowe by Allen Tullos, October 19, 1979, interview number H-0253, *Southern Oral History*, 23; Hall et al., *Like a Family*, 52; "Lowe Interview," 7.
4. Mintz, *Huck's Raft*, 156–57.
5. Ibid., 182.
6. For a similar argument see, Mink, *Wages of Motherhood*.
7. Mintz, *Huck's Raft*, 3–4, 134–35; also, Macleod, *The Age of the Child*, 22–26. See also Hall et al., *Like a Family*; Schmidt, *Industrial Violence*.
8. Friedman, *Private Lives, Families, Individuals, and the Law*; Coontz, *Marriage, a History*.
9. This chapter uses the term "social progressivism" as "a reform orientation" seeking to use government intervention to "solve social and economic inequalities viewed as the source of societal ills." See Eileen McDonagh, "Race, Class, and Gender in the Progressive Era," in Milkis and Mileur (eds.), *Progressivism and the New Democracy*, 147. For a description of various reform groups and progressive principles, see classic works such as Wiebe, *The Search for Order, 1877–1920*; Hofstadter, *Age of Reform*; Muncy, *Creating a Female Dominion*; Sanders, *Roots of Reform*, 164–65.
10. Mintz, *Huck's Raft*, 172–73; for child labor campaign as part of social and civic reform in the Progressive era that was accompanied by a strong sense of "moral outrage" on the part of progressives, see Harrison, *Congress, Progressive Reform, and the New American State*, 7.
11. Bills were selected through a manual examination of the Congressional Record Index for each year between 1899 and 1920 by searching under the index heading "child/children." The title, name, state, and party of the sponsor for each bill was recorded. In most cases the actual text of the bill was not consulted; however, the titles in most cases were explanatory of the object of the bill and of whether parental regulation or child welfare was its central focus. In all, seventy-three child welfare bills were found and analyzed.
12. Bill sponsorship data compiled by author, Congressional Record Index, 56th–66th Congress (1899–1921).
13. Mintz, *Huck's Raft*, 172; Fuller, *Child Labor and the Constitution*, 237; Pickerell, *Constitutional Deliberation in Congress*, 75–81. See also Julie Novkov, "Historicizing the Figure of the Child in Legal Discourse: The Battle over the Regulation of Child Labor," *American Journal of Legal History* 44 (2000): 369–404; Fuller, *Child Labor*, 236–38.

14. House Committee on Labor, *Child Labor Bill [Part 1]*, 63rd Cong., 2nd sess., 1914, 35.
15. Ibid., 86, 35.
16. Ibid., 95.
17. A. J. McKelway, "Child Wages in the Cotton Mills: Our Modern Feudalism," *Child Labor Bulletin* 2 (May 1913): 11.
18. *Annual Reports of the Department of the Interior for the Fiscal Year Ended June 30, 1902*, H.R. Doc. No. 57-5, at 2347 (1903).
19. Ibid., 2348–52 (Table: Statutory Provisions relating to Compulsory Attendance and Child Labor).
20. Alabama, Florida, Kentucky, Maryland, Mississippi, Missouri, South Carolina, and Texas had such exceptions in their laws, in comparison to no such provision in the laws of any northern state. Ibid., 2348, 2349, 2350.
21. See Bardaglio, *Reconstructing the Household*; Grossberg, *Governing the Hearth*.
22. Schmidt, *Industrial Violence*, 47–57; House Committee on Labor, *Child Labor Bill [Part 1]*, 124, 125; House Committee on Labor, *Child-Labor Bill*, 64th Cong. 1st Sess., 1916, 309.
23. Senate Committee on Interstate Commerce, *Interstate Commerce in Products of Child Labor, Part 1*, 64th Cong., 1st sess., 1916, 183 (Report by Eunice Sinclair, Fayetteville, N.C.).
24. Ibid., 53, 54.
25. House Committee on District of Columbia, *Regulation of the Employment of Minors within D.C.*, 62nd Cong., 2nd sess., 1920, 59.
26. Hall et al., *Like a Family*, 60–62; *Report on Condition of Woman and Child Wage-Earners in the United States in 19 Volumes*, S.Doc. No. 61-645, at 194 (1910).
27. Hall, et al., *Like a Family*, 93.
28. *Establishment of Children's Bureau*, S. Rep. No. 62-141, at 4 (1911) (Committee Report).
29. Gilman cited in Schmidt, *Industrial Violence*, 54; McKelway, *Child Wages in the Cotton Mills*, 5.
30. Cited in Schmidt, *Industrial Violence*, 77; National Child Labor Committee, H.Doc. No. 59-5485, at 1 (1906).
31. Statement of Florence Kelley, House Committee on Labor, *Child Labor Bill. [Part 1]*, 35; see also Statements of Mrs. E. K. Bushee, Senate Committee on District of Columbia, *Child Labor in D.C.*, 62nd Cong., 2nd sess., 1920, 27; House Committee on District of Columbia, *Regulation of the Employment of Minors*, 55; House Committee on Labor, *Child-Labor Bill*, 13–14; *Report on Condition of Woman and Child Wage-Earners*, S. Doc. No. 61-645, at 453.
32. Hubbard cited in Schmidt, *Industrial Violence*, 54.
33. Senate Committee on Interstate Commerce, *Interstate Commerce*, 54; House Committee on Labor, *Child-Labor Bill*, 95.
34. House Committee on Labor, *Child-Labor Bill*, 62; Hall, *Like a Family*, 102, 127–29.

35. Statement of H. R. Fitzgerald, Secretary and Treasurer, Riverside and Dan River Cotton Mills, Danville, VA, House Committee on Labor, *Child-Labor Bill*, 46–47.
36. Ibid., 62; House Committee on Labor, *Child-Labor Bill [Part 1]*, 108.
37. Schmidt, *Industrial Violence*, 3.
38. Davis, Senate Committee on Interstate Commerce, *Interstate Commerce*, 51; Parker, Greenville, House Committee on Labor, *Child-Labor Bill*, 95, 65 (emphasis added).
39. *Woman and Child Labor:* H. Rep. No. 59-2745, at 3 (1906) (Committee Report); *Annual Message of the President Transmitted to Congress Dec. 5, 1905*, H.Doc. No. 59-1, at xxi (1906); *Establishment of Children's Bureau*, S. Rep No. 62-141, 7.

4

"I Was So Glad to Be in School Here"

Religious Organizations and the School on Ellis Island in the Early 1900s

CLAIRE B. GALLAGHER

They had a school here for children. It was lovely. They sang American songs. I didn't understand a word but I picked up the tune. And I loved school. I was so glad to be in school here.
—Naomi Dorum Fader, age fourteen

Many Americans can trace their roots through Ellis Island; it remains one of the archetypal experiences in the peopling of America and the formation of the fabric of American society. From 1852 to 1954, over twelve million people were processed, detained, or denied access to the United States at this port of entry. Among them were a large number of children, either detainees themselves or the children of individuals who were infirm or waiting to be cleared for entry into the country.

In a study of the 1890 to 1932 annual reports of the commissioner general of immigration, it was noted that nearly 69 percent of the total number of aliens entering the United States had come through Ellis Island. In 1907, the peak year for immigration through this location, 1,004,756 of the 1,285,349 individuals coming through all ports into the United States passed through its gates. There are no statistics indicating what percentage of these individuals were children, but a consideration of existing photographs and a limited number of personal accounts would indicate that there were many. A 1904 article in the *Washington Post*, "Tots at Ellis Island," notes that twelve matrons were at work, and in their charge were over two hundred children from over fifteen ethnic

>> 81

groups and ranging in age from infants to twelve-year-olds. "That they [matrons] are authorities on the subject is conceded by every one who sees them on duty among the baby immigrants, thousands of whom spend from one day to four months on the island in the course of a year."[1]

Despite all that has been written about the history of Ellis Island and the immigrants who passed through it, Naomi Fader's recollection is one of the few in which a school is even mentioned. Considering the enormous numbers of children who presumably attended it, even briefly, this is remarkable. Yet photographic evidence, personal letters, newspaper articles, and reports of the religious groups who worked on the island can provide glimpses of the classroom, the organizations, and the individuals responsible for establishing and running the school, and the pedagogy and materials used by the teachers. The same evidence shows the ways in which their mission on Ellis Island moderated the religious organizations' steadfastly conservative agendas.

One of Our National Problems

Immigration was one of the great public policy issues of the era. A leading cause of concern was the literacy, or lack of literacy, among the new arrivals. The intelligence testing that had been a regular part of assessment and processing on Ellis Island for many years was, in fact, based largely on whether immigrants could read or write. The results created a general skepticism regarding the potential of the newly immigrated to assimilate into American culture and to be anything other than a burden on the country and its resources. In the 1910–11 annual report of the Woman's Home Missionary Society, an account of the good works of the Bureau of Immigrant Work began, "Immigration, as one of our National problems, has not lessened in importance over the past few years. The very word itself is freighted with obligations and responsibility." "The improbability of assimilation is a real menace," it continued. "In the transplanting of the alien to these shores the conditions are so different, the standards of living are higher, and he must needs improve physically, mentally, and morally."[2]

The settlement houses run by various secular and religious groups took partial responsibility for educating immigrants who were allowed into the country by offering kindergartens for immigrant children and adult education for their parents. Kindergartens were part of a much larger national movement; by the 1880s, there were more than four hundred kindergartens in the United States, and by the early 1900s, state compulsory education laws usually recognized kindergarten as an accepted part of public school education. Indeed, American public schools were considered, especially by the adherents of the Progressive Movement, to be a place for assimilation of immigrants into society, as well as an ideal place for them to learn English, the customs and traditions of their new home, and the principles of democracy. In the 1902 annual report of the College Settlements Association, an organization whose members saw education and the power of the neighborhood as catalysts for social change, Grace Darling wrote that "the kindergarten, with its daily work, its mothers' meetings, its excursions, gives them some idea of this new world to which they have come." She confidently asserted that "gradually the foundation is being laid for a better citizenship."[3]

But policy makers did not limit themselves to educating five-year-olds. At the turn of the century, the state of New York passed a law requiring all immigrants ages sixteen to twenty-one who were not literate in English to attend school part-time. The combination of the compulsory education and child labor laws of the early 1900s resulted in an upswing in the student population. Analyses of school enrollment statistics for foreign-born children enrolled in schools at that time indicate surprising comparisons to those of native-born children, with the enrollment rates of the five- to nine-year-old and ten- to thirteen-year-old immigrant children equaling or surpassing that of the children born in the United States. Despite opposition from those who feared rising labor costs and increased taxes, similar laws were passed elsewhere. And many of the motivations shaping the education of immigrants in the wider society emerged in the work of the religious organizations ministering to the children and adults of Ellis Island.[4]

"We Went to School, Almost Every Day"

Very few subjects in the Ellis Island Oral History Project (EIOHP) mentioned the school on Ellis Island. Angela Weinkam, who immigrated in the early 1920s, includes what is probably the most descriptive passage related to the school:

> So we were there [Ellis Island] 31 days and I remember very vividly that we went to school, almost every day. But we went to breakfast every morning as, well, everybody went in the big mess hall and everyday we'd get either an apple or an orange, everybody got that, children or adults, and then from there they would take us to this classroom and that's where I sort of started to pick up the English language. . . . They would take us to the playground and I remember being on the swings and the see-saws, and they would take us for walks on the Island, you know and at about 3:30 in the afternoon everyday we'd get a glass of milk and two, uh, graham crackers. That was everyday.[5]

The EIOHP also includes interviews with some of the employees. Josephine Lutomski was a ward maid in the women and children's infectious disease ward and lived on Island Number 1 of Ellis Island with other workers. Josephine assisted the doctors and nurses in the ward and worked with the children, making their beds, bathing them, caring for them, and reading to them from the books she got from the library that had been established by the American Library Association, through which she tried to encourage them to learn basic English vocabulary. She mentions listening and singing to music played on gramophones and it is likely that she sang to and with the children in her care. The recollections of an immigrant from that period, Constance Weiss, are consistent with those of Lutomski, but she also remembers "a large terrace where little girls would dance." It is likely that she is referring to one of the rooftop playgrounds where singing and dancing were common activities for the children in the kindergarten. The diversity of the sponsoring groups, children, teachers, matrons, and other workers, as well as all of the oral histories in which the school is mentioned, speak to the inclusive nature of the school. Attendance was voluntary, with children being recruited from the Main Hall, where families were separated for processing. The lure of being with other children, and the possibility of playing games and having fun, was the only invitation needed to follow an adult upstairs to the classroom where a child would find an introduction to new friends, a new language, and a new way of life.[6]

Weinkam's and Lutomski's recollections hint at the possibility of more than one school on Ellis Island, which in fact was the case. Elizabeth Gardiner, the chief hospital service worker in the Ellis Island Hospital from 1919 to 1922, wrote a surprising account of the institution in her work "For Foreign-Born":

> When the parents of a child arrange to have it treated at the hospital rather than have it deported, they seldom realize that the child will receive more than medical care. As a matter of fact the Occupational Therapy Department runs two schools, one for trachoma patients, one for favus and ringworm cases. It is surprisingly like other schools, the Primary, Intermediate and Advanced classes study hygiene and the three R's in English. Indirectly they learn neatness, good manners, and American ways. In the handicraft classes they are taught color craft, sewing, crocheting, knitting, leather work, stenciling, weaving, etc. The physical training hours include outdoor games, gymnastic exercises and dramatic play. In summer, all the classes are held out of doors but the chilly winds of winter drive them into their school rooms.

Gardiner does not refer to "kindergarten" or "kindergartening," but there are correlations between the activities she lists and those shown in the photographs of the kindergarten on Island 1. In addition, the Historic American Building Survey data includes a descriptive location plan of Island Number 2 on Ellis Island dating to June 1916, on which areas for an outdoor playground between Wards A and B (new hospital extension), tennis courts between Ward A and the Nurses Cottage, and several flower beds between Wards B and C and the old hospital building, all facing the water, are clearly delineated; a cinder walk encircled the complex, allowing for children to have access to fresh air and at least some exercise. It is feasible that some of the techniques employed in the kindergarten on Island 1 were also used there.[7]

The available documentation reveals that the kindergarten in the Baggage and Dormitory Building on Island Number 1 was originally located on the third floor, on the northwest side adjacent to the rooftop playground, but was moved to the second floor when the rooftop playground was moved to the southwest side of the building after 1911. It is clear that the direct proximity to the protected outdoor space was an essential part of the curriculum and instruction. The location of the classroom was also critical in recruiting children for the school. According to Bertha M. Booty, a psychologist who conducted intelligence tests with the children on Ellis Island during the early 1920s, the teacher or her assistant went through the detention rooms each morning and afternoon asking children to join them. A line of children would then be taken through a locked door separating the detention area from the rest of the complex and led upstairs to the classroom and its adjacent rooftop playground. It must be noted, however, that many mothers did not trust unfamiliar people and would not permit their children to leave their sides and attend the school.[8]

In a letter to the editor of the *Forum*, Mr. Oscar W. Ehrhorn, the former secretary of the National Republican Club, wrote that "[t]he very young children of the detained aliens are cared for during the day in a nursery which is in charge of a competent trained attendant. The older children up to sixteen years of age each day are taken to the kindergarten or out on the recreation lawn, where they are taught games and the rudiments of English." The 1984 Historic Resource Study of the Statue of Liberty/Ellis Island also mentions the nursery: "A day nursery consisting of three large rooms, one equipped with a modern porcelain bathtub for infants and all supplied with cribs, was used in part to teach sanitation and baby care." There is also an existing photograph of cribs and baby equipment that confirms this written description.[9]

Ellis Island was like a city, a congested, busy place in which extra space was difficult to find, especially when it came to teaching a large group of children. The 1904 report of William Williams, the commissioner of Ellis Island, dedicated a section to "Buildings, Grounds, and Improvements," in which he describes the "inadequacy of the Ellis Island plant for the proper transaction of the enormous amount of public business requiring attention at this immigration station." He continues, "No reasonable effort is spared to mitigate the necessary unpleasant features incident to the detention of immigrants." It is clear from his report that the government had been generous in the more than fifty contracts that had been let for improvements to Ellis Island, including a new metal ferry that would bring immigrants from their ships to the island. He is aware of the experience of the immigrant and appears dedicated to having a special concern for the children there.

He goes on to write, "At the Commissioner-General's suggestion special provision has been made for the amusement of detained children by converting a portion of the roof garden into a playground, where they may enjoy fresh air and various kinds of amusements." Over time there would be two such rooftop playgrounds, as well as one on the ground facing Manhattan, and all three would be used for classroom instruction in literacy and citizenship. Playground advocates in New York City were campaigning for more outdoor play spaces for children, which was in keeping with the pedagogy of the kindergarten. The teachers on Ellis Island were trained to incorporate sand tables, dancing, storytelling, and nature when teaching children, and the outdoor areas provided suitable spaces for them to do so. As well, a child's access to fresh air and sunshine was seen as healthy and necessary for his or her well-being and development, another aspect of the Progressive Movement's argument for more open space in urban environments.[10]

Feeding the mind was as important as feeding the body on Ellis Island, and the Red Cross and American Library Association focused on that goal. Individuals such as Florence Huxley provided access to literature and music at the library that was established by the Red Cross and was later run by the members of the American Library Association, both of which claimed Huxley as a member. An ALA newsletter editorial described her as "an accomplished librarian in the uniform and on the payroll of the YMCA, and giving her whole time to the conduct of ALA work, and ordering about several hulking and cowed-looking Y secretaries." It is clear from this that Mrs. Huxley was a powerful presence in the library on Ellis Island, presumably until its dismantling in the early 1920s when the ALA eliminated its Hospital Library Service. During her tenure she was responsible for acquisitions, and ALA records indicate materials in many languages, both in print and on records. Some oral histories mention folk music, and it is evident that children were folk dancing in the school, perhaps to the music of a record from the library played on one of the gramophones known to have existed on Ellis Island. Photographs of the library typically show individuals in line to check out books or show a book cart that was taken through the infectious disease wards for patients to take a book to read or for children to take one to keep.[11]

An essential element of the educational programming on Ellis Island was its focus on the kindergarten, which had long been seen as a vehicle for encouraging citizenship, dating to its origin in Germany and its founder, Frederic Froebel. American Progressives took up this mantel when they began to establish kindergartens throughout the United States, and the school on Ellis Island represented this effort writ large. In an address at Clark University in 1910, Patty Hill Smith, a Progressive kindergarten teacher, described its potential thus:

> Democracy itself is the most idealistic and romantic adventure ever initiated, but once the romantic venture is dreamed and started on its course, its realization will depend upon our success with the immigrant child and mother. Success with our idealistic theories of government, based upon its faith in all men of all races, and our ability to re-make them in the light of our American ideals of rights and responsibilities, will depend upon our very youngest citizens.[12]

At the turn of the nineteenth century, Phoebe Apperson Hearst, the wife of Senator George Hearst and a prominent member of the Young Women's Christian Association, presented a bill to the United States Congress that would make kindergarten mandatory for all American children. She was a noted Progressive of her time and was committed to improving the lives of women and children through access to education at all levels. Accordingly, Hearst was committed to the national movement for kindergartens, and while living in Washington established Kindergarten Colleges in the District of Columbia for both black and white women to learn the pedagogy of kindergartening, as well as kindergartens for their children to attend while their mothers studied. In addition, she started the first free kindergarten in the country, founded the Golden Gate Kindergarten Association in San Francisco and the Women's Clubs of America, cofounded the National Parent Teacher Association (PTA), and served as the president of the YWCA, engaging a young female architect, Julia Morgan, to design the national headquarters. During this time, the Y had a significant presence on Ellis Island, and several teachers in the school were members, bringing the mission of the organization within the classroom walls. Hearst was not only a member of the YWCA but also religiously affiliated with the

Methodist Church, another connection with the educational underpinnings of the school on Ellis Island.¹³

In newspaper articles, photograph titles, and various reports associated with Ellis Island before and after the turn of the century, there is an insistence upon referring to the school as the kindergarten, an odd choice considering the wide range of ages of the children being educated. It seems likely that the reference is to the pedagogy rather than to the ages of the children attending the school. Given that the population of the classroom at any one point in time represented the worst case scenario for any teacher—large numbers, high transience, and no common language spoken—the pedagogy of play seems to be a valid choice for instruction. Frederic Froebel's belief in learning through doing, while considering the development of the whole child, transcends age and is an enjoyable and creative approach, especially for students who have experienced recent trauma and anxiety. His basic curriculum included such elements as Nature Study, Handwork, Block Play, Art and Drawing, Music and Movement, and Story-telling. He was also the author of *Mother-Play and Nursery Songs*, which was the inspiration for many of the songs, marches, and stories used by the General Committee member groups, such as the Woman's Christian Temperance Union, the Congregationalist Church, and the Methodist Episcopal Church, among others, who used the melodies while changing the words to suit their underlying religious or patriotic messages.¹⁴

A typical kindergarten session would begin with a circle time in which greetings were made, songs were sung, finger plays were performed, and stories were told. In the case of Ellis Island, the teachers used common animals, folk songs and dances, marching, and sand table storytelling to connect children's previous experiences with those of their new homeland. Directly connected with the songs of Frederic Froebel are the songbooks associated with the Mayflower Band, among them works by Frances Weld Conant and Grace Wilbur Danielson. Conant and Danielson were well known for their songs for children, and in their book *Songs for Little People* there are several songs with spiritual/religious lyrics sung to tunes from Froebel's kindergarten songs, with Froebel being credited in the footnotes and acknowledgments.¹⁵

Froebel also developed what he called "The Gifts and the Occupations," in which children arranged blocks in geometric patterns, pierced cardstock in patterns, wove strips of paper, and used string and pins to make various designs. He designed sets of materials that corresponded to a set sequence of activities delineated in his two books; these were available in the United States through Milton Bradley, the company that had been approached by the nascent kindergartening societies and groups after the demonstration kindergarten at the Philadelphia Centennial Exposition made mothers, nurses, and teachers aware of them. Teachers at Ellis Island were undoubtedly trained in kindergartening techniques but had no access to the Milton Bradley supplies. They did, however, have donations of fabric, thread, cardstock, blocks, and other basic supplies through which they could lead the children in the basic kindergartening exercises. These experiences were intended to build on the children's prior knowledge in order to assist them in making connections to English vocabulary, geometry, and mathematics.[16]

Descriptions and recollections of the kindergarten program can actually help identify the location of the school, even though the location of the school was never referenced in any oral histories, the National Park Service's Historic American Building Survey does not include any drawings with spaces labeled as "school" or "classroom," and the architects on staff know of no such location. There is, however, some visual evidence that suggests the location of this space and verifies the accounts of the teachers whose kindergartening pedagogy is represented in the material culture that appears in the photographs.[17]

In the early 1920s, Frank L. Moore was hired to document some of the activities and efforts of the American Missionary Association, a multidenominational organization committed to social justice. One of the locations he photographed was Ellis Island, and his work serves as the primary documentation of the school. One of the most informative photographs is labeled "Kindergarten Room" *en verso* and shows a long, empty hallway with wooden slat benches along its sides. Walls with what appear to be institutional two-by-four-inch white subway tiles applied horizontally, and plaster above adult shoulder height, have a regular pattern of deep-set, double-hung wooden windows, and a tile floor. There is a large, dark object in the left foreground, what appear to be papers on the benches, animal pictures on the walls, some potted plants on the windowsills, and what appears to be a grouping of small chairs in the distance. At first view this photograph seems to be

Frank Moore titled this photograph "Ellis Island, Kindergarten Room, 1921," the first such reference to the hallway space as a classroom. (American Missionary Records, Series III, Amisted Research Center at Tulane University, New Orleans, LA)

Moore added a sense of human scale to the classroom space by photographing the teachers and inspectors standing along the walls. (American Missionary Records, Series III, Amisted Research Center at Tulane University, New Orleans, LA)

incorrectly labeled; this space is very long and narrow, not at all indicative of ideal classroom conditions. In a different photograph, however, the presence of adults does give a sense of scale, confirming that the space is long and narrow with relatively high ceilings, and that the benches are scaled to adults while the other furniture is child sized. There is no indication of its location on Ellis Island or of what may be adjacent to it.[18]

A comparison of the photographs taken by Moore to the drawings in the Historical American Building Survey indicates a correlation between the hallway adjacent to the baggage room in the Baggage and Dormitory Building. The relative dimensions and shape of the space, the window and door pattern, as well as a consideration of the proximity to the outdoor and rooftop playground areas are indications that this was the location of the classroom where the kindergarten existed. The animal pictures affixed to the walls, the plants growing on the windowsills, and the evidence of children's work make the argument stronger. In another photograph taken from the opposite end of the space, there are a child-scaled table and chairs, a piano, and two doorways, one leading to the baggage room. Moore's images also add credence to the premise that kindergartening techniques were employed by all the teachers (whose names are indicated on the photographs: Jenny Pratt, Miss Armaghanian, Miss Baharian, Miss Bowden, Mrs. Marmaroff, and Miss Birsneh). Although the religious affiliations of all of these women is not identified, it is not likely that all were the same; however, what is clear is that their teaching techniques were consistent with that of kindergartening.

Moore's twenty-nine photos of Ellis Island provide evidence of the specifics of kindergarten pedagogy, especially the integration of music. Children are seen dancing, singing, and doing finger plays with their teacher. They are shown working in sand tables and sandboxes in several of the images, which connects directly with the exercises described in such teaching guides as the *Mayflower Program Book* and the *Band of Hope Graded Lessons*. Froebel's occupations of paper weaving, folding, and piercing are clearly seen in a series of images of children whose work is sometimes in process, sometimes on display. Photographs taken on the rooftop playground include children following their teacher, who is using a gramophone to play records to which they are dancing,

Children's kindergarten furniture, a piano, live plants, books, and pictures of animals provide a glimpse into the pedagogy and material culture of the classroom. (American Missionary Records, Series III, Amisted Research Center at Tulane University, New Orleans, LA)

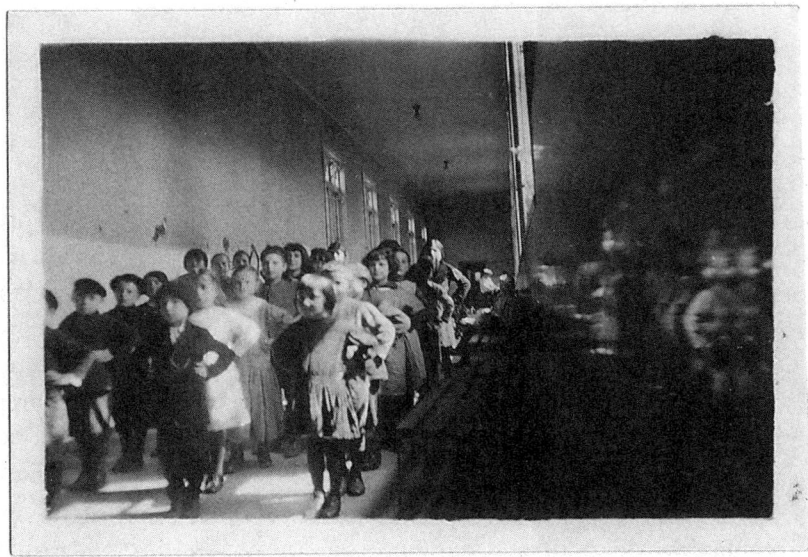

Jenny Pratt and her students march to music in the classroom. (American Missionary Records, Series III, Amisted Research Center at Tulane University, New Orleans, LA)

marching, and singing. Other images are taken in the classroom and in one of them the teacher, identified *en verso* as Jenny Pratt, is playing the piano while the children sing along; in another she leads them in finger plays, while in another she and they march together.

The teachers' accounts of large numbers of children of various ages in the classes are certainly accurate, as seen in several of Moore's photographs. In one image, children are clamoring to get in front of his camera, lending to the impression of a lively atmosphere. In another they fill the classroom, the younger children in the background in an area that appears to be designated for them, the older ones in the foreground working at a sewing task. The photographs do not give the impression that the space is a deterrent or that there are unhappy children as a result of a crowded classroom. Instead, the expression is one of play, delight, and engagement, the ideal in any learning environment. Given the degree of diversity and the student-to-teacher ratio, that alone is remarkable. That the intention of the teachers and that of their students are congruent is even more so. Whatever the specifics of the situation may have been, the outcome must have been positive and Moore's choices in the photographs he took are designed to demonstrate that.

The Eastern Gate

As the foregoing indicates, almost from the outset philanthropic and missionary groups were present on Ellis Island. All had to be approved by the Department of the Interior. A list was published each year; the one published on July 24, 1916, included thirty-two such groups, most connected with religious or ethnic organizations that had headquarters in New York City and a designated individual who was present on the island, providing a personal link to the society's services and facilities in the city. Many religiously affiliated groups, such as the Women's Home Missionary Society of the Methodist Episcopal Church, Saint Raphael's Society for German Catholic Immigrants, and the Hebrew Sheltering and Immigrant Aid Society, offered transition housing available in New York City for women and their children and their representatives that provided an environment and experiences through which the immigrants could feel safe and be among others with whom they shared a common language and culture, while having the opportunity to acclimate to American ways. In "Ellis Island at the Eastern Gate: Our Work at the Port of New York," an article published in the early 1920s by the Women's Home Missionary Society of the Methodist Episcopal Church, a routine interaction between Marie Pletzer, a missionary, and her immigrant charges was described thus:

> Their hearts beat faster as their anxiety grows, and they become confused in their answers to the Inspector's questions. After discharging one girl after another he calls into the saloon a young woman who calmly brings the group under her wing. The girls brighten and look relieved as soon as they hear her speak in a language akin to their own. . . . We make an effort to remove the stigma of detention on Ellis Island for many men, women, and girls. While the law must be enforced, it can be done with as gentle a hand as possible. Thus we keep abreast of the times in terms of loyal Christian service.[19]

Some groups were overtly committed to religious conversion of immigrants; the New York Bible Society and the American Tract Society had a strong presence on Ellis Island and distributed tracts and Bibles to immigrants in their native languages. At its Eighty-eighth Annual Meeting in 1913, the ATS "reported the distribution of a million and a half Christian books and tracts in English and an equal number in foreign languages." Likewise, the Woman's Home Missionary Society saw Bible distribution as one of its goals and provided detailed statistics in each annual report for every aspect of the Immigrant Work Bureau's operations with the exception of the categories "Number of Bibles distributed" and "Number of tracts and leaflets distributed," which were never enumerated and always listed as "Many," the implication being that there were too many to count.[20]

Children were often seen as the conduit to their parents, and missionaries often approached their education as the first step in this process, whether it was addressed through the messages inherent in the stories, songs, and games they played with them or through more overt vehicles. The Woman's Christian Temperance Union began to lobby on the local level for public kindergartens in the 1890s, later advocating for kindergarten to become part of the public school system nationally. It has been widely accepted that part of their rationale centered on the potential for influencing the content of the children's instruction, thereby creating an opportunity for disseminating temperance information to parents that would influence their votes; by extension this was also true for the children as future voters themselves. Ruth Borden argues in her historical account of the WCTU that this is only partially true, however, and that the primary reason the organization supported kindergartens was that they were an "essential service for working-class women and their children" and went far beyond an opportunity for recruiting members of the organization.[21]

The organization's archival materials are not so definitive, however. For example, the January 25, 1912, issue of *The Union Signal*, the Woman's Christian Temperance Union's primary publication, includes "A Stranger within Our Gates," an article written by Mrs. Mary B. Wilson, the National WCTU superintendent of Work Among Foreign Speaking People, the bureau under which the operations at Ellis Island were governed. In her account, Mrs. Wilson describes various efforts among immigrants on Ellis Island and Angel Island, the port of entry on the West Coast. In one vignette she says that "young [immigrant] voters" often "needed instruction along the lines of Christian citizenship, so the National Associate in this work prepared for them a neat little leaflet." This would indicate an unambiguous attempt to influence an individual's vote along religious lines.[22]

Despite their diverse religious beliefs, in order to unite their efforts to improve the lives of the women and children on Ellis Island, many of these associations formed the General Committee of Immigrant Aid, which coordinated efforts to connect immigrants with translators, pooled contributions, and shared staffing. The group began with twenty-six constituent groups, with "each group [having] its own activity designed to relieve those detained and make them realize that they have unknown friends in this country." According to Brigadier Thomas Johnson of the Salvation Army, the General Committee did not have an office on Ellis Island. Instead, each member "had their own offices. Everyone had their own . . . different offices all over the City and then we'd come together once a month and talk our business up as to what had happened, what we had been doing, and how we'd come though on our cases."[23]

The list of approved organizations on Ellis Island contains several that would be considered anything but "progressive" in mission, among them the Woman's Christian Temperance Union, the Methodist Church, the YWCA, and the Woman's Home Missionary Society of the Methodist Episcopal Church. Most were perceived as strident in their narrow attitudes toward other faiths. The WCTU, for example, was assumed to be intolerant of immigrants, particularly those who were Catholic. In the 1890s the organization published a series of articles in *The Union Signal* describing foreigners, Irish and Germans among them, as the "strength and bulwark of the liquor power" and advocating for stricter immigration laws that would restrict the numbers of offensive immigrants. Although the WCTU officially accepted Catholics as members, the group as a whole was militantly Protestant, and that was palpable to those who did not share their religious beliefs. Yet their sometimes hard-line ideology seems to have moderated a bit in their work among the children of Ellis Island.[24]

Indeed, the pedagogy applied to religious groups on the island duplicated standard practices in secular kindergartens. A study of the materials used by the Congregationalist Church reveals a striking similarity to a typical Froebel kindergarten. The Congregationalists' children's group was called the Mayflower Band and there was a specific guide to instruction entitled *The Mayflower Program Book: A Week-Day Course in World Friendship and Training Services for Children Six, Seven, and Eight Years of Age*. Here one could find a specific sequence for a day's lesson, of which there are twenty-six, to be held on Saturday mornings or after school on a selected weekday: "1. Aim (a traditional lesson objective), 2. Equipment, 3. Games, 4. Song-cheer (The Mayflower Band), 5. Story, 6. Marching Song, 7. Story (continued), 8. Plans for Work (rationale for work), 9. Games, 10. Hour of Work (gifts to make)." This structure aligned with that of a typical kindergarten, although the songs and stories for the Mayflower Band were religious in content. The *Mayflower Program Book* also specified materials, many, such as weaving mats, cut-outs, and pasteboard shapes, coming directly from the Milton Bradley catalog. The guide describes qualifications for the staff for a band as including one teacher and "a large core of assistants one of whom is a pianist, for the play and work periods." The overarching goal of a Mayflower Band is also clearly stated to be one in which "children make and give gifts and learn empathy for and acceptance of other people and their needs." In one example, the girls and boys made scrapbooks (picture books) and toys to send during the hour of work and sent them to the Italian Mission in New York, which had a direct connection with Ellis Island. These scrapbooks probably became part of the instructional materials in the classroom on Ellis Island.[25]

Sand tables were used frequently in Mayflower Band lessons, each of which had a specific title; program 11, for example, is entitled "Our Guests." This particular week's activities include a sand table story in which objects are arranged in the sandbox or table in order to tell a story of the immigration of a boy from Italy. In another example, "Children of the West: The First Americans," the sand table is used to make a picture of an Indian scene, including models of canoes, teepees, and other related items of Native American life. In "Children of the South: Cotton Plantation," the sand table is used to plant a cotton field and experience the raising and harvesting of cotton. All of these lessons were intended to help the children gain empathy for foreigners.[26]

Acting out stories was another technique common to both Froebel's kindergarten and the Mayflower Band. In a play written by Mrs. E. C. Cronk entitled "Visitors from Ellis Island: A Little Play for Boys and Girls," new immigrant children are seen in their ethnic dress, each one brought into the scene by one of the Mayflower Band members, who holds the child's hand. Discussion centers around misconceptions and slurs related to the ethnic group and how, since the Mayflower Band member now knows what this group has contributed to America, he/she will never say or do such things again. The two main characters in the play are Lady Liberty and Uncle Sam, whose dialogue engages the children in discussion about their new foreign friends. The play concludes with all the children being led by Uncle Sam and Lady Liberty in the Pledge of Allegiance to the American flag as well as the Pledge of Allegiance to the Christian flag, thereby combining both religious and patriotic purposes, overtly demonstrating newfound empathy, acceptance, and enculturation.[27]

The Methodist Episcopal Church had its own organization for children. In the instructional materials for children in this group, many songs and activities are credited to Froebel. In fact, in the lesson plan books and other written materials used in training teachers to teach in the program, there are lists of materials to order and references to the Milton Bradley catalogue, the source of Froebel materials and kindergarten supplies. In the case of those teaching on Ellis Island, however, there was no money for buying these materials so they were improvised; many were provided by the member organizations of the General Committee of Immigrant Aid, who all donated to the schoolroom in one form or another. In the case of groups such as the Methodist Episcopal Church, the associated children's bands often made items in Sunday school, such as picture books, that were then donated to the children on Ellis Island, thereby increasing empathy for the foreigners. Other groups donated fabric, toys, food, soap, and other small items given as gifts. One of the most valuable donations and services was the expertise of the small group of women who served as teachers for children who chose to attend the school they conducted.[28]

This study of the ways in which the huddled masses of children who passed through Ellis Island in the late nineteenth and early twentieth centuries were schooled shows several convergences and a few paradoxes. Although relatively few immigrants or administrators even mentioned the school's existence, it was nevertheless one of the notable experiences of the children who spent a few days or weeks in its narrow confines. Progressive-era concern about immigrants' literacy intersected with the growing kindergarten movement. And traditionally conservative religious organizations found themselves educating the immigrants whose religions they abhorred and whose ignorance they mistrusted with the same methods promoted by Progressive educators.

NOTES
1. Comparative Tables—Immigration through all the Ports of the United States and New York, EL-MS, Box 35, Ellis Island Archives; *Washington Post*, June 5, 1904.
2. Bertha M. Booty, *A Psychological Study of Immigrant Children at Ellis Island*, Mental Measurement Monographs, Serial Number 3 (Baltimore, MD: Williams and Wilkins, 1926); The Woman's Home Missionary Society, *Annual Report* (Cincinnati, Ohio, 1910–11), 186.
3. College Settlements Association, *Annual Report* (1902), 34–35.
4. Mintz, *Huck's Raft*, 174; Susan Cotts Watkins, ed., *After Ellis Island: Newcomers and Natives in the 1910 Census* (New York: Russell Sage Foundation, 1994), 224; Nina C. Vandewalker, *The Kindergarten in American Education* (New York: Macmillan, 1923), 194–96.
5. Interview with Angela Weinkam, February 4, 1986, Ellis Island Oral History Project Microfilm (hereafter EIOHP), Reel VII.

6. Interview with Josephine Lutomski, February 10, 1986, EIOHP, Reel VIII; interview with Constance Weiss, January 22, 1986, ibid., Reel VI.
7. Elizabeth Greene Gardiner, *For Foreign Born* (1921), Elizabeth Greene Gardiner Papers, Department of Manuscripts and University Archives, Cornell University, Ithaca, NY.
8. Booty, *Psychological Study of Immigrant Children at Ellis Island*.
9. *The Forum*, August 1927; Historic Resource Study, Statue of Liberty, Ellis Island National Monument/New York–New Jersey, p. 13, http://www.nps.gov/history/history/park_histories/index.htm#stli; Amm0019, Frank L. Moore photographs, American Missionary Series III, #419, Amisted Archives, Tulane University, New Orleans, LA.
10. Report of the Commissioner of Ellis Island to the Commissioner-General of Immigration, September 15, 1904, in Reports of the Department of Commerce and Labor, 1904 (Washington, DC, 1905), 834.
11. *Bulletin of the American Library Association* 13 (July 1919): 158.
12. Patty Hill Smith, "The Relation of the Kindergarten to Child Welfare," in *Proceedings of the Child Conference for Research and Welfare* (New York: Stechert, 1910), 41.
13. "The Phoebe A. Hearst Kindergarten Work in Washington," *Kindergarten Review* 11 (May 1899): 558.
14. Frederic Froebel, *Mother Play and Nursery Songs: Poetry, Music, and Pictures for the Noble Culture of Child Life, with Notes to Mothers*, Elizabeth Peabody, ed. (Boston: Lothrop, Lee, and Shepard, 1878).
15. Frances Weld Conant and Grace Wilbur Danielson, *Songs for Little People: For Use in the Sunday-school, the Kindergarten, and Home* (New York: Abingdon, 1915).
16. Henry W. Blake, *Paradise of Childhood: A Practical Guide to Kindergartners* (Springfield, MA: Milton Bradley, 1986); *Milton Bradley's School Aids and Kindergarten Materials* (Springfield, MA: Milton Bradley, 1891).
17. Robert Arzola to the author, October 11, 12, 2012; Lisa Davidson to the author, June 11, 2012.
18. The Moore photographs are from the American Missionary Records, Series III, Amisted Research Center at Tulane University.
19. "Ellis Island at the Eastern Gate: Our Work at the Port of New York," The Woman's Home Missionary Society, Methodist Episcopal Church, Cincinnati, Ohio, 1922, EL-MS, Box 26, IM-119, Ellis Island Archives.
20. "Half-English, Half-Foreign," *Continent*, June 26, 1913; The Woman's Home Missionary Society, *Annual Report* (1910–11), 187.
21. Ruth Borden, *Women and Temperance: The Quest for Power and Liberty, 1873–1900* (New Brunswick, NJ: Rutgers University Press, 1990).
22. *Union Signal*, January 25, 1912.
23. HRS (draft), ch. vi, Box 34, Ellis Island Archives; interview with Brigadier Thomas Johnson, January 30, 1985, EIOHP, Reel I.

24. *Union Signal*, January 1, 1891.
25. Jeanette Perkins Brown, *The Mayflower Program Book* (Boston: Pilgrim Press, 1920).
26. Ibid., Program 11, 86; Program 11, 106–14.
27. E. C. Cronk, *Visitors from Ellis Island: A Little Play for Boys and Girls* (Philadelphia: Women's Missionary Society of the United Lutheran Church in America, 1921).
28. "The Phoebe A. Hearst Kindergarten Work in Washington," *Kindergarten Review* 11 (May 1899): 558.

5

The Trajectory of Benevolence

Progressivism in the Little Colonel *Books*

SARAH E. CLERE

Although now long out of fashion, the *Little Colonel* series, by Annie Fellows Johnston, was wildly popular among turn-of-the-twentieth-century girls, having sold more than one million copies by Johnston's death in 1931. Primarily set in the fictional village of Lloydsboro Valley, Kentucky, forty years after the Civil War, the series follows the exploits of Lloyd Sherman, nicknamed "the Little Colonel" because of her resemblance to her irascible grandfather, a Confederate veteran. The romantic trappings of the series, most notably its southern backdrop and the didactic fairy tales Johnston inserts in nearly every volume, captured the imaginations of numerous children. The thrust of the series, however, proves surprisingly realistic, representing the shifting contours of childhood and adolescence over the course of the Progressive Era as Johnston depicts the growing influence of the middle class and the increasingly public roles played by its girls and women. In the books, however, as in society at large, the middle class constitutes itself and solidifies its authority by firmly shutting its borders to a sizable portion of America's populace. Furthermore, the growing societal influence of female characters often proves directly proportionate to the control they exert over the lives of their less-enfranchised neighbors, particularly ethnic others. The series perfectly represents the tensions of the Progressive Era and the cost of middle-class white America's tenuous reunification at the cusp of the twentieth century as goodwill and optimism collided with patterns of assimilation and control.[1]

David Blight has noted the difficulty of delineating "the myriad ways sectional politics and the emergence of Jim Crow (in law and life) melded" between the 1880s and World War I "into an uneasy national compromise" linked to "the cultural nostalgia rooted in the alienation born of rapid industrialization." The *Little Colonel* books provide one of the numerous mechanisms through which the fractured United States continued to reconstruct itself in the wake of the Civil War. At first glance they appear to be a valentine to the Lost Cause. The elderly Colonel (clad in white during the summer months) is a picturesque southern gentleman; gracious living at the ancestral plantation, Locust, is celebrated; and, most significantly, the position of African American "servants" appears little changed from the days of their enslavement. In her 2010 book, *Creating a Confederate Kentucky*, Anne E. Marshall devotes a significant amount of space to the *Little Colonel* books. Referring to the series as a "happily nostalgic literary creation of Kentucky's Confederate past," she interprets Johnston's books as reinforcing Lost Cause ideology: "The Little Colonel, her family, and her friends lead enviable lives of leisure filled with house parties, boarding school high jinks, and European vacations. They enjoy a gentle existence buffered from insecurities by a stable social arrangement that entails powerful yet chivalrous men and well-behaved, maternal women." The consciousness of the books, however, is more national than regional. Beneath the pseudo-antebellum trappings, Johnston's series works to erase sectional divisions and depicts a reconstituted United States through a reinforcement of unifying structures, such as class and whiteness, that move beyond region.[2]

The series began in 1895 with the publication of *The Little Colonel* and ended in 1912 with *Mary Ware's Promised Land*. A 1935 movie. *The Little Colonel*, starring Shirley Temple and Bill "Bojangles" Robinson, both attested to the continued popularity of Johnston's books and introduced them to a new generation of readers. *The Little Colonel* (1895) is a slender volume that was initially written as a stand-alone story. The book narrates five-year-old Lloyd Sherman's reconciliation of her grandfather with her mother, whom he disowned after she married a northerner. Beyond its status as a representation of children's increasing familial and cultural capital, the understanding achieved by the Confederate Colonel and his northern son-in-law makes *The Little Colonel* one of the reconciliation narratives so popular in the decades following the Civil War. Romantic reconciliation themes that smoothed over sectional differences could and did coexist with progressivism's forward-looking optimism. Blight explains how nostalgia for an idealized past often influenced contemporary debates: "[T]he reform fervor of the Progressive Era, with its quests for order, honesty and efficiency and its impulse against monopolism, compelled Americans to look inward and forward, but [it] did so in a culture full of sentimentalized remembrance."[3]

A nonsoutherner herself, Johnston grew up in central Indiana and began writing professionally after the death of her husband in order to provide for her three stepchildren. The setting of the initial book was inspired by a trip she took to Pewee Valley, Kentucky, in 1891. The privileged lives its inhabitants enjoyed piqued Johnston's imagination, and years later she recalled that her first visit to what would become the fictional Lloydsboro Valley was like "stepping between the covers of an old romance." Pewee Valley, however, lacked a storied antebellum history; its significant development did not begin until 1851 when the railroad arrived, turning the tiny rural community into a suburb of Louisville. By Johnston's first visit, Pewee Valley was essentially a summer community where well-off Louisville residents had vacation homes. The luxury and comfort that appeared to be characteristic of the antebellum South were in reality emblematic of the social and material aspirations of the swelling middle class. "A commuter village in Oldham County" at the time the *Little Colonel Books* are set, Pewee Valley's fictional transformation into Lloydsboro Valley reflects the rise of suburbia and the fetishizing of green space and fresh air in the wake of America's increasingly polluted cities.[4]

* * * *

Johnston herself was more concerned with writing books that would enable her to support her stepchildren than with refighting the Civil

War, writing of the series in 1928, "Little did I dream it would expand into twelve volumes." Her continuation of the saga of Lloyd and her community represents her awareness of the dynamics of the children's book market and her attempt to capitalize on the original volume's success. Following Sheri Inness's helpful distinction, the *Little Colonel* books are books in a series, rather than series books; that is, the characters grow older in realistic ways from book to book. Rather than continuing Lloyd's story where the first book left off, the second volume, *The Little Colonel's House Party*, jumps six years to show Lloyd as an eleven-year-old. At about three times the length of *The Little Colonel*, it establishes the format for the remaining books. Once Lloyd gets married in *The Little Colonel's Knight Comes Riding* and presumably passes into the adult world, the focus of the last three volumes shifts to her younger friend Mary Ware, who is still a teenager. The books thus reflect Johnston's awareness of what Stephen Mintz refers to as the "emergence of the popular concept of adolescence," particularly as it pertained to girls.[5]

The chief architect of the modern idea of adolescence at the beginning of the twentieth century was psychologist G. Stanley Hall, a household name to many middle-class parents. Fearful of changing gender roles and the challenge to white hegemony posed by immigrants and African Americans, *fin de siècle* Americans fixated on the minutiae of white boys' physical development and their socialization into suitably masculine behavioral modes. According to Christa De Luzio, Hall's philosophy somewhat contradictorily "professed the universality of developmental categories, while it upheld current notions of inherent difference and hierarchy between various groups of social subjects." In other words, Hall made the experiences of white middle-class males the normative standard by which to measure all other youths, regardless of their gender, ethnicity, or class status. De Luzio argues convincingly for Hall's interest in female adolescent development as both a corollary to male maturation and a significant phenomenon in and of itself, remarking,

> The changes modern girls were experiencing and facilitating in their own lives at the turn of the century also influenced Hall's thinking. Of great interest and concern to Hall in this latter regard were white middle-class

girls' pursuit of equal opportunities in secondary and higher education, as well as their involvement with leisure activities and experimentation with modes of self-expression as part of a distinctive youth culture.

These concerns recur throughout the *Little Colonel* books (for instance, Lloyd attends not one but two boarding schools), which continually depict young women's attempts at self-fashioning. A collection of essays published in 1914 by the National Congress of Mothers and Parent-Teacher Associations entitled *Parents and Their Problems: Child Welfare in Home, School, Church, and State* contains both an article written by Hall and an essay endorsing the *Little Colonel* series as "useful in moral instruction," indicating how the work of the pioneering psychologist and popular author interacted within the received culture of progressive parenting.[6]

The publication and marketing of the books themselves clearly reflect the period's heightened interest in adolescent development. The series' particular popularity relied not only on an audience of young women with disposable income but also on the blessing of various adult arbiters of youth culture—now not only parents but other professionals, including teachers, librarians, and ministers. *The Little Colonel's House Party* initiates this concern with middle-class adolescence by showing three of Lloyd's friends from around the country attending a house party at her Kentucky home. The house party allows Johnston to cater to the fantasies of her young readers, who could read about the guests' enjoyment of their luxurious surroundings and various leisure pursuits, from riding to charades. The four girls themselves are surprisingly modern; their differing backgrounds allow Johnston to depict a broad cross-section of the American middle class. An exchange between Joyce, a midwestern girl whose attorney father has died, leaving the family penniless, and Eugenia, a wealthy New Yorker, allows Johnston to champion the emergent middle class. After Eugenia remarks in a lofty tone that "sometimes schools that advertise themselves as being awfully select are no better than those horrid public schools," Joyce defends public schools, saying that in the Midwest they are "considered better than the private ones" with "better teachers and more progressive methods." At many points *The Little Colonel's House Party* privileges such seemingly egalitarian views, basing social class on intelligence and affiliation rather than wealth and social prestige; however, the crisis of the novel shows how the boundaries of the middle class can quickly become inflexible. Three of the girls defy Lloyd's mother's admonition that they not go to a nearby gypsy camp because the gypsies "are a rough, low set of people—gamblers and horse thieves." Their violation of maternal authority results in all four girls contracting measles, and one of them nearly going blind, illustrating the vulnerability of young middle-class white women to contagion and disease spread by ethnic others.[7]

The books' treatment of its characters' economic fortunes also tests the boundaries of the middle class. Characters exhibit a surprising degree of economic mobility, albeit heavily structured by race and social class. Rather than accruing from unspecified hereditary sources, families' wealth often comes from business investments, extractive practices such as mining, or success within professions such as law, medicine, or the military, exemplifying Robert Wiebe's assertion that the new middle class of the Progressive Era coalesced along professional lines. The American West and even Mexico are frequently mentioned as places of economic opportunity, and the series' male characters prove more interested in keeping pace with the national and international nature of modern industry than in reviving the local economies of the plantation-era South. Although the lifestyles of Lloydsboro Valley's inhabitants appear to be ones of static ease, a closer look at the economic structures that underpin characters' wealth reveals the boom-and-bust nature of turn-of-the-twentieth-century business practices. In *The Little Colonel*, Lloyd's parents undergo a brief period of poverty, due to some risky, but ultimately shrewd, investments by her father, who tells her mother that he has "the inside track" in a concern out west and that the firm he "went security for in New York is on its feet again." Even old money is not allowed to rest on its laurels. A character in *The Little Colonel's Knight Comes Riding* is lauded by his young sister-in-law because rather than simply living a life of leisure, he "looks after the details of his own business as a man should. He knows all about the mines he has stock in down in Mexico, and he studies mineralogy and labour problems and investments, and has an office that he goes to regularly every morning." The books are surprisingly frank about the reversals of fortune middle-class characters can suffer. The cure for poor economic outlook is the market economy, which will eventually reward diligence, rather than more fanciful nineteenth-century contrivances, such as an older relative leaving a fortune.[8]

As their economic values indicate, the books are not quite as provincial as they first appear; the patina of the Old South conceals a world that has much in common with the lives of middle- and upper-class child readers from other parts of the country, including the supposedly alien North. Even the books' undercompensated African American labor, seemingly a hallmark of the southern United States, had its northern counterpart in the recently arrived Irish and other immigrants. Lloyd's cosmopolitan life at times appears remarkably similar to that of a middle- or upper-class girl from New England at the beginning of the twentieth century. She travels throughout the United States and Europe and goes to an exclusive school in Washington, D.C., to be "finished." The ready attentions of African American custodians ensure that she has ample time for both learning and leisure. The domestic situation was not that much different for middle-class northern girls, who were liberated from household drudgery by the emergence of a cheap immigrant workforce and their families' social aspirations. Affluent Lloyd is rarely seen doing any household labor, and what domestic work she does is charitable in nature. In *The Little Colonel's Christmas Vacation*, kept home from boarding school for a term by a bout of illness and finding time hanging heavily on her hands, she cooks lunch for a poor neighboring family. Her plan to clean the home of another needy neighbor entails her actually doing no cleaning at all but rather supervising May Lily, a young African American woman who "swept and scrubbed and scoured" in her stead. Lloyd's experience reflects Jane Hunter's determination that among affluent families, domestic labor at the *fin de siècle* was seen as a mechanism to "structure the lives and enhance the character of prospering girls," rather than a fulfillment of household labor needs.[9]

Johnston frequently directs her main characters' (and by extension her readers') visions outward toward an American, rather than a purely southern, identity, recognizing that the unification of white Americans was essential in order to combat the influences of immigrants and African Americans at home and increase national standing abroad. A number of volumes of the series are set primarily in other locales, among them Washington, D.C., Arizona, and Switzerland. In *The Little*

Colonel's Holidays (1901), Lloyd travels only as far as the nearby city of Louisville, but finds herself in the home of U.S. Army general Walton, who died during the Philippine-American War. Walton's real-life counterpart was General Henry Ware Lawton, a soldier who began his career as a Union officer during the Civil War and was a veteran of the Indian campaigns and the Spanish-American War before his death in the Philippines. When Lloyd is surprised by the rush of emotion the war hero's portrait elicits, his widow replies, "It is a part of patriotism," causing Lloyd to say wonderingly, "I didn't know I had any. . . . I always took grandfathah's side, you know, because the Yankees shot his arm off. I hated 'em for it, and I nevah would hurrah for the Union. I've despised Republicans and the Nawth from the time I could talk." Mrs. Walton directly refutes Lloyd's declaration of unconditional loyalty to the memory of the Confederacy:

> "Don't say that Lloyd. . . . What have we to do with that old quarrel? Its time has long gone by. I, too, am a daughter of the South, Lloyd, but surely such lives as his have not been sacrificed in vain." She pointed impressively to the portrait. "That, if nothing else, would make me want to forget that North and South had ever been arrayed against each other. Surely such lives as his by their high loyalty should inspire a love of country deep enough to make America the guiding star of the nations."

This passage calls into question Marshall's assertion that despite the "occasional reference to the theme of reunion" in the *Little Colonel* series Johnston "creates a Kentucky whose allegiances and whose historical memories are entirely Confederate." In her analysis, Marshall creates this impression by quoting only Lloyd's initial reaction to the portrait and omitting Mrs. Walton's response. The words of this older, wiser woman, also a fellow southerner, render Lloyd's expressed loyalty to the Lost Cause anachronistic, indicating the modern, forward-looking dimensions of the *Little Colonel* books. Johnston, using Mrs. Walton as a mouthpiece, implies that Lloyd is an impetuous young girl whose sectional loyalty must be channeled into the service of a larger American identity. Mrs. Walton's checking of Lloyd also implies a larger rhetorical adult presence, which presides didactically over the lives of the books' young characters. Her expressed wish that America be "the guiding star of the nations" reflects the United States' increasing international awareness and involvement in the years leading up to the First World War; it also shows that Johnston herself thought that the overdue cultural reconciliation of North and South was essential for America to meet its global potential in the Progressive Era.[10]

This explicit evocation of nationalism in a work targeted at white American girls indicates that America's international rise depended on its female as well as its male citizens. In *The Little Colonel's Hero*, Johnston makes her most compelling case for America's international involvement, seeing no contradiction between cooperative humanitarian endeavors and American military imperialism. Johnston's precarious rhetorical position anticipates the propaganda surrounding America's entry into World War One on the side of the Allies, which characterized military force as an instrument of benevolence. The "hero" of the story is a St. Bernard who served as a rescue dog in the Red Cross before becoming Lloyd's pet due to circumstances too improbable and convoluted to delineate. The book is effectively a paean to the Red Cross framed by a trip the Little Colonel and her parents take to Switzerland. When Lloyd first meets Hero and begins conversing with the elderly German army officer who has trained him, her companion is shocked that she has never heard of the Red Cross. The officer's incredulity increases when he learns that Lloyd is ignorant, not only of the Red Cross but of Clara Barton, the Civil War nurse who founded the American arm of the organization in 1881 and headed it until 1904. Through praise of Barton and the International Red Cross, Johnston explicitly advocates a unified America's abandonment of isolationism and involvement in international affairs. Praise of Barton and her linkage with the Red Cross recurs in multiple incidents throughout *The Little Colonel's Hero*. In addition to the elderly officer, a German soldier in the Franco-Prussian War, Lloyd and her friends meet Madame, whose husband fought on the French side of the same engagement; Madame also lauds the Red Cross and Clara Barton. Further references to Barton focus on her role in the American rather than the International Red Cross. On the boat ride back to the United States, numerous passengers tell the girls how Barton and the American Red Cross helped them in the wake of various disasters. These accounts span all regions of the country, from the 1886 Charleston, South Carolina, earthquake to the

1889 Johnstown, Pennsylvania, flood, casting the Red Cross as an organization that helps Americans from all regions, including the South, and Barton as a symbol of national cooperation.[11]

So taken are Lloyd and her friends by the glowing descriptions of the Red Cross's work that upon their return to Lloydsboro Valley, they organize a play to raise money for the organization. The full text of the play, entitled *The Rescue of the Princess Winsome*, appears in the book and runs to some twenty-seven pages, including four songs, which come complete with music composed by Johnston's sister. Sue Lynn McDaniel notes that a number of children's organizations actually performed Johnston's play and donated the proceeds to charity in the manner of Lloyd and her friends. In her autobiography Johnston frequently expresses pleasure at the larger societal impact of her books and takes particular pride in her play's success: "It is good to hear of the charitable work started by the play of the Princess Winsome which has been given in many places." In an example of the marketing savvy of Johnston and her publisher, L.C. Page and Company of Boston, the play, along with the other moralistic fairy tales embedded in the *Little Colonel* books, was available for separate purchase as part of "The Johnston Jewel Series." Considering the period's lack of widespread access to quick methods of facsimile reproduction such as the mimeograph machine, it seems reasonable to conclude that putting on a charitable performance of *The Rescue of the Princess Winsome* may have involved purchasing multiple 75-cent copies of Johnston's play. This double-barreled appeal to the pocketbooks and the idealism of young, mostly female adolescents exemplifies Joe Sanders's designation of the Progressive Era as "one of the early high points of consumer culture in US history" during which "girls' shopping and buying became increasingly important as both an economic and a cultural phenomenon."[12]

Despite her obvious recognition of the increasing consumer power and cultural sway of young American women, at the end of *The Little Colonel's Hero* Johnston sharply restricts Lloyd's participation in public life. The last page of the book presents a saccharine forecast for the Little Colonel's future: "She knows she can never be a Joan of Arc or a Clara Barton, and her name will never be written in America's hall of fame, but with the sweet ambition in her heart to make life a little lovelier for everyone she touches, she is growing up into a veritable Princess

Winsome." Johnston offers American girls a stark choice between the evidently mutually exclusive roles of Clara Barton and Princess Winsome. While this limited vision of Lloyd's future proves particularly jarring given the book's illustration via Barton of exactly what American women are capable of, Johnston's restrictive parameters may have reflected her recognition that the heteronormative, domestic lives many of her female readers expected to lead were not yet conducive to the activities of a Clara Barton. After all, during the early years of the twentieth century even professional women such as teachers were still routinely forced to leave their jobs once they married; Johnston's own professional writing career and involvement in public life did not begin until the death of her husband.[13]

Lloyd's desire to "make life a little lovelier for everyone she touches" illustrates the realistic limits of female empowerment for marriageable girls of the middle and upper classes at the beginning of the twentieth century. The careful circumscription of Lloyd's future reflects cultural pressure to keep young women in the home even as the home itself was coming under increasing scrutiny, and professionals from physicians to social workers were beginning to undercut homemakers' status as experts on domestic matters. Although Johnston injects national and international events into her books, Lloyd's civic involvement is not supposed to reach beyond her own community, reflecting Carolyn Carpan's assertion that "[t]he ideals of Victorian domesticity, womanliness, and marriage still permeated girls' series fiction throughout the Progressive Era, even as new roles for middle and upper-class girls were possible." Lloyd's role models are her mother and other Pewee Valley women who engage in organized charitable work. The adult women's efforts at reform did not extend beyond a fairly local circumference, but this would have been typical for the 1890s and early 1900s, emblematic of what Nancy S. Dye calls the "local emphasis of progressivism," which preceded the national networks of women's organizations that would emerge over the next two decades. The "Kings Daughters," one organization mentioned in multiple books, exists today as the International Order of the Kings Daughters and Sons. In the *Little Colonel* books, the Kings Daughters is a Protestant "circle" whose members perform charitable acts for the ill and indigent.[14]

In imitation of the adult clubwomen they see around them, Lloyd and her friends form a number of clubs dedicated to good behavior and good works. In the early books of the series Johnston does not show any effort to translate philanthropy directly into municipal policy. As with the glowing depiction of Clara Barton, however, the books often gesture toward this possibility, while keeping their girl characters confined in more traditional roles. For example, in *The Little Colonel in Arizona* when Lloyd, vacationing near Phoenix, encounters a student from a nearby Indian boarding school, she exclaims,

> "That's an Indian ploughing there! An Indian in a cadet unifawm, with brass buttons on it. Doesn't it seem queah? Jack says it's the unifawm of the school, and that they have to weah it when they hiah out to the fahmahs. This is paht of their education. I like them best in tomahawks and blankets. It seems moah natural."

Soon after she encounters the young man plowing, Lloyd tours the school where he is a student and sees Indian children engaged in various "civilized" activities such as tailoring clothing and practicing finger exercises at the piano. This particular boarding school, described in appreciative detail by Johnston, is probably a representation of the Phoenix Indian School, which, like many of its peer institutions, required its male students to wear military uniforms and work for neighboring white farmers, while its female students were hired out to white women as domestics. Margaret Jacobs has written extensively about how federal policies surrounding Indian boarding schools in the United States, including the Phoenix Indian School, were heavily influenced by white female reformers' ideas regarding gender roles and family structures. Lloyd's older, romantic view of American Indians contrasts with the progressive ideals of assimilation and absorption the boarding school system embodied. As with Mrs. Walton's condemnation of Lloyd's southern partisanship, Johnston inserts a progressive attitude as a counterpoint to Lloyd's romantic one. Although she does not show her books' white female characters working actively on behalf of these entities, the affirmative depictions of the American Red Cross and the Phoenix Indian School indicate Johnston's awareness and approval of national reform projects.[15]

White maternal benevolence, fittingly enough, is first modeled for Lloyd by her mother. The initial example of charitable largesse involves

Betty, Mrs. Sherman's goddaughter and the daughter of her childhood friend. An orphan who lives with distant cousins in a rural community and does the work of a hired girl, Betty is a variety of the genteel orphan living in circumstances that are beneath her. The series contains a preponderance of orphans and half-orphans, illustrating that Mintz's assertion that "Nineteenth Century literature was obsessed with orphans" held true for the early years of the twentieth century as well, perhaps reflecting progressivism's interest in child welfare. Betty is worthy of being raised to, if not an equivalent social position to that of Lloyd, one that is definitely within the middle class. One of Mrs. Sherman's first charitable acts for her goddaughter elicits the following response from Lloyd: "Now I see what you meant, mothah, . . . about the different ways of givin' things. It can't hurt anybody's pride if you make them feel that you give it for love's sweet sake. That was a beautiful way you did it, mothah, and I'll never fo'get it."[16]

While Betty is treated like a member of Lloyd's family, charity is administered to other characters in a less delicate manner. Johnston is very conscious of class distinctions among white people, and the *Little Colonel* books contain at least three distinct categories of white poverty: well-bred people such as Betty who have fallen on hard times, honest denizens of the working class, and the "poah white trash," whom no amount of uplift can redeem. In *The Little Colonel's Holidays*, Lloyd and her friends reunite a hired girl named Molly (Betty's replacement as her cousins' drudge and a member of the middle category of poor people) with her little sister Dot, who was kidnapped by their alcoholic father. Lloyd finds the younger sister while engaged in a task of charitable uplift, delivering American Beauty roses to sick children in a Louisville hospital. The reunion between Molly and Dot takes place at Christmas, allowing a Dickensian exploitation of the gulf between the wealthy and poor. Building on the holiday's sentimental associations, Johnston has the gravely ill Dot die just as the candles on the Christmas tree are burning out.[17]

Viewing the death of a child in a positive light seems unimaginable to a twenty-first-century reader, but Mrs. Walton, who has four beloved children of her own, describes Dot's death as "beautiful," and even Molly seems resigned to the loss of her sister:

Oh, Mrs. Walton, now that I know that she's comfortable and happy, I can't feel so bad about her as I used to. She's so safe now. No matter what happens, the saloons can't hurt her, now. There'll be no more hungry days, no more beatings, and it will always be such comfort to me to think she had such a good time in the hospital. For six weeks she had plenty to eat, and everybody was good to her. . . . She had white grapes and roses even in the winter-time, and she had *ice-cream!* All she wanted. And I made up my mind this morning that when I'm old enough I am going to be a trained nurse and help take care of poor little children the way she was taken care of here.

Molly's condemnation of the "saloons," which, according to the novel, inveigled her father into a life of drunkenness and broke apart her once-happy family, indicates not only support for temperance but the larger idea that social conditions bear some responsibility for poverty and misfortune. Her desire to be a "trained nurse" reflects the medicalization of nursing and its transformation into a paid occupation for young, working-class women. The bulk of her exclamation, nevertheless, endorses older, Victorian ideas of benevolence. Molly's rhapsodic list of the luxuries her sister enjoyed suggests that the gifts of prosperous, well-meaning women can make up for a lifetime of abuse and neglect. Lacking any discernible personality traits beyond sweetness and gratitude, Dot becomes little more than a vehicle for charitable activity and a lesson for the book's well-off children regarding the symbolic meaning of Christmas. Unlike the gifted and well-born Betty, Molly will never be eligible for the middle class. Her acceptance of Dot's death hinges on her sister's brief tenure as a protected and indulged child, and she obviously views Dot's enjoyment of some of the pleasures of middle-class childhood as compensation for her truncated life. The improbable account of the finding of Dot and the sentimental depiction of her death paradoxically allow *The Little Colonel's Holidays* to mirror realistic progressive trends, showing women's benevolent activity expanding to the realm of the urban institution. In addition to hospital volunteer work, the book's adult female characters offer their support to a "free kindergarten" targeted at children living in in the city of Louisville's tenement district.[18]

By the end of the series in 1912, Johnston envisioned an even broader reach for women's charitable involvement. In *Mary Ware's Promised Land*, Lloyd's friend Mary becomes a secretary to Mrs. Blythe, a socialite and tenement reformer, who, like many of the books' other characters, has a real-world prototype, the author's sister Albion Fellows Bacon. Bacon's biographer notes, "During the midst of Albion's housing reform campaign Annie even modeled the character of tenement crusader Mrs. Blythe . . . after her younger sister." Horrified at the conditions those who rent the city's tenement apartments must endure, Mary Ware becomes a crusader in her own right, helping Mrs. Blythe to influence local elections and move a tenement reform bill through the state legislature. There are, however, still distinct limits to women's civic activity. Mary Ware, eager to reassure a friend that her employer's involvement in public life is still within the realm of ladylike behavior, writes, "Don't think that Mrs. Blythe has gone in personally for politics or anything like that, because she hasn't. But she has waked up a lot of influential people to work for her cause, and induced one of the foremost men in the senate to introduce the bill." When Mary determines to renounce marriage in order to devote herself to tenement reform, Mrs. Blythe cautions her against such a decision, citing her own experience: "Because I have a home of my own, and a recognized social position, and am a happy wife and mother, people listen to me far more readily when I go to them with a plea for less fortunate homes and wives and mothers." Mrs. Blythe's remark indicates the first point in the series where Johnston specifically advocates maternalism—the idea that middle- and upper-class women's experiences as wives and mothers fit them to set social policy for their less fortunate sisters. Revisiting *The Little Colonel's Hero*, published in 1902, and comparing Lloyd's future with that of Mary Ware, exemplifies the evolution of Johnston's thinking. Unlike Lloyd, who "knows she can never be a Joan of Arc or a Clara Barton," Mary Ware realizes that she has been "called to a destiny even greater than that of the Maid of Orleans. This battle, once won, would give not only this generation of helpless poor their chance for health and decent homes, but would lift the handicap from their children and all their children's children who might come after them." In 1902, little girls could not aspire to anything like the significance of Joan of Arc; by 1912 young women could accomplish even greater objectives. *Mary Ware's Promised Land* also depicts benevolence extending to an expanded category of European Americans. The book mentions the plight of Irish and eastern and southern European immigrants. It also advocates concrete solutions to social problems rather than nebulous "help."[19]

The growth and development the series affords its young white characters and the expansion of ideas of social engagement it illustrates fall apart with respect to African Americans. From 1895 to the series' end in 1912, their status does not change; unlike recent immigrants or even American Indians, they are not seen as capable of progress or assimilation. Detailed analysis of the *Little Colonel* books' African American characters serves little purpose, since Johnston makes use of the broadest, most simplistic stereotypes. Black characters appear only as domestic servants, speak in exaggerated dialect, and are superstitious, simple-minded, and completely loyal to their white "families." The stasis in which they exist highlights the maturation of Lloyd and her friends. Over the course of the series, the white children grow in knowledge and poise, while the black children grow only in body. May Lily, who makes mud pies with Lloyd in the first book of the series, *The Little Colonel*, and "swept and scrubbed and scoured" in *The Little Colonel's Christmas Vacation*, becomes Mary Ware's cook in *Mary Ware's Promised Land*. In *The Little Colonel's House Party*, a young African American girl named M'haley gives Lloyd's friend Eugenia a chicken to take back with her to New York City. Of course this action elicits much merriment among the white characters. When questioned as to why M'haley is giving Eugenia such a gift, M'haley's friend Tildy explains, "Cause Miss 'Genia, she give M'haley her hat wid roses on it ovah to the ole mill picnic, when it fell in de spring an' got wet." In *The Little Colonel, Maid of Honor* (1906) Eugenia gets married, and M'haley, who is to be maid of honor in her mother's wedding, is once again the beneficiary of the white girl's castoff finery. When the newly wed couple are pelted with shoes for good luck, M'haley snatches them, exclaiming, "Them slippahs is mates! . . . and I'm goin' to tote 'em home for we-all's wedding." Just as the African American wedding, described in the most offensively racist terms imaginable, serves as a foil for the white wedding, so M'haley, still as ignorant as she was as a child, highlights the maturity of Lloyd and her friends.[20]

Over the span of the *Little Colonel* series, Annie Fellows Johnston keeps pace with the tide of progressivism as it affected white women and girls of the middle class. Her characters move from initially helping close friends and family to eventually aiding members of the surrounding community. Their reach eventually extends to anonymous institutions and finally to broader civic reform movements. Johnston's failure to depict any corresponding upward trajectory with regard to her African American characters also reflects progressive trends. Reforms often failed to include African Americans or targeted them specifically in particularly harmful ways. Ultimately, the *Little Colonel* books showed their contemporary child readers the importance of social consciousness, but in a very limited context.

NOTES

1. Arthur W. Shumaker, "Annie Fellows Johnston" in *Notable American Women, 1607–1950: A Biographical Dictionary*, vol. 2, Edward T. James, Janet Wilson James, and Paul S. Boyer, eds. (Cambridge, MA: Harvard University Press, 1971), 280.
2. David W. Blight, *Beyond the Battlefield: Race, Memory, and the American Civil War* (Amherst: University of Massachusetts Press, 2002), 127; Anne. E. Marshall, *Creating a Confederate Kentucky: The Lost Cause and Civil War Memory in a Border State* (Chapel Hill: University of North Carolina Press, 2010), 138, 140.
3. Blight, *Beyond the Battlefield*, 126; Annie Fellows Johnston, *The Little Colonel* (Boston, MA: L.C. Page, 1904).
4. Johnston, *The Land of the Little Colonel: Reminiscence and Autobiography* (Boston, MA: L.C. Page, 1929), 3; "Pewee Valley," in *The Encyclopedia of Louisville*, ed. John E. Kleber (Lexington: University Press of Kentucky, 2001), 699; Sue Lynn Stone, "Annie Fellows Johnston," in *Encyclopedia of Louisville*, 451.
5. Johnston, *Land*, 3; Sherrie A. Inness, "Introduction," in *Nancy Drew and Company: Culture, Gender, and Girls' Series*, ed. Sherrie A. Inness (Bowling Green, OH: Bowling Green State University Popular Press, 1997), 2; Stephen Mintz, *Huck's Raft: A History of American Childhood* (Cambridge, MA: Harvard University Press, 2006), 186.
6. De Luzio, *Female Adolescence in American Scientific Thought, 1830–1930*, 91, 92; G. Stanley Hall, "Must Your Child Lie?" in *Parents and Their Problems: Child Welfare in Home, School, Church, and State*, ed. Mary Harmon Weeks (Washington, DC: National Congress of Mothers and Parent-Teacher Associations, 1914), 285; Norman Coleman, "Some Definite Needs of Moral Instruction," in *Parents and Their Problems: Child Welfare in Home, School, Church, and State*, 283–84; Johnston, *The Little Colonel's House Party* (Boston: L.C. Page, 1919), 105, 116.
7. Johnston, *The Little Colonel's House Party* (Boston, MA: L. C. Page, 1919), 105, 116.

8. Robert Wiebe, *The Search for Order: 1877–1920* (New York: Hill and Wang, 2001), 112–13; Johnston, *Little Colonel*, 101; Johnston, *The Little Colonel's Knight Comes Riding* (Boston, MA: L.C. Page, 1910), 101, 39.
9. Johnston, *The Little Colonel's Christmas Vacation* (Boston, MA: L.C. Page, 1909), 305; Jane H. Hunter, *How Young Ladies Became Girls: The Victorian Origins of American Girlhood* (New Haven, CT: Yale University Press, 2002), 22.
10. Johnston, *The Little Colonel's Holidays* (Boston, MA: L.C. Page, 1923), 175.
11. Johnston, *The Little Colonel's Hero* (Boston, MA: L.C. Page, 1908), 70, 162–68.
12. Johnston, *Hero*; Sue Lynn McDaniel, "The Little Colonel: A Phenomenon in Popular Literary Culture," *Register of the Kentucky Historical Society* (Spring 1991): 15–16, http://digitalcommons.wku.edu/dlsc_fac_pub/4; Johnston, *Land*, 131; "A Glimpse of the Juvenile Book World," in *The Bookman*, vol. 28, ed. Arthur Bartlett Maurice (New York: Dodd, Mead, 1909), 385; Joe Sutliff Sanders, *Disciplining Girls: Understanding the Origins of the Classic Orphan Girl Story* (Baltimore, MD: Johns Hopkins UP, 2011), 95.
13. Johnston, *Hero*, 273.
14. Johnston, *Hero*, 273; Carolyn Carpan, *Sisters, Schoolgirls, and Sleuths: Girls' Series Books in America* (Lanham, MD: Scarecrow, 2009), 19; Nancy S. Dye, "Introduction," in *Gender, Class, Race, and Reform in the Progressive Era*, ed. Noralee Frankel and Nancy S. Dye (Lexington: University Press of Kentucky, 1991), 2.
15. Johnston, *The Little Colonel in Arizona* (Boston, MA: L.C. Page, 1908), 255; Owen Lindauer, "Archaeology of the Phoenix Indian School," *Archaeology* (March 27, 1998), http://www.archaeology.org/online/features/phoenix; Margaret Jacobs, *White Mother to a Dark Race: Settler Colonialism, Maternalism, and the Removal of Indigenous Children in the American West and Australia* (Lincoln: University of Nebraska Press, 2009), 332–33, 339.
16. Mintz, *Huck's Raft*, 157; Johnston, *House Party*, 95.
17. Johnston, *Christmas Vacation*, 300; Johnston, *Holidays*, 207–8.
18. Johnston, *Holidays*, 227, 229, 167.
19. Johnston, *Mary Ware's Promised Land* (Boston, MA: L.C. Page, 1923), 186; Robert Graham Barrows, *Albion Fellows Bacon: Indiana's Municipal Housekeeper* (Bloomington: Indiana University Press, 2000), 85; Johnston, *Mary Ware*, 247–48; ibid., 295; Johnston, *Hero*, 273; Johnston, *Mary Ware*, 219 .
20. Johnston, *Little Colonel*, 24; Johnston, *Christmas Vacation*, 305; Johnston, *Mary Ware*, 310; Johnston, *House Party*, 261; Johnston, *The Little Colonel, Maid of Honor* (Boston, MA: L.C. Page, 1907), 215.

PART II

Managing Change

Children, Youth, and Families

From 1908 to 1921, Lewis Hine traveled the country on behalf of the National Child Labor Committee (NCLC), photographing thousands of children at work in factories and mills, on street corners and in tenement apartments. From time to time he had to sneak into manufacturing plants, canneries, or cotton mills to get pictures, but occasionally he could get the young workers to pose for what may have been the first photograph ever taken of them. Published in NCLC pamphlets and books, displayed in exhibits, and used to illustrate lectures on child labor, his iconic photographs document one of the biggest moral and economic issues of his day. They featured barefoot boy and girl "doffers" in southern cotton mills, dwarfed by the giant looms on which they changed the spindles; grimy-faced boys as they emerged from coal mines; tiny children who look as though they are barely able to walk working alongside their parents and older siblings in dingy apartments; devil-may-care newsboys. Sometimes Hine recorded the names and ages of the children in hand-written captions, and he occasionally remarked on a child's sickly appearance, lack of education, and pitiful wage.[1]

>> 121

John Tidwell, Cotton Mill Product. (Library of Congress Prints and Photographs Collection)

The boy in this photo, John Tidwell, is a doffer in Avondale Mills near Birmingham, Alabama. Hine calls him a "Cotton Mill Product" and comments disapprovingly that "[m]any of these youngsters smoke." Young John might be anywhere from ten to sixteen years old, but, at least in this picture, on an afternoon when the drudgery of mill work was broken for at least a few moments by this Yankee photographer, John projected an aura of confidence, independence, even cockiness. The two boys looking on seem almost uncomfortable to be in the picture. Even though they realize that they are not Hine's real target, you can see the tension in their shoulders and their hesitant half-smiles. John, on the other hand, seems at ease, as though he had made a joke or wisecrack just before he turned to face the camera. For whatever reason, he seems content, perhaps even satisfied, with his lot in life.

That is not quite what Gilded Age and Progressive Era reformers expected of the children they were trying to "save." To a greater or lesser extent, the youth featured in the essays in part 2 share at least some of the spirit displayed by John Tidwell. At the very least, they show that, like children and youth in any time and place, they were not simply objects to be manipulated by adults. They had their own needs and ideas, and they would absorb the lessons and values that they found useful.

NOTE

1. The most recent biography of Hine is Kate Sampsell-Willmann, *Lewis Hine as Social Critic* (Jackson: University Press of Mississippi, 2009).

6

Willful Disobedience

*Young People and School Authority in the
Nineteenth-Century United States*

JAMES D. SCHMIDT

When Zeb Gardener came home from school one spring day in 1895, his grandmother knew something was not right. He did not eat dinner and complained that his leg hurt. Thirteen-year-old Zeb, it turned out, had taken a severe beating from George Long, his teacher at the North Carolina school he attended. Mr. Long "whipped me for shooting a boy with a small crossbow," Zeb later testified. "The boy held up his hand for me to shoot at and I shot him with a small arrow, which had a pin in the end of it. We were not mad at each other." Cut and badly bruised, Zeb walked on crutches for nearly a month, but he and his family did not take the thrashing lightly. They went to the local authorities, who indicted the teacher on assault charges. Convicted by a lower court jury, Long took the case to the North Carolina Supreme Court. From his point of view, the punishment had been necessary and proper to maintain good order. "I told him that I was very sorry that I had to whip him," Long recalled, "but that I had expressly commanded him not to shoot the bow on the ground, and that he had, almost immediately, violated my instructions." The high court agreed, noting that "the authority of teachers to correct their pupils for disobedience and the limitations thereon have long since been settled."[1]

Like many principles, the authority of teachers was anything but "settled" in the late-nineteenth and early-twentieth centuries. The Gilded Age and Progressive Era witnessed an outpouring of legal challenges by young people and their families to the power of schools and school teachers to inflict physical punishment, expel or suspend students, or enforce an ever-evolving set of rules for school governance. This essay examines corporal punishment and the questions about school authority suggested by these cases. These clashes, I argue, helped to shape daily expressions of power in the modern school system.

The records of these litigations reveal conflicts embedded in class and gender but also in contested notions of the role of schooling in a democratic society. While teachers and administrators often debated the methods, they nonetheless agreed that obedience was both the heart of the school day and the overall purpose of schooling in a polity committed to the rule of law. Students and their families certainly shared these notions, but they often expressed differing visions about the nature and limits of schoolmasters' power. Seemingly minor disputes about, for example, studying geography or participating in a school play, turned into major examinations of power when the violence of physical punishment entered the picture. Confronted with students who did not cheerfully obey, schools adapted. Indeed, student and parent resistance to corporal punishment pushed schools more and more toward suspension and expulsion as means of school governance by the early twentieth century. By looking inside schools during the period when they came to dominate the lives of young people, then, we can see that students themselves took an active and sometimes ironic role in the making of school authority.[2]

* * * *

Discussion of corporal punishment in the household and in society, of course, predated the Gilded Age and Progressive Era. Indeed, the long imprint of the ancient world, especially biblical proverbs regarding childrearing, provided a touchstone for much of the nineteenth-century discussion. By the post–Civil War era, however, biblical authority often came in for direct scrutiny as not in keeping with the spirit of the age. In other words, while the Word remained the truth in postbellum America, that truth was increasingly under assault. That it should be so reflected, in part, the rise of what in religious history is called "the higher criticism," an approach to the Bible that reads it in historical context. More important was the conundrum of republican government raised by the American and French revolutions. The legitimating ideology of republicanism rested on, in Jefferson's famous articulation, the "consent of the governed." But how could that consent be secured? In the late-eighteenth and early-nineteenth centuries, republican thinkers looked to the schools. An educated populace would submit to authority, but it would do so willingly. In a widely circulated essay penned in 1786, Benjamin Rush called for "absolute authority" in the schools, envisioning them as places to "prepare our youth for the subordination of laws and thereby qualify them for becoming good citizens of the republic." Authority of this nature might be gained by force of reason or by just plain force, but the goal was the same. By the early antebellum period, alternatives to pure and simple caning started to appear in religious and educational periodicals. In one particularly ingenious example, a correspondent in 1821 related an elaborate legal process of arraignment and trial before punishment was meted out. Aping the emergent American trial system, it turned out, produced a "cheerful submission" that carried over into home and street.[3]

The conflicts of the later nineteenth century were also influenced by early-nineteenth-century experiments in governance, both inside and outside of schools. These changes formed part of a broader Atlantic school reform movement that began in the eighteenth century and continued in the nineteenth. In turn, school reformers were influenced by Atlantic debates about sanguinary punishment and Britain's "bloody code." Together, these twin ideological strains would push along the debates about school governance initiated by the republican impulse. From one direction, elites worried about the madding crowds of growing Atlantic cities, especially burgeoning seaport towns. In Britain, the rapid growth of London and other mercantile and industrial centers prompted a movement toward charity schools as a way to ensure proper submission of the laboring classes. As more young people began to enter such schools, questions of discipline invariably arose, but in the wake of the American Revolution, they did so in an altered context. The revolution had prompted a new look at Britain's horrifically violent penal code, and by the 1780s, debates raged about capital punishment throughout the newly minted states. The American reaction to the Terror of the French Revolution in the 1790s raised further concerns about the role of violence in governance. By the turn of the nineteenth century, then, an ideological and historical stage had been set upon which debates about corporal punishment in schools would play out. The spread of the Lancasterian, or monitorial, system in the Early Republic raised further questions about the efficacy of corporal punishment in an even more direct manner. Established by Joseph Lancaster, a British educator, the system relied on the orderly recitation of lessons in huge classrooms overseen by a hierarchical system of monitors chosen from the advanced students. Though critics decried the regimented nature of the plan, monitorial schooling caught on quickly in the early United States.[4]

Not only did debate about corporal punishment precede the postbellum era, but legal challenges did as well. Law records and newspaper reports of legal matters in the Early Republic are sketchy, but it appears that the first assault cases involving corporal punishment arose in the 1820s. The earliest one I have found is *Commonwealth versus Patrick Coad*, an action tried in Philadelphia in 1821. The conflict concerned Coad, a schoolmaster, and Edwin Greble, a fifteen-year-old student at his school. When Edwin responded to Coad in ways the teacher interpreted as insolence, he grabbed the boy by the collar and gave him several licks with a knotted rope. Edwin responded by pulling a knife and vowing to "stick" schoolmaster Coad if touched again. Edwin's father pressed charges, but a jury of townspeople acquitted the schoolmaster. In arguing his innocence, Coad maintained that "it was his duty, as well as his legal right, to inflict adequate and reasonable punishment, and to maintain his authority among his scholars." Indeed, far from "exceeding the bounds of moderation," the schoolmaster averred, "he had not in this case, carried severity to its proper and salutary length."[5]

The Coad case both illustrated the quotidian struggles of the schoolhouse and reverberated outwards into elemental debates about morality, authority, and society. In the narrow sense, Edwin Greble did not want a beating and his father agreed. In a broader sense, Coad was a stand-in for deep-seated conflicts over authority in a republican society. Commenting on the case, the *Baltimore Morning Chronicle* made this matter explicit. "Unbroken and undisciplined boys" arrived at the schoolhouse as "in every moral sense, orphans," the paper opined. "The preceptor has not only to instruct, but to break . . . these youths to habits of obedience." How exactly said "breaking" was to occur was the rub. A near consensus on the need for discipline and obedience, in school and in society, was obtained, but debate raged on the role of school violence in effecting that salubrious outcome. In the 1840s, that discussion famously surfaced in Boston where noted reformer Horace Mann, then secretary of the Massachusetts State Board of Education, battled Boston's teachers over the right to deploy the rod. Even Mann, however, conceded that "order is emphatically the first law of a schoolroom."[6]

Simultaneously, legal challenges to corporal punishment had begun to find their way out of the local level and into the exalted halls of state supreme courts, where the words of bench-bound solons would carry much more weight than those of a local justice. The first and most important of such cases arose not in reform-minded New England, but in the slave South. It involved not the typical rowdy teenage boy but a young girl of six or seven. Rachel Pendergrass had suffered a switching at the hands of her teacher in 1837 near the town of Caswell, North Carolina. The beating had left marks that disappeared in a few days, but apparently Rachel's parents went to the authorities, who charged the teacher with assault and battery. The matter led North Carolina justice William J. Gaston to solidify the salience of *in loco parentis* in school authority but at the same time qualify that authority with the proviso that corporal punishment must not involve malice. The Pendergrass cases foreshadowed the approach that jurists would take toward corporal punishment for decades to come: that it was legal with limitations. This compromise was not without opponents on the bench, and the most forthright during the antebellum era was William Z. Stuart, who used his short stint on the Indiana Supreme Court to write stinging denunciations of corporal punishment in two cases that came before the court in 1853. If teachers must resort to the rod, "the nurseries of the republic are not the proper element," Stuart declared. If schoolmasters were not restrained, "those whose feelings are outraged will have no apology for taking redress into their own hands." As we shall see, Stuart was more than a little prescient on this score.[7]

* * * *

In the decades after the Civil War, conflict over corporal punishment and the authority of schools and schoolmasters exploded. Students and their parents challenged the right to physical discipline both in the courts and in the streets. Simple suits for assault and battery were the most common form of opposition, but occasionally parents and older siblings took matters into their own hands, just as Stuart had predicted, resulting in numerous assaults and some actual murders of school teachers. While opposition appeared all over the country, many of the more violent responses took place in the South, where lingering codes of honor and manly fighting prompted extralegal solutions to schoolroom imbroglios. Although dramatic, these violent incidents had less influence on the actual daily operation of school authority than did more traditional legal means of redress. Suits against teachers, whether brought in civil court by families themselves or in criminal court by the state, prompted careful examinations of wider cultural and local community assumptions about how schooling in a democratic society was supposed to work. These efforts worked in parallel with the movements of progressive reformers, refashioning the locus of authority in the educational system. Slowly, the personal, patriarchal command of the master in his schoolroom gave way to a more anonymous, bureaucratic power lodged in the school itself, even if that power was wielded by its chief of operations: the principal. Opposition to corporal punishment also led to a significant shift in the actual forms of enforcing school discipline. Expulsion grew as a means of counteracting the baneful influence of the incorrigible. Removal might be to the streets or, by the turn of the century, to a truant school. At the same time, educators began to explicitly explore play and sports as alternatives to corporal punishment in maintaining school discipline. In all of these discussions, a common thread persisted: authority was tantamount.

These changes, which ran throughout the Gilded Age and Progressive Era, took place in an era when the respectable classes worried more and more about vagrant youth. Certainly, jeremiads about the decline of discipline in the younger crowd antedated the nineteenth century. Unruly youth was a common theme of Puritan divines and puritanical legislators from the seventeenth century onward. Still, the growth of urban order and disorder in the nineteenth century produced new cries and crises that spawned new forms of juvenile discipline. From the Children's Aid Society of the antebellum period to the juvenile court movement of the Progressive Era, middle-class reformers extracted wayward boys and girls from their sullied environments and lodged them in spots where wholesome discipline could be applied, either in an imposing institution or with a nice farm family. Such extreme measures dealt with the worst offenders, but daily order could not be supplied by these means. Republican virtue and liberty required a more systematic application of force, which came in the form of truancy and compulsory-attendance laws. Although limited compulsory attendance in schools had been a part of the earliest child labor statutes since the 1820s, Massachusetts created the first true compulsory attendance laws in American history, first with a truancy law in 1850 and then, more signally, with a compulsory attendance statute in 1852. By the turn of the twentieth century, thirty-two states and territories had adopted some form of compulsory attendance legislation. Certainly, these statutes did not automatically herd children into schoolhouses, but they did announce a new standard of the social good, one that would come of age in the twentieth century.[8]

By the postbellum period, when legal conflict over corporal punishment expanded, a widespread debate about the role of physical punishment in schools occupied local and state boards of education across the country. Bills abolishing the rod passed state legislatures in various states, but much of the discussion occurred on the local level. A particularly lengthy and influential battle took place in the city of New York. In 1865, a group of parents lodged a series of complaints against teachers for "cruelty in inflicting corporal punishment." The school board investigated and found that while some principals had limited or abolished the practice voluntarily, more than one hundred thousand cases of corporal punishment had been recorded in New York's schools in the previous year. Over the next few years, the board enacted a series of bylaws intended to constrain the rod and encourage its voluntary abandonment, a move that culminated in system-wide abolition in 1870.

The leaders of this movement saw abolition as another step in the long progress of the city's schools, a history that included free schools, night classes, and such innovations as music classes that "added taste and refinement in recreation." The end of whipping would mean that classrooms would be "controlled . . . by the influence of kindness and capability alone" and that school children would be spared "the unnecessary degradation and pain peculiar to corporal punishment." Teachers had opposed abolition all along, and by 1873, they marshaled their forces for an assault on the antiwhipping rule, presenting a lengthy indictment of discipline via moral suasion. Their remarks clarify the heart of the contest: authority. "Wilful [sic] and defiant disobedience is much more common than heretofore," they charged. More to the point, "Insolent behavior and saucy and sneering looks and remarks, and indifference and disrespect toward all school authority have greatly increased under the present system." The conflict between teachers and reformers on the board continued into the Progressive Era, for simple rules in district manuals did not end whipping entirely and because teachers frequently mounted campaigns to recapture their lost physical power.[9]

The boundaries of that authority remained porous as the era of widespread and compulsory school attendance grew. In more extreme cases, violence in the classroom was met with violence, ending in serious injury or death for teachers who had dealt the first offending blow. In a particularly dramatic case in Tennessee, Earnest Powers, a boy of fifteen or sixteen, stabbed and killed his teacher, Elbert Wattenbarger. The conflict began as a schoolyard row in which Earnest and Charlie Stanton hurled rocks at each other. When Charlie's father complained the next day, Mr. Wattenbarger attempted to extract a promise from the boys that they would no longer engage in rock throwing. Charlie assented, but Earnest said it would depend on the circumstances, after which Wattenbarger met his insolence by getting a switch. As the teacher aimed his first blow, Earnest pulled a knife, slicing Wattenbarger once above the eye, and then fatally thrusting the blade into his heart.[10]

Violence of this sort often occurred at the time of the attempted whipping, but families also extracted vengeance in the hours or days after. In a Missouri case a few years after the Wattenbarger murder, Clarence Mosier was gunned down in the streets of Saratoga by Charles Heath, whose sixteen-year-old daughter Lou had been a pupil at

Mosier's school. Lou was no demure young lady. On February 21, 1907, Lou violated a school rule, and in return, Mosier inflicted a whipping. Lou, for her part, whacked Mosier over the head with an iron poker and then retired to her home. Later that evening, Charles Heath rounded up the local school board and sought, as "the largest taxpayer in the county," to secure a guarantee that Mosier would not whip his children. The next day Mosier administered another whipping while Charles was attending a local sale and making promises he would soon keep: "If he would whip one of my kids," Charles vowed. "I'd fill him full of lead." When Charles's son John showed up at the sale to report the second flogging, the elder Heath's dander rose further. "I told him not to whip that girl," he exclaimed. "God damn him, I told him not to whip that girl. I'll go over there and fix it with him for it." And he did. Marching over to the schoolhouse, he called out the teacher. The two exchanged words, but Mosier then headed for his own house for dinner. Heath followed, pelting the schoolmaster with rocks and then pulling a pistol. Mosier quickly grabbed the gun, commanding Heath not to shoot him. Heath seized the weapon back, cried, "'Damn you,' and fired the fatal shot."[11]

Murder and assault cases of this kind, which were by no means uncommon, represent an extreme kind of resistance to corporal punishment. Students such as Earnest Powers or Lou Heath or aggrieved parents such as Charles reacted in these ways for a variety of reasons. Many of these more violent reactions happened in the South, where codes of honor and masculinity clearly colored the proceedings. In the Heath affair, class also seems to have entered into Charles's considerations. As "the largest taxpayer in the county," he evidently believed a teacher who had been working in the local area only seven weeks should pay attention to him. The teachers in both cases, however, strove to maintain classroom authority with violence. They, too, resided in a state of transition. As the heads of their small-town schools, they embodied the physical power of masters past. Their patriarchal clout relied upon and reflected lingering notions of household authority of a sort increasingly antiquated in the larger, bureaucratized schools of the nation's burgeoning urban centers.

In the main, resistance more often concerned the severity of punishment or the import of the student's alleged offense, and it took the form of court challenges, proceedings that both illuminated the nature of school authority and slowly altered it. In turn, these conflicts arose because the American school system evolved during a period in which law was becoming the "modality of rule." That is, legal process began to become the hegemonic mode of conflict resolution, replacing older forms lodged in premodern notions such as moral economy and community sanction. As school building and school attendance grew over the course of the nineteenth century, schools articulated elaborate sets of rules—the legal codes of the schools themselves—to govern the behavior of students. Rules of this nature blurred the meaning of *in loco parentis*, for schools increasingly came to supplement, if not replace, the household and the church as centers of moral authority in local communities, raising fundamental questions about the extent of the power of individual teachers and of schools themselves. Students and their families repeatedly tested those boundaries, especially when their breach resulted in corporal punishment. These litigations, in turn, refashioned the rules and the broader nature of the power of schools and teachers.[12]

The limits of school authority were on display quite clearly in *Morrow v. Wood*, a Gilded Age litigation in Wisconsin that both probed the meaning of *in loco parentis* and resulted in a surprising, and perhaps rearguard, outcome for school authority. Morrow was a teacher at a Grant County school in the dairy state's southwestern corner. Wood sent his twelve-year-old son to school at the commencement of the winter term in 1872, wishing him to concentrate on the three Rs, particularly 'rithmetic. Ms. Morrow believed the younger Wood needed knowledge of the wider world and set him to studying geography, a learning outcome to which the elder Wood objected. Morrow insisted, claiming that "she had the right to direct and control the boy in respect to his studies, even as against his father's orders." When her pupil chose to obey his father instead, the teacher enlightened him with the rod, and Mr. Wood brought charges. In the proceedings, the local court judge issued a sweeping statement of school authority, telling the jurors that "when a parent sent his child to a district school he surrendered to the teacher such authority over his child as is necessary to the proper government of the school, the classification and instruction of the pupils, including what studies each scholar shall pursue."

Proper respect was due to parental wishes, but in conflicts, parents must accede.[13]

The Wisconsin Supreme Court vehemently disagreed. "We do not really understand that there is any recognized principle of law, nor do we think there is any rule of morals or social usage, which gives the teacher an absolute right to prescribe and dictate what studies a child shall pursue, regardless of the wishes or views of the parent," Justice Orasmus Cole wrote. As a former abolitionist who figured prominently in the famous fugitive slave case of *Ableman v. Booth*, Cole knew something about conundrums, and such was how he understood the younger Wood's position. "The situation of the child is truly lamentable," Cole declared, "if the condition of the law is that he is liable to be punished by the parent for disobeying his orders in regard to his studies, and the teacher may lawfully chastise him for not disobeying his parent in that particular." Resolution of such potential paradoxes was best left in the hands of reasonable parents. A father was "as likely to know the health, temperament, aptitude and deficiencies of his child as the teacher." Certainly, Cole acknowledged, schools had every right to lay down rules and regulations for their internal governance, but Mr. Wood retained "his right to direct what studies his boy should pursue that winter." In short, Morrow "entirely exceeded any authority which the law gave her, and the assault upon the child was unjustifiable."[14]

If cases such as *Morrow v. Wood* tested the authority of teachers within the classroom, others probed the extent of a school's powers beyond the school grounds. As school authority expanded along with the system itself, schools promulgated rules governing student behavior after hours. Following in this trend, the local school in the tiny town of Bougechitto, Mississippi, decreed that students must remain at home between 7:00 and 9:00 p.m. to attend to their studies. In October 1908, sixteen-year-old Henry Germany violated this regulation by attending a religious meeting with his father. Having learned of the boy's transgression, teachers at the school "gave him his choice of submitting to corporal punishment or confinement in the schoolroom for forty minutes during the noon hour for the period of five days." Henry refused both, the school expelled him, and William Germany, his father, brought suit. Both the local authorities and the Mississippi Supreme Court concluded that the rule was a violation of parental rights. Justice Robert

Burns Mayes was particularly incensed. "Certainly a rule of the school, which invades the home and wrests from the parent his right to control his child around his own hearthstone, is inconsistent with any law that has yet governed the parent in this state," Mayes intoned, "and the writer of this opinion dares hope that it will be inconsistent with any law that will ever operate here so long as liberty lasts, and children are taught to revere and look up to their parents." Like Justice Cole, Mayes was not willing to cede power over social and moral life to the school system. "In the home the parental authority is and should be supreme, and it is a misguided zeal that attempts to wrest it from them," he wrote. That the case involved a religious gathering in the deeply religious Deep South clearly figured into Mayes's thinking. If this rule was valid, Mayes reasoned, why could schools "not prescribe a rule which would forbid the parent from allowing the child from attending a particular church, or any church at all, and thus step *in loco parentis* and supersede entirely parental authority?" Fathers still mattered, in heaven and in the home.[15]

While religious conviction might present a clear-cut case of schools overstepping their authority, other off-grounds infractions were not so plainly decided. In 1877, for example, the Supreme Court of Missouri upheld the right of schools to expel a student for attending a party. Fighting presented an even more obvious instance. In 1887, the court of appeals of Texas affirmed the right of James Hutton to give W. K. Nugent a whipping for off-grounds fisticuffs. Nugent, age nine, had engaged another boy away from the schoolhouse. Hutton, in turn, applied nine licks to Nugent's legs with "a switch of reasonable size." In this case, Hutton acted the role of the fatherly authority figure, and the court picked up on the cultural cues. "It was merely an ordinary whipping with a small switch, such as many parents inflict upon their refractory boys, and as such should perhaps be more common among parents and teachers," Justice Samuel P. Willson pointed out. Two years earlier, the Supreme Court of Missouri had reached a similar conclusion, clarifying why such an extension of school authority seemed necessary and proper. "The effects of the scholars using to and with each other obscene and profane language, quarreling and fighting among themselves on the way to their homes, would necessarily be felt in the school room," the justices wrote. Far from being independent of the schoolhouse, it would "engender hostile feelings between scholars, arraying one against the other, as well as the parents of each, and destroying that harmony and good will which should always exist among the scholars who are daily brought in contact with each other in the school room."[16]

In reaching this conclusion, the Missouri court had reasoned backwards from other infractions, especially truancy. In fact, in the Gilded Age and Progressive Era, the Supreme Court of Missouri heard several cases involving school governance and became something of a leading authority on the matter, defying the common pattern of important judicial pronouncements emanating from the Northeast. In part this occurred because the Missouri state legislature had explicitly authorized schools to "make and enforce all needful rules and regulations for the government, management and control of such schools and property as they shall think proper not inconsistent with the laws of the land." In line with rule-making powers being constructed elsewhere, direct legislative authority forced a discussion of what constituted proper exercise of these powers. In addition to this fact, the Missouri state constitution of 1875 had implied a legal right to education. In 1880, the court considered the extent of that right. The case grew out of a suspension in Jefferson City for a student who had violated a simple rule about attendance: "Any pupil absent six half days in four consecutive weeks, without satisfactory excuse, shall be suspended from school." In considering the appeal, Justice William Barclay Napton reviewed contemporary arguments about truancy and its punishment. Truancy, Napton noted, was often treated as a minor infraction, important only to pupils and their parents. Moreover, he acknowledged, the "right to go to the public school" could not be taken away by a local school board, for such a rule would be "subversive of the object of our system of common schools, which was designed to throw open and leave open the doors of the school to all children of the proper age, and give them an opportunity of acquiring such education as will fit them for the after duties of life." All this was true, but "this right of attending school necessarily requires, when the school is joined, and whilst such attendance continues, a submission to the regulations of the school." If not, Napton laconically continued, schools might as well recast attendance rules to read, "Any pupil is at liberty to go a fishing during school hours and be absent a half day or a whole day, and as many days as he pleases, provided he conducts himself decently when in attendance on school." As Huck knew, idling away time on the river was not a proper activity for a respectable boy. In brief, Napton declared, "Taxes are not collected to pay teachers to sit in front of empty benches or to hunt up truant boys."[17]

As the age of compulsory attendance dawned, Napton's pithy comments pointed to a central conundrum. State law and truant officers aimed to fasten young people in schools, but growing restrictions on corporal punishment pointed toward their exclusion as a principle means of school governance. This outcome arose from the general public debate about corporal punishment in the Gilded Age and Progressive Era, but it also came from legal challenges by students and their families. An early case in Iowa addressed this question in a peculiarly pointed way, for it involved a young woman a bit past age twenty-one. Ada Buemer missed several classes at her school, each time providing notes from her parents. Finally, Buemer's teacher, a Mr. Minzer, reached a breaking point with her nonattendance. Ada later recalled in court what happened next, in a passage worth quoting at length for what it reveals about the heart of common contests over attendance and the schoolmaster's authority. Telling her tale in court, Ada recalled,

> I said: "Don't you remember I brought you an excuse from father excusing me from afternoons this winter." He said: "None of your sass, or I will take the hickory to you." I said: "Don't strike me." My reason for making that remark was that he reached for the whip as he spoke. The whip was about six feet long, and was about a half an inch in diameter at the largest end. He broke a piece off that end . . . and whipped me with the top part. . . . It was not more than four feet long. . . . Think he struck me a dozen times . . . over my shoulder. . . . I felt the blows. . . . They produced marks that stayed there two months. . . . Think the whip broke to pieces. . . . He raised on his tiptoes every time he struck. . . . I went to my seat and got my cloak. He said: "Do you understand me now?" I said: "No, sir, I do not understand you." . . . I made this remark because I did not know what he whipped me for.

Minzer found himself convicted for assault and battery as a result of this confrontation, and on a second trip to the Supreme Court of Iowa, the case turned on a direct discussion of the role of punishment in enforcing school authority. School rules must be obeyed, Justice William H.

Seevers noted, but a whipping was not the proper response to nonattendance. "Until compulsory education is established we are unwilling to sanction the rule that a teacher may punish a pupil, as in this case, for not doing something the parent has requested the pupil to be excused from doing," he ruled. "The remedy in such case is not corporal punishment, but expulsion."[18]

Drawing a clear distinction between physical punishment and physical exclusion pointed to the eventual resolution of the conundrums of corporal punishment decades later, but no such outcome appeared at hand as the twentieth century dawned. As we have seen, debate about the rod raged on into the Progressive Era, even as reformers inched toward their goal of casting whipping as a "relic of barbarism." The court contests pursued by students and their parents pushed this process along, but the outcomes of these litigations restricted both schools and their charges. In an 1882 Massachusetts case, for instance, the high court of that state refused to countenance a suit that involved a student sent home as a temporary disciplinary measure. "To hold that, whenever a teacher sends a child home as a punishment, the parent may treat it as an expulsion, and sue the city or town, would lead to vexatious litigation and impair the discipline and usefulness of the schools," the court concluded. In 1897, the Supreme Court of Georgia upheld the suspension of an entire family of children because their mother had stormed into a schoolroom and upbraided the teacher. About a decade later, the Kentucky Court of Appeals upheld a suspension for a student who had been kicked out of the Walton Community Graded School for "insubordination." He had refused to take part in the school play.[19]

As expulsion became a more and more common alternative to corporal punishment, schools also experimented with other novel means of discipline. The Progressive Era witnessed an expansion of school athletics, and in some instances, leaders of this movement tied sports directly to discipline. George F. Wingate, founder of New York's Public Schools Athletic League, noted in 1908 that not only had athletic contests improved the physique of boys but at the same time "the discipline of the schools themselves has been immensely bettered." A year later, the *Trenton Evening Times* reported the progress of daily play as a form of discipline in New York's schools, connecting the move directly to the school board's 1907 refusal to reinstitute physical punishment. "The rod has given place to the baseball bat and the dreaded ruler to the basketball," the paper declared. "Compulsory play has replaced corporal punishment." It seems that chaos reigned at an Upper East Side school until one Ms. Kirtland, "a basketball enthusiast," took charge. Armed with no more than the round ball, Kirtland "punished with play" and effected "a swift reformation of the recalcitrant brood." Other schools were following suit, the *Times* exulted, even going so far as to subject students to classes in folk dance. Boisterous games of basketball fit nicely with the ongoing playgrounds movement of the era, but other forms of discipline took less cheery forms. Increasingly, incorrigible youth were simply removed from school and society to such places as the New Jersey State Industrial Home for Girls, where, a 1908 investigation revealed, the beatings continued, accompanied by hypodermic injections of narcotics.[20]

For all of these progressive measures, corporal punishment persisted in many parts of the country and so, too, did the court challenges and local debate it engendered. In Savannah, Georgia, for example, national newspaper coverage about the Progressive Era struggles in New York City sparked a southern version of that controversy. Responding to events up north, one Colonel Mercer, president of the Savannah School Board, pushed for reinstatement because teachers "very often have boys to deal with who are unmoved by moral suasion." Throughout the autumn of 1907, the town debated the issue. "For twenty years the small boy has been immune from the application of the birch," noted the *Augusta Daily Chronicle* in commenting on events southward, "but all signs now point to the passage of the immunity, and he stands in a fair way to catch it when he is naughty." The board followed Mercer's lead, but two years later, the issue was hardly closed. Even as local ministers preached on moral suasion, the local paper came out in favor of the rod. "The lack of corporal punishment in schools has deterred the manliness and worth of many a child, especially when that child is upheld by a sympathetic parent," the *Savannah Tribune* opined. If the public policy debate did not cease, neither did the trips by students and their parents to local courtrooms. In 1893, a Russellville, Oregon, teacher faced charges after he whipped several boys for "over-indulgence in snow-balling." J. L. Cook of Youngsville, Louisiana, was cleared of assault in 1908 when a local judge ruled that the beatings he inflicted "had not exceeded his authority in the degree of chastisement." After a whipping at the Maple Shade Public School near White Horse, New Jersey, in 1909, Hazel Skirm took her teacher to court at the insistence of her aunt.[21]

As with most of the history of American education, change occurred slowly, incompletely, and, most importantly, locally. One final, particularly telling, example of the complex relationships among corporal punishment, school authority, legal challenges, and state and local policy making comes from the small Kansas town of Newton, where a court challenge in fall 1905 led directly to a local campaign for abolition. The matter of corporal punishment had been "discussed in nearly every home in the city" after a female teacher had whipped five boys with a rubber hose, a method many schools were then adopting because, in the word of Newton principal D. F. Shirk, "soft rubber hose will cause pain but not leave marks." Anabel Wilson, a teacher and lifelong resident of the area, had whipped the boys for "low deportment," recounting a series of infractions that included "throwing ink, whispering, breaking ranks, throwing chalk." For their parts, the boys all confessed in court to "deserving" their punishment, but the trial turned, as in so many cases, on its severity. Principal Shirk admitted that the hose had grown hard with age, and all of the boys and their parents reported black and blue backsides that lasted for some days. The amount of force actually applied by Wilson was also the issue. As Wesley Billeter, whose mother, Lucy, brought the case, put it, "[T]he blows were hard. [They] hurt so bad I couldn't sleep." Moreover, Wesley understood proper limits. "I may have needed a whipping but I got a beating," he concluded.[22]

Wesley's case focused local attention and led to political action. When the hearing began, the district courtroom "was filled to overflowing soon after court opened. A large part of the audience was made up of women, who evinced a deep interest in the proceedings." Some of those women went a step further and petitioned the local school board to overturn its rule requiring corporal punishment for low deportment and abolish the practice altogether. "Corporal punishment has long been regarded as a relic of barbarism," their petition declared, and "more than two hundred mothers and sisters" of the district affixed their names. The board "respectfully" received the petition but noted its irritation that instead of settling the conflict with the school board as requested, the boys and their parents had taken the matter to court. From this basis, the board issued a bland statement upholding the need for corporal punishment but assured the petitioners that "steps will be taken as will guarantee the protection of our children and the subservance [sic] of the best interests of the schools."[23]

The Newton case exemplified many of the ongoing conflicts over school governance and authority in the Progressive Era. For her part, Anabel Wilson echoed countless of her peers when she admitted that the boys would "deliberately disobey me after being spoken to." Personal authority remained at least part of the conflict. But the political context was changing. Following the lead of Chicago and other local officials, the state had created a juvenile court system in March of 1905. With the commencement of the 1905–1906 school year, the district administration in Newton had also initiated a "vigorous enforcement of the truancy law," paying particular attention to the sections of the school law that made parents responsible for the good behavior of their progeny. Parents could, however, sign away that authority, after which the misbehaving children would be turned over to the truancy officer and the juvenile court. Indeed, Wesley Billeter had been hauled before the juvenile court and placed in charge of the truancy officer because he "threw some eggs." All parts of this story connected because enforcement of the truancy laws resulted in the largest attendance "in the history of the county." More students meant more discipline problems, and the Newton school board saw corporal punishment as a viable alternative to expulsion or suspension. "The denial of corporal punishment in extreme cases has proven a menace to discipline of the school," the board noted, "and has deprived many suspended children of the privileges of the schools." Better to wield the rod than suspend the child, the board reasoned.[24]

* * * *

Such direct lines of causation between the court cases and policy discussions were unusual, but the legal challenges mounted by students and their parents acted in tandem with the movements of reformers to keep corporal punishment and school authority at the forefront of public discussions about the nature of education in a democratic society. That debate predated the Gilded Age and Progressive Era, and it outlived that time as well. Still, the growing adoption of compulsory schooling, the increase in school populations, and the multifaceted ruminations in educational circles about teaching methods upped the ante. Free schooling had once meant both free of charge and free of compulsion. Boys and girls who went to the schools of the Early Republic had to submit to masterly authority when there, but nothing made them undertake submission in the first place. As we have seen, even the authority of the schoolmaster had limits. By the turn of the twentieth century, students, parents, and reformers had reshaped the nature of that school authority even further. Corporal punishment, while still widely deployed, was under siege. Expulsion and new forms of more "positive" school governance had become commonplace. In the end, however, these changes did not erase the underlying dilemmas of a school system designed to inculcate obedience to duly constituted social, political, and legal authority. A century of struggle had shown that the daily submission of young people at school was anything but cheerful. That legacy would persist.

NOTES

1. *State v. Long*, 117 N.C. 791 (1895), 791–94, 799.
2. The only sustained treatment of this issue is the now classic Glenn, *Campaigns against Corporal Punishment*, esp. 103–12.
3. See Henry Kiddle and Alexander Jacob Schem, *The Cyclopædia of Education: A Dictionary of Information for the Use of Teachers, School Officers, Parents, and Others*, 3rd ed. (New York: E. Steiger, 1883), 185, for a summary of how ancient authority was interpreted in the late nineteenth century; Kaestle, *Pillars of the Republic*, 7; AMICUS, "A Successful Experiment," *Christian Herald and Seaman's Magazine*, December 1, 1821, 8, 14.
4. Sundue, *Industrious in Their Stations*, esp. chs. 3, 5; Steven Robert Wilf, *Law's Imagined Republic: Popular Politics and Criminal Justice in Revolutionary America* (New York: Cambridge University Press, 2010); Rachel Hope Cleves, *The Reign of Terror in America: Visions of Violence from Anti-Jacobinism to Antislavery* (New York: Cambridge University Press, 2009), 215–17; Kaestle, *Pillars of the Republic*, 40–42; "The Advantages of the Lancasterian System of Education," *Almoner*, September 1, 1814; "The Lancasterian System of Education," *Vermont Republican*, May 21, 1821.
5. *Franklin Gazette*, reprinted in *Independent Chronicle & Boston Patriot*, September 29, 1821.
6. *Baltimore Morning Chronicle*, reprinted in *Norwich Inquirer*, December 10, 1821; Horace Mann, *Fifth Annual Report of the Secretary of the Board of Education*,

Massachusetts Senate Executive Document 4 (Boston: Dutton and Wentworth, 1842), 57.
7. *State v. Pendergrass*, 19 N.C. 365 (1837), 365–66; *Cooper v. McJunkin*, 4 Ind. 290 (1853), 291–93; *Gardner v. State*, 4 Ind. 632 (1853), 634–35.
8. U.S. Office of Education, *Report of the Commissioner of Education for 1901* (Washington, DC: U.S. Government Printing Office, 1902), 1014–15; Lassonde, *Learning to Forget*, ch. 2. Surveys of compulsory attendance laws and lawmaking can be found in numerous federal and state government reports from the late nineteenth and early twentieth centuries. I have taken the particulars of the 1852 Massachusetts law from *The Executive Documents of the House of Representatives for the First Session of the Fifty-first Congress* (Washington, DC: Government Printing Office, 1890), 471–72.
9. *Reports on Corporal Punishment in Board of Education* (New York: Board of Education, 1877), 3, 12, 15.
10. *Powers v. State*, 117 Tenn. 363 (1906), 366–68.
11. *State v. Heath*, 221 Mo. 565 (1909), 570–75.
12. On the legal transformations, see esp. Christopher L. Tomlins, *Law, Labor, and Ideology in the Early American Republic* (New York: Cambridge University Press, 1993), ch. 1; and Laura F. Edwards, *The People and Their Peace: Legal Culture and the Transformation of Inequality in the Post-Revolutionary South* (Chapel Hill: University of North Carolina Press, 2009).
13. *Morrow v. Wood*, 35 Wis. 59 (1874), 61–65.
14. Ibid., 65–66.
15. *Hobbs v. Germany*, 94 Miss. 469 (1909), 473–79.
16. *Dritt v. Snodgrass*, 66 Mo. 286 (1877); *Hutton v. State*, 23 Tex. Ct. App. 386 (1887), 387; *Deskins v. Gose*, 85 Mo. 485 (1885), 489.
17. *Constitution of the State of Missouri, 1875, with All Amendments to 1909* (Jefferson City: State of Missouri, 1909), 53; *King v. Jefferson City School Board*, 71 Mo. 628 (1880), 629–31.
18. *State v. Minzer*, 50 Iowa 145 (1878), 146–47, 152, ellipses in original.
19. *Davis v. City of Boston*, 133 Mass. 103 (1882), 106; *Board of Education of Cartersville v. Purse*, 101 Ga. 422 (1897); *Cross v. Trustees of Walton Graded School*, 129 Ky. 35 (1908).
20. *Daily People*, June 23, 1908; *Trenton Evening Times*, November 7, 1909; *Trenton Evening Times*, December 6, 1908.
21. *Augusta Daily Chronicle*, October 13, 1907; ibid., October 27, 1907; *Savannah Tribune*, December 5, 1908, May 5, 1909, November 20, 1909; *Portland Oregonian*, February 26, 1893; *New Orleans Times-Picayune*, June 19, 1908; *Trenton Evening Times*, March 19, 1909.
22. *Vindicator* (Coffeyville, Kansas), November 17, 1905; *Evening Kansan-Republican* (Newton), October 7, 1905; October 16, 1905.
23. *Evening Kansan-Republican* (Newton), October 23, 1905; November 7, 1905.
24. *Evening Kansan-Republican* (Newton), October 16, 1905; October 24, 1905; November 7, 1905.

7

The Contested Meanings of Child Marriage in the Turn-of-the-Century United States

NICHOLAS L. SYRETT

On January 16, 1913, Joseph Campbell of Maiden, North Carolina, wrote a letter to the register of deeds for Lincoln County: "This is to notify you that you are not to issue license for my daughter Susie Campbell to marry any one, she being under lawful age." W. H. Sigmon, the register of deeds, responded the next day to ask that Campbell write immediately with Susie's exact age. He explained that he was legally obligated to issue a marriage license to any two people who both claimed under oath to be eighteen years of age and that some were under the mistaken impression "that 21 is the lawful age." Campbell replied that Susie was "not quite 16 years of age." He continued, "Any certificate purporting to be from me will not be genuine." The certificate to which he referred would have been his written permission allowing Susie to marry. While North Carolina statute did not forbid a girl of Susie's age from marrying (fourteen was the marriageable age for girls), state law did mandate parental consent for those below the age of eighteen and also made obtaining a marriage license "under false pretenses" a misdemeanor for those below eighteen.[1]

Encapsulated in this brief exchange we see a father calling upon the state to control a daughter; a county official explaining that there are limits based on chronological age to the control a father might actually have over his child; and a father's allusion to his daughter willfully disobeying him through forgery, asserting her right to do as she pleased despite his authority. The three issues were being fought out on the terrain of marriage, which Joseph Campbell clearly believed his daughter planned to enter into without his permission, and which would have emancipated her from his control had she been successful.

While it is unlikely that after this exchange Susie Campbell was able to marry in Lincoln County, she may have done so elsewhere, and indeed the numbers of underage marriages were not insignificant at the turn of the century. This article uses a variety of sources—newspaper stories, court cases, archival materials from reformers, parents, and county officials—from the period roughly between 1880 and 1920 to explore the meanings of child marriage for the children who married, the society in which they lived, and the parents and, eventually, reformers who objected to the practice. This is the era in which childhood and adolescence were legally and culturally solidified: through juvenile courts, mandatory schooling campaigns, municipal curfews, child labor prohibitions, statutory rape laws, and many other innovations that used precise chronologic age markers to regulate young people. I argue that one of the consequences of children marrying was that their doing so contested their very status as children. Marriage allowed children, especially female children, to have sex legally in a society that, after the mid-1880s, was regulated by statutory rape law. Marriage also emancipated children from their parents and legally ended their status as minors. It also clearly allowed some poor and working-class girls to gain material wealth and opportunities they would not have had without marriage. Marriage could thus have real benefits for some children, particularly so in a society that was increasingly regulating them on the basis of chronologic age. The institution allowed children to defy their categorization as children.[2]

The plentiful newspaper stories about individual child marriages during the period also indicate that Americans were increasingly coming to see childhood as incompatible with marriage and its attendant responsibilities and rights, sex chief among them. While there is not room to explore the issue here, evidence indicates that the marriage of girls in earlier eras did not garner nearly the same amount of attention that it would attract by the late nineteenth century. Reading news accounts of child brides and boy husbands (the latter represented out of proportion to their actual incidence in the population) tells us about how Americans were recalibrating their understandings of childhood and adolescence to demarcate them as separate stages of life in need of protection. And so do reactions by parents and reformers. While some parents continued to consent to their children's marriages, many were opposed to such unions and attempted to exert what they may have seen as a waning parental authority in order to prevent their children from marrying. They used the law to do so. And by the 1910s and '20s, social workers and other reformers attempted to strengthen the law to give parents and the state more power to control an apparent increase in underage marriages. Their fixations on very precise ages demonstrate how numerical boundaries were becoming more entrenched in understandings of where childhood was thought to end and adulthood to begin. Combining the perspectives of adults and children allows us to see how the cultural and legal categories of childhood and adolescence were forged at this moment, though not without continued resistance by the very people identified by the categories.

One of the reasons there may have been so much resistance at this moment was the newly developed category of adolescence. While psychologists and social workers distinguished adolescence both from childhood *and* from adulthood, within the realm of the law, those in their teenage years were usually lumped in with children, not with adults. When state legislatures raised the statutory age of marriage during this period, the result was to treat teens like children. And yet, by the 1900s and 1910s, experts believed that adolescence was also a period of transition away from childhood in a wide variety of ways, one of which was sexual. In the debates about child marriage we see parents, reformers, and lawmakers insisting that adolescents should be regulated in ways similar to children; adolescents themselves resisted, asserting that they were really more akin to the adults they were becoming.[3]

* * * *

Common law, which the United States inherited from its past as a colony of England, allowed for the marriage of a boy of fourteen and a girl of twelve. However, as historians have demonstrated, by the middle of the nineteenth century, many states had either passed statutory law that raised those ages, or had mandated that persons below certain ages—usually eighteen for girls and twenty-one for boys—must obtain parental consent before marrying. What this meant was that, depending on the state, girls between the ages of twelve and eighteen, and boys between the ages of fourteen and twenty-one, could legally marry with parental consent.[4]

The laws, however, were only as strong as their enforcers, and as social workers pointed out, many license issuers were notoriously lax about enforcing these laws, meaning that licenses were often issued to those who did not qualify for them, either because the issuer did not care to ask the proper questions or because the parties applying had lied outright, a common tactic, or had simply forged parental signatures. Most judges, following the common law, ruled that once a marriage was solemnized it remained legally binding even if the license was issued illegally. Those states where the marriage could be voided if the parties had contracted for it illegally demanded that one of the parties actually sue for nullification; if both parties remained satisfied with the union, the marriage stood. What this meant was that many child wives and husbands, though *illegally wed*, remained *legally married*.[5]

On the basis of census records, social worker and marriage reformer Mary Richmond calculated that there were approximately 667,000 people living in the United States who had either been married as a child or been married to a child between 1890 and 1925. She suggested that this was almost certainly an underestimate. Richmond's calculations counted those below sixteen as children, meaning both that she classified some adolescents as "children" and that those sixteen and older were not her primary concern. By contrast, many laws did prohibit sixteen- and seventeen-year-olds from marrying without parental consent, demonstrating that this was a period of flux in the numerical fixing of childhood, adolescence, and the onset of adulthood. While the published census makes calculating exact numbers difficult, it is clear that 11.71 percent of girls aged fifteen to nineteen were married women in 1880; 9.4 percent of that same group, in 1890; and 10.96 percent, in 1900. By 1910, more precise numbers are available. At that time, 1.2 percent of fifteen-year-old girls were married, 3.7 percent of sixteen-year-olds, and

8.7 percent of seventeen-year-olds. In 1920, the percentages for fifteen-, sixteen-, and seventeen-year-old girls were 1.4, 4.2, and 9.8, respectively. These figures count those who were married at the time the census was taken; many of these young wives may have married one or two years earlier. The statistics show the percentages increasing slightly over time, and certainly as the ages of the children go up, but they also vary a good deal by race and region. African American girls and those who lived in rural areas were more likely to marry early. Indeed, 14.1 percent of seventeen-year-old black girls were also wives in 1910, 16.9 percent in 1920. Because marriage below certain ages was illegal in many states, these numbers must be taken as a conservative estimate. The point, however, is that while early marriage was not typical, it also was not rare.[6]

Social workers like Mary Richmond, who would become one of the leaders of the marriage reform movement, believed that children who married were exploited by their husbands, often for sex, or had foolish and backward parents who allowed or encouraged them to marry against their own best interests. Historian Stephen Robertson has demonstrated that many girls were pressured into marriage to "right the ruin" of premarital intercourse and pregnancy. The accounts that I include here run counter to these narratives, portraying girls who are either actively consenting to marriage or pursuing marriage against their parents' wishes. Neither version of the story gives us a complete picture, of course, given that hundreds of thousands of underage girls married during these years. Some chose marriage and some were exploited in it. Some did make impetuous decisions to marry, just as millions of legal adults did and continue to do. This essay examines those girls and boys who actively chose marriage and places them in the context of a society that was rapidly reevaluating what it meant to be a child in the first place.[7]

The Benefits of Marriage

One of the best ways to understand the motivations of children who married is to look at court records. Though ending up in a court put them in the minority, their cases can tell us something about why they might have chosen to marry in the first place, as well as the reactions by those around them, especially their parents. Married children's reasons for being in court varied. Sometimes they reconsidered and attempted to have their marriages annulled. At other times parents sought such an annulment or sued the clerk who had issued the marriage license. Parents who were angry about losing the labor of their children or worried that they were being exploited by new spouses sued clerks because doing so was a way of claiming monetary damages and publicly affirming that they had been wronged. In most states this was also their only recourse. As Michael Grossberg has demonstrated in the realm of legal history, the overall trend judicially was to uphold minor marriages, even when they had been entered illegally. But that does not tell us much about why minors might have found marriage attractive in the first place. Marriage protected the sex spouses had with each other in states that criminalized sex between minor girls and adult men. Following the purity campaigns that commenced in the mid-1880s, sex between an adult man and a girl below the age of fourteen, sixteen, or eighteen, depending on the state, was a crime. If the two were married, it was not. Marriage also legally emancipated minors from their parents, freeing them from parental oversight and from having to labor on behalf of those parents. Further, judges interpreted the common law to mean that marriage made legal adults out of children; they literally ceased to be children under the law. As I have argued elsewhere, it is clear that children used the law of marriage and the support of judges, however unwitting, to become sexually active adults, independent of their parents.[8]

A number of cases illustrate this phenomenon. In October 1881, Josephine Gibbs and Thomas Brown were married in Richmond County, Georgia. Soon afterward Josephine's mother attempted to regain custody of her daughter through a writ of habeas corpus. She claimed further that Josephine was under the age of fourteen, the legal age of marriage in Georgia. In an era before the widespread use of birth certificates, the Georgia Supreme Court first had to determine Josephine's age and then decide whether to uphold the marriage, as a lower court judge had done. The court's decision was that Josephine was fourteen and that the marriage was thus valid; the justice thus affirmed the lower court's decision to allow Josephine to stay with her husband. Often in cases like this the daughter/wife is discussed in terms of her "custody": whether she is to be "returned" to her parent or "given" to her husband. While legally a minor girl and a wife were both denied most of the perquisites of citizenship, these words also tend to obscure the choice that a girl like Josephine had made in the first place. The decision to marry emancipated her from her mother's control and allowed her to live with her husband. Another Georgia case ten years later was decided in much the same way. There, the court found that the husband defendant, charged with kidnapping, had "without fraud or force . . . obtained the voluntary consent of the lady to run away and marry him." The fourteen-year-old "lady" and her new husband consummated the marriage and judges upheld the validity of their choices, noting that "since the law makes the child capable of giving her consent to a marriage, this consent must count for something." Part of the process for the court was deciding whether or not the young bride had been forced or coerced into her marriage. They found that she had chosen freely and that as a result of her marriage, "the law makes her a grown woman, and deals with her as such." A final Georgia case, this from 1911, illustrates the ways that some couples attempted to use marriage to escape an abusive household. In this case, *Crapps v. Smith*, a thirteen-year-old girl married and her father commenced a habeas corpus proceeding to have her returned to him. The girl's lawyer alleged that there was mistreatment at home and that this was one of the reasons why custody should be awarded to her husband. While the appeals judge in this case did not affirm the marriage because she was under the statutory age of fourteen, he did explain that if the "young couple," who "seem to be very much in love," waited until the next winter when she "will unquestionably be fourteen" before getting back together, "this will ratify the former attempt at matrimony and render it a legal marriage." While it is unlikely that the girl's father would have been any more excited about the union only a few months later, marriage clearly offered this young bride a way to escape the abuse she claimed she faced in his home.[9]

In 1899 in Hennepin County, Minnesota, Alexander Scott, thirty-two, married Sadie Lowell, who was just shy of her fourteenth birthday. Despite the fact that she desired to live with her husband, her parents took her from him; he promptly swore out a writ of habeas corpus to have her returned to him. The court ruled in the Scotts' favor, explaining,

> The marriage of the wife, even without the father's consent, emancipated her from the custody of the father, and he was not legally entitled to

detain her if she elected to return to the husband. . . . A wife—and this girl must be regarded as such for the purposes of this case—certainly has the capacity to consent to live with her husband.

The court inquired into Sadie's desires in the matter; in a piece titled "She Loves Scott: Child Bride Expresses Her Preference in Court," the *Minneapolis Journal* recounted that Sadie replied to the judge's query, "Well, I would like to go with him."[10]

Two New York City cases, though atypical in that they featured underage grooms and not underage brides, nevertheless illustrate the ways that young people used marriage to be with their lovers despite the wishes of their parents. In 1918, Albert Marone, who at the time was below the age of consent, was married to a twenty-year-old woman in New Jersey. Although they lived in New York, they had gone to New Jersey to marry precisely because it would be easier there. As his guardian ad litem, Albert's mother, Angelina Marone, sued to have the marriage annulled. The court ruled against her: "[I]n this case both the plaintiff [Albert] and the defendant [Catherine Marone, his wife] object to the annulment of the marriage. Each has testified that not only since the action was commenced, but up to the time of the trial thereof, they have continuously cohabited as husband and wife." Because county marital records in New York State are sealed to all but the parties involved for one hundred years, we have no access to the testimony of the Marones. We cannot know why marriage was so important to them or why Angelina Marone so opposed it; all we know is that they were successful.[11]

But in a 1916 case that made its way to the Supreme Court of New York State, *Herrman v. Herrman*, we have a better sense of the motivations of the parties involved. It is clear that Philip Herrman's parents found out about his courtship with Dorothy Gates, a chorus girl, before they married. Philip's father, James Herrman, visited Gates at her home and urged her to cease her relations with his son. She was eighteen and Philip was seventeen and still in school. It seems likely that Philip's parents believed that Dorothy was unsuitable company for their son precisely because she was a chorus girl. James repeatedly emphasized that Philip was "a schoolboy" and under the age of eighteen: "I notified her that he was in school and was home on the Christmas holidays, and I forbade her to have anything to do with him whatsoever, that he was only just past 17." The testimony of Philip and Dorothy diverges on whether or not they had sex prior to marriage, although both agree that they had intercourse several times afterwards. Both agree also that Dorothy told both Philip and his father that she was pregnant and that this may have precipitated the marriage, but the testimony is inconclusive on this point, and she never gave birth to a child. What we do know is that both Philip and Dorothy filed defense briefs opposing the annulment. Because they had had intercourse following the marriage, and following Philip's eighteenth birthday, the judge ruled in their favor, ending the Herrmans' effort to annul the marriage. And whether or not Dorothy had used marriage in hopes of bettering her station in life— clearly the implication of Philip's parents—Dorothy and Philip had also used marriage to defy his parents and be together.[12]

There are also plenty of cases throughout the court system brought by children themselves seeking to annul their own marriages. It is apparent that many of these unions were not happy ones. Be that as it may, what remains clear is that children entered the marriages in the first place, even if they later proved unsuccessful, and they did so either without their parents' knowledge or against those parents' wishes. Many of these children benefited from the legal ramifications of their marriages in that they had sex legally and they became emancipated adults.

Newspaper accounts also demonstrate this trend, often in cases where the law was not directly involved in adjudicating the validity of the marriages. While the reporters clearly found the marriages noteworthy because of the spouses' ages (which I discuss below), the stories demonstrate that the children entered them willingly. In 1902 Ella Nora Green, thirteen, and her husband-to-be, Frank Maines, sixteen, executed an escape from Petersburg, Kentucky, that involved wading to a sandbar in the Ohio River and then stealing a boat so that they could make it to Indiana and marry in Lawrenceburg, all while being pursued by her father. In 1913, Mrs. Annie Marham Cochran, seventeen, refuted claims that she had been held a prisoner by her husband, reporting instead that her mother had held her captive in San Francisco to prevent her being with her new husband. And in 1908, Frances Pinkerton, fifteen, wed John McKnight, a 65-year-old Civil War veteran, in West Chester, Pennsylvania, claiming, "It's so nice to be called Mrs." She further explained that "I'd rather be an old man's darling than a young man's slave." Or, as seventeen-year-old Alma Chester Thomas put it in 1909 of her 42-year-old groom,

> Why shouldn't I have married him? Did not I promise to marry him when I was a weenty 'teenty little girl with pigtails, when he used to carry me around in his arms and—yes, before that time. He nursed me when I was a baby and I have practically grown up knowing him and I feel more safe with him than I [do] with some of those youngsters who don't know their minds two hours at a time.

Perhaps the more common scenario in these articles was simply that of a couple who believed themselves in love, married without parental permission, and only later attempted to convince the bride's (and sometimes the groom's) parents not to legally contest the marriage. Sometimes they were successful, sometimes not. If they were of reasonably similar ages the newspapers usually represented the decision as one of mutual consent.[13]

Others clearly married for different reasons and left their marriages as soon as they found they did not serve their purposes. In 1905, for instance, Eureka Sherman, fifteen, of Des Moines, sought a divorce from her husband because he wanted to kiss her too much. As Sherman explained,

> "He was just a regular baby over it all. He wanted me to sit on his lap all the time, but I just couldn't stand it. I have had more troubles than a woman twice my age. I married him to secure a home for my mother after my father died, and for a while I thought we would get along all right, but I had to leave him because he wanted to kiss me to death."

In the same year, Myrtle Beattie Grubbs, seventeen, sued her husband, Dr. A. M. Grubbs, seventy-six, for divorce in McKeesport, Pennsylvania. She had entered into the marriage voluntarily but declared at the time of divorce, "'He's too old, anyway. I don't want to live with him.'" Mrs. Thomas Hubbard, a child of less than eighteen, married her husband, sixty, and then ran off with his horse trainer after only three months, taking two thousand dollars in cash belonging to the husband.

Far from him exploiting her, it seems she was biding her time with him until someone better came along.¹⁴

Representation

While it is clear that children were no strangers to marriage during these years, examining how their society reacted to the marriages tells us much about changing norms of childhood and the more recently developed category of adolescence. The same newspaper stories that demonstrated some children's enthusiasm for marriage also indicate a profound unease with the idea of young people as being capable of marriage. In July of 1872, a *San Francisco Bulletin* reporter wrote from Visalia, California, that he had happened upon a child bride of twelve, married three years earlier to a man of fifty. "Mrs. Lou Peyson, the little matron, is very small even for her age, wears short dresses, and conducts herself in most matters precisely as the child she is." In emphasizing the brides' childishness, many accounts stressed that they were still in short dresses, not being old enough yet to have graduated to the longer frocks that fully grown women wore. In 1897, the *St. Louis Republic* reported that Clementine Pope, aged fourteen, "is a beautiful child, possessing a striking figure in her short dresses." She was married in April to sixteen-year-old H. H. Brown. Marie Cecelia Kartese, married at thirteen to Michael Jones, twenty-two, in New York City in 1905, was described as "a small frail little creature." "Up until yesterday Miss Kartese had worn short dresses, all white." The *Wilkes-Barre Times* reported in 1908 in a case of one child-bride citing another's seduction of her own husband in divorce proceedings that "[b]oth the child wives looked like school children, their dresses scarcely reaching their shoe tops. The two had been playmates before marriage."¹⁵

The pastimes of child brides were also sometimes discussed in these articles as a way to denote their youth. For instance, in 1908 fifteen-year-old Mrs. Lucy DiAngelis, though a married woman, still enjoyed playing with children, and on one occasion was pretending to be a highwayman when she accidentally shot and killed six-year-old Elizabeth Dumbrosio. Helen Stobba, fourteen, due to marry her twenty-six-year-old fiancé the next week, confessed that she did not intend to give up playing with her two favorite dolls after her wedding: "'I admit I like to play with dolls, and my getting married won't make me care less for them,'" she said. In one of the more disturbing stories, the *Philadelphia Inquirer* reported that Captain John W. Morse, forty-five, was wed to fifteen-year-old Nora Theresa Shaughnessy in June of 1904. The reporter explained that the wedding "is the culmination of a romance dating back five years ago, when the captain saw little Nora, who was only ten years of age, playing in Penn Treaty Park, which is in front of her home. He had amused himself then by tossing pennies to the child and her little playmates." Nora would become stepmother to Morse's three children from a previous marriage, the youngest of whom was five years her senior. One of Nora's bridesmaids whispered to the reporter that "the white silk gown of the bride concealed a copper penny hung about her neck by a ribbon, and that it was one of the same identical pennies tossed to her by her husband five years ago."[16]

In all of these instances the girls are portrayed as being just that: girls, not prematurely developed young women who happened to be chronologically younger than they appeared or acted. This emphasis on their girlishness was clearly one of the ways newspapers were able to sell the story in the first place; through publishing the accounts, reporters indicated that they thought there was something strange about the unions. And that is not surprising, given that this is the moment when childhood and adolescence became more cordoned off from the world of adults. Through myriad different procedures already examined by other historians—child labor laws, age grading in schools, sexual age-of-consent laws, juvenile justice programs, and psychological and medical theories of adolescence—and those previously unexamined, like municipal curfew laws, Progressive reformers called upon the state to dictate appropriate behavior for children. In so doing they increasingly used chronological age as a marker of childhood and of adolescence, creating the very categories of people they were attempting to protect. And in emphasizing the childishness of young brides, and indeed reporting on them at all, newspaper reporters were responding to the new ideals of adolescence as a protected stage of life.[17]

It also bears noting that what sounds to our ears like clear cases of pedophilia—Captain Morse grooming little Nora Shaughnessy from her tenth birthday into his fifteen-year-old bride—were celebrated openly in church weddings and reported in major newspapers. These were men marrying children but with little of the shame and embarrassment we might associate with doing so today. In the late nineteenth and early twentieth centuries, there were ample numbers of American men who thought these marriages perfectly appropriate and families and communities around them who, to varying degrees, accepted and supported these decisions. There were competing understandings of childhood in play: one that understood girls below a certain age as inappropriate for marriage and another that did not. The two discourses met—and clashed—in these accounts. Some could see those who were members of the newly invented category of "the adolescent" as childlike, while others saw them as more like adults. That both interpretations remained common indicates the novelty and liminality of the category itself.

Parental Opposition

There is no way to know what a majority of parents thought about their children marrying. Some probably encouraged it, particularly for daughters who might be marrying a man who could provide for them. Some simply consented, particularly if they lived in areas where early marriage was the norm; the parents themselves might well have married young. Others were clearly opposed, as with the many who sought to annul their children's marriages, either because marriage would deprive them of a daughter's or a son's service, because they feared their child was being married for his or her money (or the parents' money), or because, like many Americans, they had come to believe that marriage as an adolescent was inappropriate.

From the early nineteenth century onward, one of the ways that many states regulated the marriage of minors was to demand that they obtain parental consent before marrying. For those states with such statutes, girls, usually below eighteen, and boys below twenty-one needed to obtain the written consent of their parents before a county clerk or register of deeds could issue them a marriage license. Those clerks and registers thus became a key site where parents could call upon the state to help them regulate their children; local government acted as a wedge to maintain parental authority. Some county clerks and registers of deeds kept the paperwork that allowed them to issue marriage licenses to minors as well as the letters, like the one with which I began, that denied that consent. While it would be impossible to gauge which was more common because we do not know the method by which these county officials saved what they did and what made its way to the archives, a sampling of North Carolina denials of consent allows us to see the way that parents, usually fathers, spoke of their children's plans to marry. We can see the willfulness of children in pursuit of their goal and parental resistance to that goal. The frequent insistence upon chronological age, while necessary under the statute, is also indicative of a moment when numerical age was used as a means to argue that children, adolescents in particular, should not be allowed to be self-determining, that they still belonged under the authority of their parents.

In 1902, J. C. Capel wrote to his county register of deeds, "I am informed that my daughter (Edna) and Andy Bowers are expecting to run away and get married. This is to notify you that Edna is only 17 years old and that I am opposed to the marriage." In 1906, the register of deeds for Stanly County in Albermarle, North Carolina, wrote to his colleague in Montgomery County to let him know that Frank Blalock, a Montgomery resident, feared that his seventeen-year-old son, Littleton, was about to elope with "one Miss Hinson." Blalock had requested that neither register issue the license. On April 3, 1912, Livvie Burns wrote to the register of deeds of Halifax County to ask that he refuse to issue a marriage license to James Gibbs, who intended to marry her daughter, Lizzie, who was fourteen. These were fairly straightforward requests made by parents who suspected that their children might be contemplating marriage with specific people and who opposed those unions, either because of the prospective spouse, the age of their child, or both. They were able to call on county officials to help them stop the unions because their children were young enough that they required parental consent. But that they wrote to the officials at all indicates that they feared their children were on the verge of defying parental wishes. Doing so through marriage would effectively terminate the rights that parents had in their children, and it was at least partially for this reason that parents sought to bar the children from marrying.[18]

Other requests were more curious. In December of 1914, a parent named A. M. Lutz wrote to the register of deeds of Lincoln County, "I hereby forbid you to issue marriage license to my son Fred A. Lutz to mar[r]y any one without my consent in writing, as he is only 16 years old." A. M. Lutz did not specify a prospective bride, but was quite clear that Fred did not have permission to marry, no matter who she was. Two years earlier, in July of 1912, a parent named C. A. Spencer similarly forbade the marriage of daughter Pearl Spencer, "she being only 14 years of age," "to any one." Exceptional among notices of this kind is a 1917 missive that seems to have been mass-produced. Printed on cheap newsprint, it is headed "WARNING" and explains, "I hereby forbid any one to issue marriage license, convey or assist in anyway, for the marriage of my daughter, Candas, who is only 15 years of age. S. R. Beam, Bessemer City, North Carolina." Beam sent the notice to the register of deeds for Lincoln County, though he lived in Gaston County; he may have had the notices produced and sent in bulk in order to prevent his daughter from marrying in any county in the state. It is unclear, however, whom any of these parents thought their children might be attempting to marry. Perhaps they did not say because they felt it necessary only to name their own children, but some of the letters are quite clear that sons and daughters be forbidden from marrying "any one," suggesting either that the children had a number of possible options or that the parents simply suspected that marriage might be seen by their children as a way to escape their own households, an escape they hoped to prevent.[19]

Some parents did not fully understand the state statute and attempted to bar their children from marrying even when they were legally entitled to do so. In March of 1913, Mrs. L. B. Conrad wrote to the register of deeds of Lincoln County to forbid her son Russell from marrying Linda Ward. She noted that he was nineteen years old, which in North Carolina entitled him to marry without parental permission. Others used the phrase "not of age," or "under the lawful age," as Joseph Campbell had, though they did not specify what they believed that age to be. Combining both of these trends—prohibition of a child legally entitled to marry and a blanket denial without reference to that child's actual prospective spouse—in January of 1913, a parent named P. V. Cobb wrote to the register, "If any body comes for Grover Cobb license. Do not let them have them, he is not but (18) eighteen years old. I don't much think he will come but if he does be sure and don't let him have any." Because Grover seems to have been eighteen, his parent, probably his father, was incorrect in his belief that he could forbid his son from marrying, but noteworthy here is that he is not even sure Grover wanted to marry. This seems to have been a preventative measure in case Grover should decide he might want to avail himself of the option. Even the remote possibility of marriage was worth attempting to prevent for this North Carolina parent.[20]

Another parent, F. L. Little, in an almost illegible note, gave consent for his or her child to marry because "they are going to Run of[f] to S. C. anyway to marry if they don't mar[r]y here." While this letter is not dated, if it comes from the same period as the other letters filed along with it, it was a moment in which South Carolina had just instituted an age of consent to marriage. In 1912 the state updated its statute, mandating consent for those below age eighteen and prohibiting the issuance of a license to boys below eighteen and girls below fourteen. Even if this letter was sent after 1912, it is plausible that Little's child simply did not know that the law had changed and assumed that there was still no age of consent to marry in South Carolina. Either way, Little was resigned: a parent giving consent but only because he knew he had no chance of stopping his child, that child being willful enough to run to another state if s/he did not have parental permission.[21]

Filed in among these letters forbidding officials to issue licenses are also many letters of consent, both for children who legally did not require it and for those who did, some as young as fourteen.[22] There are also scribbled memos where a register has simply noted two names and ages with the words "Forbidden" or "Consent." Presumably these were moments when parents visited in person to make their wishes known and the register kept a record so that he would remember when the actual applicants came to his office. Also included are boilerplate refusals of consent on official stationery, signed with an X; these seem to have been written by a register of deeds and then signed by a parent who was concerned enough to come to his office but unable to write a letter to convey his or her wishes. Taken as a whole, they attest both to a high degree of interaction between local residents and their county officials regarding their children and, more importantly for our purposes, to a concerted effort to control those children and in many cases to deny them the right to marry as they seem to have wished. While few parents said precisely why they forbade the marriages, most made mention of their children's ages and asserted their rights as guardians of minors to make those decisions for them. These documents are clear evidence of children's resistance to parental authority, and their use of marriage in order to do it. But this resistance and heightened oversight make most sense when read in the context of a society increasingly understanding childhood and adolescence as separate and protected stages of life, cordoned off from adulthood and fundamentally incompatible with the rights and duties of marriage. In partial acknowledgment of this, C. C. Rowe wrote his local register in 1914, "Please do not issue any marriage license to any one for Rose Bud Lowe my daughter. She is only a child and don't know what she is doing. There is to[o] many children getting married now so turn any one down that ask for papers for her."[23]

Apparently agreeing with C. C. Rowe, by the late 1910s Progressive reformers began trying to regulate what they saw as a rash of child marriages. The majority of activism around the issue, and thus the most public face of child marriage in the twentieth century, took place during the 1920s, beyond the temporal scope of this essay. The urgency with which reformers approached the issue was related both to their escalating concerns about precocious sexuality and youth culture in that decade and to growing fears about the instability of marriage and leniency of divorce law. That said, national organizing around child marriage prevention had begun at least by 1918 and was clearly in reaction to precisely the phenomena I have already been describing: perceptions of a rise in child marriage coincident with, and caused by, a belief that marriage was fundamentally incompatible with the state of childhood, itself increasingly defined in terms of chronological age and extended through the teenage years. In 1918 the American Association for Organizing Charity, a nationwide network of social welfare agencies (what would later become the Family Service Association of America), commenced a survey of family welfare organizations in various states to determine their marriage laws. The next year they established a standing committee on marriage laws, which met regularly to ascertain problems, advise local activists how best to change state laws, and present strategies on how to assist their local license issuer in preventing child marriage. Reformers aimed to tackle the problem in two ways: by helping children and families through social work, fostering "proper" homes that would themselves discourage early marriage; and by amending the laws and better enforcing the existing laws to make it impossible for children to marry even if they were so inclined. They planned to raise the marriageable age and the age under which children required consent; to implement new laws to require documentary proof of age at a license bureau and waiting periods between application and issuance of license; and, for some, to lobby for a constitutional amendment allowing the federal government to regulate marriage and for accompanying legislation that would standardize marriage law among the states so that couples denied a license in one state could not simply cross state lines and marry elsewhere.[24]

While the strategies themselves were not all new in relation to early marriage, the fact that they attracted a national constituency was, as was the fact that they were primarily focused on protecting children instead of the institution of marriage itself. That activists across the United States embraced one or more of these reforms indicates that they saw childhood, as a cultural and legal category, as being fundamentally incompatible with marriage, which itself was a rite and right of adulthood. But what had changed was not that people of certain ages were marrying—"child marriage"—so much as a belief that marriage below those certain ages constituted a problem, because those ages now had greater cultural currency, and because the invention of adolescence had effectively lengthened childhood, especially in the realm of the law. And as the people demarcated by those ages—children and adolescents—were increasingly controlled and regulated on the basis of chronological age, some of them rebelled against the strictures placed upon them, using marriage to do so. The children themselves probably did understand marriage to be something that adults did, but it is also the fact that marriage legally transformed them into adults, granting them a means to defy their parents and assume a certain amount of autonomy over their own lives. Child marriage was thus, depending on one's perspective, a grave social ill, a willful defiance of parental authority, or a means to an end: the end of childhood itself.

NOTES

1. Joseph Campbell to Register of Deeds of Lincoln County, January 16, 1914 [though almost certainly 1913, given the response and the other correspondence in the folder]; W. H. Sigmon, Register of Deeds for Lincoln County, to Joseph Campbell, January 17, 1913; and Campbell to Sigmon, n.d., all in folder marked "Marriage records concerning parental consent," Lincoln County Miscellaneous Records (folder cited hereinafter as LCMR), CR 060.928.4, North Carolina State Library and Archives (hereinafter NCSLA). On the laws, see Fred S. Hall and Elisabeth Brooke, *American Marriage Laws in Their Social Aspects: A Digest* (New York: Russell Sage, 1919), 101–2; Geoffrey May, *Marriage Laws and Decisions in the United States: A Manual* (New York: Russell Sage, 1929), 315–16; *Revised Code of North Carolina, 1854* (Boston: Little, Brown, 1855), chap. 69, page 393; Thomas B. Womack, LL. D., Needham Y. Gulley, and William B. Rodman, *Revisal of 1905 of North Carolina: Prepared under Chapter Three Hundred and Fourteen of the Laws of One Thousand Nine Hundred and Three*, 2 vols. (Raleigh, NC: Uzzell, 1905), I: 998.

2. On the emergence of adolescence and the codification and glorification of childhood during this period, see G. Stanley Hall, *Adolescence: Its Psychology and Its Relations to Physiology, Anthropology, Sociology, Sex, Crime, Religion, and Education*, 2 vols. (New York: Appleton, 1904); Kett, *Rites of Passage*, chaps. 8–9; Odem, *Delinquent Daughters*, chap. 1; Zelizer, *Pricing the Priceless Child*; Chudacoff, *How Old Are You?* chaps. 3–4; Mintz, *Huck's Raft*, 156, 168, 172–78, 180–83. On curfews, see Lucius Cannon, "Curfew: Texts of the Ordinances of Some of the Cities of the United States," *Saint Louis Public Library Monthly Bulletin*, August 1919, copy in American Social Health Association Papers, SW 45, Box 210, Folder 1, Social Welfare History Archives, University of Minnesota (hereinafter SWHA).

3. On the ways that adolescence prolonged childhood, see Kett, *Rites of Passage*, chap. 8, esp. 217, 238; Mintz, *Huck's Raft*, 196–98. For the canonical text of the movement, see Hall, *Adolescence*.

4. William Blackstone, *Commentaries on the Laws of England*, 4 vols. (Oxford: Clarendon, 1765–69), I: 424–25; Brewer, *By Birth or Consent*, chap. 8; Grossberg, *Governing the Hearth*, 69, 74, 76, 79, 88, 96; idem, "Guarding the Altar: Physiological Restrictions and the Rise of State Intervention in Matrimony," *American Journal of Legal History* 26:3 (June 1982): 197–226; Hall and Brooke, *American Marriage Laws*, 32–34, 37.

5. Hall and Brooke, *American Marriage Laws*, 34; Grossberg, *Governing the Hearth*, 107–8.

6. Mary E. Richmond and Fred S. Hall, *Child Marriages* (New York: Russell Sage, 1925), 57–58; Susan B. Carter, et al., *Historical Statistics of the United States: Earliest Times to the Present*, vol. 1, part A, Population (New York: Cambridge University Press, 2006), 77; United States Census Bureau, *Census Reports, Vol. II: Population, Part II* (Washington, DC: Government Printing Office, 1902), lxxxix,

255; idem, *Sixteenth Census of the United States*, vol. 4, part I, U.S. Summary (Washington, DC: Government Printing Office, 1942), 21; idem, *Fourteenth Census of the United States*, vol. 2 (Washington, DC: Government Printing Office, 1921), 392–93.

7. Richmond and Hall, *Child Marriages*; Robertson, *Crimes against Children*, chap. 5.
8. Odem, *Delinquent Daughters*, chap. 1, esp. 14–15; Grossberg, *Governing the Hearth*, 107–8; Nicholas L. Syrett, "'I did and I don't regret it': Child Marriage and the Contestation of Childhood in the United States, 1880–1925," *Journal of the History of Childhood and Youth* 6 (Summer 2013): 341–58.
9. Gibbs v. Brown, 68 Ga. 803 (1882); Cochran v. The State, 91 Ga. 763 (1892); Crapps v. Smith, 9 Ga. App. 400 (1911).
10. State ex rel. Scott v. Lowell et al., 78 Minn. 166 (1899); "She Loves Scott," *Minneapolis Journal*, October 21, 1899, 4.
11. Marone v. Marone, 105 Misc. 371 (New York County, 1918).
12. Herrman v. Herrman, 93 Misc. 315 (New York County, 1916). Transcript is in *New York Supreme Court Cases and Briefs*, 176 App. Div., New York State Archives, Albany, NY; quotation on 28–29.
13. "Wade the Ohio to Elope," *Anaconda Standard*, September 16, 1902, 5; "Child Wife Found and Tells of Her Thwarted Love," *San Jose Mercury News*, August 1, 1913, 3; "Girl of 15 Weds Veteran of 65," *Pawtucket Evening Times*, August 14, 1908, 10; "School Girl Drops Her Books to Wed," *Fort Worth Star Telegram*, March 14, 1909, 21. For the common scenario, see, for instance, "Weds Girl of 15," *Morning Oregonian*, April 11, 1907, 14; "Police Find Child Bride," *Duluth News Tribune*, July 31, 1908, 8; "Imogene Glenn Is Taken to Seattle," *Olympia Record*, September 18, 1908, 1.
14. "Child Bride Revolts at Connubial Kisses," *Fort Worth Star Telegram*, August 19, 1905, 2; "Doctor, 76, Sued for Divorce by Wife, 17," *Philadelphia Inquirer*, October 26, 1905, 1; "Child Bride Eloped with Horse Trainer," *Pawtucket Evening Times*, May 17, 1901, 3.
15. "A California Bride," *Daily Picayune*, July 17, 1872, 2; "She Is a Beautiful Child," *St. Louis Republic*, April 16, 1897, 7; "13-Year-Old Girl Weds in Gotham," *Duluth News Tribune*, September 14, 1905, 4; "Bride of 13 Accuses Child Wife in Her Divorce Petition," *Wilkes-Barre Times*, May 14, 1908, 13.
16. "Little Girl Killed by Child Bride," *San Jose Mercury News*, May 2, 1908, 4; "Child-Bride Clings to Dolls," *Bellingham Herald*, August 14, 1909, 7; "Takes a 15-Year-Old Bride after Five Years' Romance," *Philadelphia Inquirer*, June 30, 1904, 2.
17. See note 2, above.
18. J. C. Capel to Register of Deeds of Montgomery County, November 24, 1902; J. M. Vanhoy to same, July 23, 1906, both in folder marked "Marriage Permissions," Montgomery County Miscellaneous Records (hereinafter MCMR), CR 067.928.2, NCSLA; Livvie Burns to J. C. Williams, April 3, 1912, folder marked

"Marriage Licenses," in Halifax County Miscellaneous Records (hereinafter HCMR), 1761–1927, CR 047.928.5, NCSLA.

19. A. M. Lutz to Register of Deeds for Lincoln County, December 11, 1914; C. A. Spencer to W. H. Sigmon, July 26, 1912; Notice from S. R. Beam, June 23, 1917; all in LCMR.
20. Mrs. L. B. Conrad to Register of Deeds of Lincoln County, March 13, 1913; J. A. Bowman to Register, December 24, 1914, both in LCMR; J. B. Stowe to Register of Deeds, March 16, 1912, HCMR; V. Cobb to Register of Deeds, January 21, 1913, LCMR.
21. F. L. Little to Register of Deeds, n.d., LCMR. On the age of consent in South Carolina, see *Code of LN.Cws of South Carolina* (Charlottesville, VA: Michie, 1912), 1040; Hall and Brooke, *American Marriage Laws*, 114.
22. The letters of consent outnumber the denials but it may be that some registers of deeds only kept the consents. Only a handful of counties kept either consents or denials. The youngest consent I have found is for a girl "not quite 15 years." John Pemberton, marked as colored, to P. H. Morris, April 17, 1878, MCMR. Pemberton signed with an X. In 1878 the statue mandated only that girls below the age of fifteen, not eighteen, have a father's permission. See *Battle's Revisal of the Public Statutes of North Carolina* (Raleigh, NC: Edwards, Broughton, 1873), 301.
23. C. C. Lowe to Register of Deeds for Lincoln County, July 15, 1914, LCMR.
24. Letters from various charity organizations to Helen Kempton, Associate Secretary for American Association for Organizing Charity, August 1918, Box 13, Folder 38, Family Service Association of America Files, SWHA; Richmond and Hall, *Child Marriages*.

8

Sex, Abortion, and Prostitution in the Lives
of Gilded Age Chicago Girls

MARY LINEHAN

In 1909, Chicago social reformer Jane Addams wrote, with some sadness, about young women in her city. She noted that this was the first time in history that girls were valued more for their contributions to the economy than for their purity. She recognized that adolescents struggled to announce their presence in the world and to validate their individuality. Addams knew that if girls did not find legitimate outlets for their youthful passions they would confuse "joy with lust, and gaiety with debauchery." In turn, reformers and lawmakers would "resort to all sorts of restrictive measures." Though her analysis was limited to working-class girls and viewed all premarital sexual expression as "malignant and vicious," Addams sensitively described a conundrum of adolescent life in industrial Chicago.[1]

Forty years before Addams, in the wake of the Great Chicago Fire and in the face of rapid urban and industrial development, some girls acquired unusual freedom and took the opportunity to make their own sexual choices. Labeled "bad girls" in the press, they were a cross-class and cross-cultural subset of adolescents between twelve and twenty. Though they may not have been able to articulate it, they shared a new sexual ethic with some adults who placed sexual expression at the heart of life and accorded girls the same right as boys to sexual freedom. The girls' exploits alarmed those who sensed that traditional American life was being subsumed by the city and feared conventional Victorian morality was waning. At first, these girls were depicted as lawless and depraved. By the mid-1880s, however, the story changed. The *Chicago Tribune* began to portray sexually active girls as innocent victims in need of protection. This new narrative served the needs of a class of lawmakers and moral reformers who built their careers controlling and circumscribing the sexual lives of girls to construct an extended and protected childhood.[2]

This essay argues that whether they were rebelling against Victorian morality, contemplating what to do about an unplanned pregnancy, or engaging in sexual commerce, Chicago's bad girls made their own choices—from limited and often grim alternatives—and asserted agency and independence. The words "choice" and "freedom" are used in this essay to connote girls' wishes for (or expectations of) the same control over their sexuality that boys had. When the church, government, or reformers tried to limit these choices, they were aided by the *Chicago Tribune*'s insistence on promoting a narrative in which sexually active girls were helpless victims. By the end of the century, even as girls manipulated the press and reformers, a large and repressive mechanism to control the behavior of bad girls was put in place in Chicago.

* * * *

The Victorian morality that bad girls rebelled against placed strong proscriptions on girls' behavior. From an early age, family, church, school, and society impressed upon girls that there were many things they could not do. Good girls did not have premarital sex, did not encourage male passions, did not engage in sex for recreation or pleasure, did not question authority, did not pursue individual goals, and did not have financial aspirations of their own. A lapse in any of these standards would deny girls the right to the promise of future happiness and protection through marriage. Though never universal, this Victorian ideal was easier to impose in smaller towns where girls stayed close to home. It was much easier to be a bad girl in a big city.[3]

Gilded Age Chicago was a large and diverse city of almost one million. At this unique point in time, many girls had unprecedented freedom and opportunity. Tens of thousands did not live at home. Some worked for wages. Others attended school or engaged in commerce. They all traversed the city on a daily basis, exposing themselves to new people, new experiences, and new temptations. In this world, Victorian strictures seemed unduly limiting to some girls. Moreover, born in the shadow of the Civil War and the Great Fire of 1871, they grew up steeped in loss. Girls were keenly aware that life was transitory and could end early. As one explained in a *Tribune* editorial, her generation "enjoy[ed] everything that is bright and dangerous," because "I think there are some rather sharp corners to turn in life. If I can find happiness now, I want to secure it." This pursuit of pleasure and their new freedom of the streets led some girls to a sexually permissive subculture that rebelled against Victorian morality.[4]

When nineteen-year-old art student Isabella Rittenhouse came to Chicago in 1884, she quickly flouted many of the rules of good girl behavior and courted two young men at the same time. She did not think Ned's art was any good, doubted his financial prospects, and disapproved of his drinking. But, he was "bohemian" and "very exciting." In her diary, Isabella fantasized about Ned's kisses and his inappropriate comments about her figure. Yet, knowing that the young artist wanted to marry her, she also went out with Elmer. Even though she had to "try hard" to treat him "pleasantly," Isabella encouraged Elmer and went with him on trips to Milwaukee and to the theater. He never called without a dozen roses and a five-pound box of chocolates. She recognized Elmer as a "steady generous boy," but Ned was "more fun." She used Elmer to play with Ned's emotions. At the same time, Isabella had goals and ambitions for herself that did not include a wedding to a starving artist. While she was eager to encourage Ned's passion and to enjoy his "hard" kisses, such intimacies were for her pleasure only, not a prelude to marriage.[5]

Other girls were even more sexually adventurous in their search for freedom. In December 1882, fourteen-year-old Annie Loftus Jackson, the daughter of a railroad executive, disappeared. She was the tenth "missing girl case" that month. Annie sought out 27-year-old medical student George Buddington and willingly accompanied him to a downtown hotel. When he left for class, the girl conned the hotel out of train fare to St. Louis. There, she met a "very kind man" and spent several days in a hotel with him. As Christmas approached, Annie decided to return home. The baggage man on the train was "kind," so she got off the train in Pullman and went to a hotel with him. The *Tribune* noted that the girl was "very independent" but never expressed shock at Annie's sexual spree. Such behavior by teen girls was not unthinkable. Despite the strictures of Victorian morality, in 1882, Illinois set the age of consent at ten. After that age, unless a girl or woman struggled to the limits of her endurance, it was assumed she had consented to every sexual encounter.[6]

The seeming increase in unapologetic sexual activity among girls coupled with other factors to bring a change to the law. An 1870 decision by the Illinois Supreme Court affirmed that children had rights. This gave impetus to a reform movement that wanted those rights curtailed. It emphasized children's developmental differences from adults and the state's obligation to ensure that all young people had a protected childhood. New theories of adolescence contributed to this concept of an extended childhood. This added an element of horror to an 1885 report on child prostitution in England that inspired twenty-four U.S. states to raise their age of consent by the end of the decade. Two laws passed by the Illinois General Assembly in the summer of 1887 were intended to grant adolescents the same protection available to girls under ten. One made fornication with any "unmarried female of chaste life and conversation" a felony. The other applied to men over the age of fifteen, "who shall have carnal knowledge of any female person under the age of fourteen with or without her consent." They would be tried as rapists and faced a potential life in prison.[7]

These laws were paternalistic attempts to extend childhood and protect girls. They also served to clarify for men which female bodies were available to them. After July 1, 1887, girls under fourteen were off limits and legally protected from the sexual advances of men or the consequences of their own sex play with chosen partners. Even older teens were recast as passive and helpless to resist male desire. As bad girls blatantly rejected older notions of propriety, reformers, the state, and the *Tribune* contributed to an alternative narrative of innocence and victimization in which girls required special protection.

The 1888 case of Linnie Sinclair reflects all of these changes. The paper never allowed the seventeen-year-old the independence and sexual impulses it accorded Annie Jackson under the old laws. The *Tribune* described Linnie as "an attractive girl . . . [with] an expression that is almost childish in its innocence." Her lover (age thirty) was accused of abduction and fornication and the paper fretted that Linnie was too fragile and modest to hear the evidence, even though the bulk of the testimony concerned her own activities. The defense established, without objection, that Linnie and her friend May were in the habit of picking up men in saloons, drinking with them, and going to their rooms. The night before she met Little, Linnie admitted to drinking and kissing another man until two in the morning. Nonetheless, the *Tribune* denied her any choice or agency in her sexual activities.

The evidence presented did nothing to prove the claim that Hugh Little "deflowered the girl of womanhood's highest charm." Linnie met him at a beer garden, drank beer and whisky with the man, and willingly went to Little's room. When questioned by the boardinghouse keeper, Linnie claimed to be of age. After spending two days and a night with the man, she sent a messenger to her parents requesting clean clothes. Her outraged family sent the police, who found her singing and dancing. When the police told Linnie that her parents were angry and that she could be sent to the Erring Women's Refuge or House of the Good Shepherd for her dalliance, the girl changed her story. She then admitted to being under age and claimed Little had "seduced" her with the promise of marriage. The *Tribune* had no doubt who was telling the truth. The girl, "the personification of innocence," became a helpless victim in the press. Her sexual partner spent eight weeks in jail, lost his job, and "nearly" broke his mother's heart. The jury, having heard the exculpatory evidence, still voted eleven to one to convict Little for violating Linnie's perceived purity.[8]

While many rightly worried about the Victorian double standard of sexual morality that indulged male licentiousness, bad girls found a way to create an alternative double standard. They learned they could capitalize on assumptions about girls' purity and manipulate the age-of-consent law. By doing so, rebels like Linnie avoided punishment or interference with their freedom. Not only did they assert the same right to choose enjoyed by boys; bad girls also found a way to even the field as to who bore the social ostracism for premarital sexuality.

Given the extant sources, most stories about girls' challenges to Victorian morality are hetero-normative. The experiences of girls who, in another age, might identify as transsexual, bisexual, or lesbian are largely hidden from history. In the Gilded Age, these categories were being debated and delineated, making this era particularly crucial to the study of these girls' lives. The glimpses of such girlhoods as do emerge, however, show the same desire for independence and free sexual choice that motivated heterosexual girls.

Gender passing was another form of sexual rebellion. Some girls believed life was fairer for boys and they passed as boys to pursue adventure, money, and freedom. Girls who dressed, thought, and acted like boys were labeled "inverts." They were pitied for a mental defect it was believed they could not control. It was widely assumed, though not always true, that inverts had sexual desire for other girls. The idea that she might have passionate feelings for another girl was frightening to the child involved. She was not likely to know anyone else who shared her secret. This was the context of Silvia Hammond's adolescence.[9]

At thirteen, Silvia ran away from her Ohio family to live life as Sidney. She met the standards then identifying inverts: "her inclinations are of a masculine tendency" and "she is of heavy stature, dark-featured, and decidedly plain." Those who knew her as Sidney described the girl as being very strong, hard-working, and quite religious. But, Silvia's story contained other implications. She liked to view pornography and read erotic novels. She had also had a romance with a farmer's daughter in Ohio. Silvia came to Chicago when that relationship became "too complicated." It was, apparently, not easy for the girl to forget her first love. One of the factors that led to Silvia's exposure was the bitter tears she shed when the Ohio girl sent a letter. Clearly the young woman was in a troubled state about a relationship that, at a minimum, suggested same-sex desire. Given the attention paid to her "exceptionally good" morals and character, the *Tribune* was also troubled by the implications of Silvia's story. Still, in 1885, rather than address her sexuality—as the paper did with heterosexual girls—they simply announced that Silvia had been sent home to her parents with the vague hope that she "will stay home and behave herself."[10]

By 1896, implications of same-sex desire elicited a different reaction. Rachel Mogstad (eighteen) and Bessie Youngren (seventeen) grew up in a world where love between two girls was possible, at least among the elite, but such relationships were increasingly viewed as abnormal. An 1895 article in *Ladies Home Journal* warned girls not to have a "girl sweetheart" because if they "wasted" their love, they would have nothing left for "Prince Charming when he comes to claim his bride." That same year, three novels appeared in which "mannish" lesbians murdered the objects of their desire. In 1892, for the first time, a Chicago medical journal used the word "homosexual." As economic changes made it more possible for girls in love to forego marriage to men and remain true to each other, culture and science increasingly attached a warning and a label of deviance to love between girls.[11]

Despite these proscriptions, Rachel and Bessie sought the same independence and freedom as the other rebellious girls of their generation. They took the significant step of renting a room together at 352 Grand Boulevard. Rachel, who preferred to be called Ray, was studying to be a midwife and Bessie worked as a nurse. Although active in the Lutheran church with a wide spectrum of friendly acquaintances, the girls were unusually devoted to each other. By the spring of 1896—perhaps alarmed by the new notions of deviance—Bessie's parents encouraged her to date a young man. She obliged, but on Independence Day the girls committed suicide together. Ray's last words were spoken to Bessie's beau. She told him, "you don't know the reason and nobody ever will."

But from the facts of their story, the *Tribune* concocted a narrative that took away the girls' agency and made them victims of something inexplicable. Although two thousand people attended her funeral, the paper claimed that Ray was lonely and overly sympathetic to women because of her studies. This made her "jealous" of the boy Bessie was pressured into dating. Ray's "firmer will" convinced the other girl that suicide was the only solution to their "strange connection." They were willing to grant the more "mannish" Ray an "infatuation" with Bessie, but that was the extent of the paper's acknowledgment of same-sex desire. Even then, the *Tribune* offered a "clarification." The girls were not "degenerates." They were bright, industrious, ambitious, and had "good names." Religious girls, Ray and Bessie were so pure and innocent that they could not comprehend the concept of homosexuality, much less be driven by "freakishness."[12]

Like their peers who exploited young men, enjoyed premarital intimacies, or engaged in sexual adventures, girls who seemed to choose other girls as sexual partners pushed the boundaries of Victorian sexual culture. In so doing, they responded to a sexual ethic that recognized freedom of choice for young women. Such girls displayed tremendous independence and agency. Yet, even as the *Chicago Tribune* told their stories, it presented the girls as helpless and innocent victims. This complemented their middle-class readership's need to understand modern girls as childlike and in need of protection. Just as the paper turned sexual defiance and rebellion into passivity, it turned girls' control of their bodies into need and dependence.

Girls who were sexually active with male partners faced the risk of an unplanned pregnancy. Like their sexually rebellious peers, these girls saw their world as one of freedom and alternatives and demanded respect for their decisions. They also relied on a subculture of other girls to support their choices. Just as adolescent sexual expression gave rise to reformers' attempts to control their behavior through legislation, girls' reliance on abortion as their first choice for birth control led to state intervention. Ultimately, this control was reinforced by the *Tribune's* narrative of female helplessness and innocence.

Theoretically, pregnant teens had the choice to give birth. But, for most of the late nineteenth century, there were limited services for unwed mothers. Built at great public cost in 1877, Cook County Hospital refused care to such girls. The best option was the Erring Women's Refuge—primarily a home for ex-prostitutes—which provided the only free obstetrical care for single women. However, they required girls to stay for two years, attend religious services, and keep their babies. At the end of that time, the only jobs that paid uneducated girls enough to support a child were prostitution and domestic service—the latter often taking place under the close supervision of a judgmental matron. Moreover, the refuge predicated its services on the ideal that girls instinctively wanted to be mothers and wives. This was not always true.[13]

Another option for pregnant girls was to get married. In Chicago, it cost two dollars to be married by a justice of the peace, and in 1887 business was brisk. According to one justice, the majority of such marriages occurred when "the christening and the wedding are nearer to each other than the laws of God and man allow." While this attests to the extent of premarital sexuality among city youth, and marriage was one choice girls did have, it was not everyone's ideal. Madeleine Blair, seventeen and pregnant in 1887, rejected a marriage proposal. Her lover was "too controlling" and she was "as unmolding as any girl could possibly be." Life had too much to offer and she did not want to sacrifice her "individuality" for marriage and forced motherhood—particularly as her reaction to the baby was that "I did not want that ['thing'] within me." American girls at this time were generally not expected to view the fetus as a living soul or a potential child, but as an obstruction to their normal menstrual cycle. Thus, Madeleine was not alone in viewing her pregnancy as an impediment to her personal economic and emotional survival. Girls did not necessarily have the innate maternal desire the Erring Women's Refuge and other middle-class reformers demanded.[14]

For such girls, abortion was the preferred choice and a crucial element of the new sexual culture. The Comstock laws had rendered birth control costly and virtually inaccessible. Abortion was critical to fully separating sexual desire from procreation. Even though Illinois passed the nation's first anti-abortion law in 1867, popular morality continued to regard the procedure as a necessity for women and girls in a variety of circumstances.

In 1873, Rosetta Jackson (sixteen) came to Chicago to help her married sister care for a new baby. Soon, neighbors began to gossip that Rosetta was "very intimate" with her forty-year-old brother-in-law, William Flagg. While his wife stayed home, he accompanied Rosetta to church, to dinner in restaurants, and on picnics. By April 1874, she was pregnant. While Flagg "appeared to be respectable," he had an ongoing relationship with a prostitute who referred Rosetta to an abortionist, Charles Earll. He prescribed aborticants for the girl, but when those failed he performed two surgical abortions. Nine days after the second procedure, Rosetta died of infection. Earll buried the fetus in the back yard, listed the cause of death as typhoid, and shipped the body back to Wisconsin. Chicagoans heard her story only because she died.[15]

While not condoning or excusing Rosetta's actions, the *Tribune* conceded that such procedures were generally performed "without fatal consequences." The Cook County coroner's reports showed an average of eight deaths a year as a result of abortion. Given the illegal nature of the operation, such statistics may not be complete, yet, even extrapolated, they are comparable with the number of women who died in childbirth. Physicians insisted, "there is hardly a family in which there are not attempts made to prevent childbirth." Police reports, which may have been exaggerated, claimed that Dr. Henry Stafford performed 130 successful abortions each year, Dr. Franklin Brooks operated on fifteen girls in one week, and Dr. B. R. Reynolds had six abortion appointments in a single afternoon. A woman physician, who did not perform abortions, told investigators she received three hundred requests a year from girls and women who expected her to sympathize on the basis of female solidarity. Though the *Tribune* decried the city's "addiction" to abortion, newspapers were one of the chief ways pregnant girls learned about the accessibility of this option.[16]

Papers carried ads by physicians, like Franklin Brooks, who promised "special attention given to all private diseases . . . particularly obstetrics" and "*Menstrual Obstructions* greatly and speedily relieved." When a Christian newspaper criticized the *Tribune* for running such thinly veiled advertisements for illegal aborticants, the editors replied that their doctors were "medical experts of the highest character." Not only did the paper endorse known abortionists; it also provided directions. In writing about Brooks, it identified his office as a "rickety, old two-story dwelling, No. 191, upon the north side of Kinzie Street, between Green and Peoria." The article also told girls how long the procedure and recovery took, what aftercare was available, and how much money to bring.[17]

Investigative journalists at the *Chicago Times* carried an exposé of abortion in its December 1888 editions. From the study, girls learned that "society women" and middle-class mothers were the women who most frequently terminated their pregnancies, further legitimizing this choice. Girls were told that there was a "widespread sympathy for the plight of unmarried, pregnant women." The paper listed the names of forty-eight doctors who, in violation of the law, were willing to provide an abortion or a referral. This not only confirmed the girls' choice; it also instructed them in the type of appeal most likely to arouse the sympathy of doctors and get them to circumvent the law. Media was not the only way girls learned about accessible abortion options.[18]

Before choosing to undergo the procedure, girls conferred with each other, with their boyfriends, and, sometimes, with their families.

Girlfriends were not ashamed to discuss their own abortions and readily exchanged advice and referrals. Friends raised money to pay for the procedure, went with each other to the appointments, and nursed each other through convalescence. A surgical abortion, ordinarily, required a two-week recovery. During that time, most girls were in pain, sickly, and unable to work. Without the support of girlfriends, this would be an unbearable ordeal. Because abortion was a familiar part of the female life experience, however, girls helped each other out. Nellie Ryan was only in Chicago three weeks when she found other young women who provided and cared for her during her abortion. Pregnant teens knew they could rely on other young women to be empathetic and to provide for them. They were not—in most cases—helpless or alone.[19]

Lovers were less reliable allies. If both partners had a stake in covering up an affair—such as in Rosetta Jackson's case—boyfriends had an expected role to play. They found the provider, paid for the services, and attended to their girlfriend during and after the procedure, as William Flagg did. But such emotional and financial support could not be counted on. When Mary Crekoffer announced her pregnancy, the father told her to "get rid of her trouble." Eventually, he took her to a doctor who provided drugs that effectively terminated the pregnancy. The "doctor," however, was a Blue Island Avenue saloonkeeper and the drugs left Mary an invalid.[20]

If a family did not disown a pregnant daughter, girls could find an important ally in their mothers. Many older women had personal experience with the burdens an untimely pregnancy placed on women and the double standard that absolved the young men of any blame or punitive consequences. Illegitimacy destroyed a girl's reputation, caused her great unhappiness, and limited her future and marital prospects. It also could cause the social and financial stigmatization of the girl's entire family. Meanwhile, the boy and his family were left unscathed. For these reasons, sixteen-year-old Mary Morgan's mother took her to Dr. Earll for an abortion. The Morgan family intended to quietly deal with the problem pregnancy. However, the police happened to be conducting an investigation of Earll. Officers allowed the abortion to be performed, then arrested Mary and her mother and forced them to testify against the abortionist. The Morgans did not receive the privacy that typically attended a successful abortion, but Earll abortions were not always successful. The police were investigating him because the doctor's procedures had resulted in the deaths of at least six women. Nonetheless, he was one of the busiest providers in Chicago. He was also the cheapest.[21]

While unplanned pregnancy and abortion knew no class barriers, the rationales and experiences of girls varied greatly according to economic status. Elite girls who planned on an education and a prosperous marriage regained a sense of freedom and personal control over their lives through abortion. Licensed doctors assured these girls that they were "perfectly safe" and that abortion was a natural choice ("the only thing to do when one gets into trouble is to get out again") and a popular one ("thousands are doing it all the time"). They performed medical and surgical abortions in comfortable and clean surroundings for around a hundred dollars. Working-class girls, like Madeleine Blair, worried about their own economic survival through the pregnancy and beyond. They saw their own mothers overburdened and aged by maternal responsibility and they wanted something better for themselves. For these girls, abortion was far from a comfortable or controlled experience and was almost prohibitively expensive. For this reason, most such girls began with drugs from the pharmacy. If these did not work, girls were forced to undergo a surgical procedure at a later and more dangerous stage of pregnancy. For twenty dollars, doctors provided instruments and do-it-yourself instructions. Midwives charged fifty dollars. The regular, licensed physicians of the elite were out of the question for working-class girls. But, there were unlicensed specialists like Charles Earll. He charged fifteen dollars for a surgical abortion and was willing to barter.[22]

Girls unable to procure even a cut-rate abortion probably ended their pregnancies by themselves. Just as they exchanged names of providers and gave each other advice and support in the planning process, girls were there for each other during this option. The *Tribune* noted that books circulated among young girls on how to commit an abortion and they contained "elaborate descriptions." The methods included injecting oneself with vinegar or ice water, taking extract of ergot mixed with santonin, drinking tansy tea, and skipping rope. A physician testified that girls used whalebones, quills, lead pencils, and knitting needles to terminate pregnancies. These methods were not generally safe and not always effective, but compared to the expense of an assisted procedure, self-abortion seemed to be a reasonable choice and a responsible way for a girl to take care of herself.[23]

Over time, however, the *Tribune* obliterated the meaning of abortion to girls and popularized the image of desperate, victimized girls. It cast them as uneducated in proper morals, impoverished, alone, and in need of rescue. In the paper's preferred narrative, girls had abortions because boys, like Etta Pfau's lover, "forced her to submit to him." Victimized in their sexual relationships, girls were also victims when they sought abortions from "quacks" like the doctor who gave Olive Stokes, "a young colored girl," aborticants, but also raped her. Girls were triply victimized when the law failed to file charges or dismissed the cases against the men who harmed the innocent. In the paper's narrative, sexually active girls who became pregnant were hopeless, helpless, and in need of deliverance from their "misery." This was hardly the experience of most girls who chose to have an abortion.[24]

The words and actions of girls in Gilded Age Chicago suggest that if a girl became pregnant she had some choices, the network of support she needed, and the ability to take care of herself. They establish that sex and procreation were not inextricably linked and that maternal instinct was not necessarily innate in women. Despite laws meant to limit their options, sexually active girls were successful in getting their needs met. They conveyed to providers their desire to terminate an untimely pregnancy and expected to have their wishes fulfilled. Abortions were frequent, relatively safe, easily accessible, and popularly accepted as a woman's right. Young women had the agency and ability to make difficult choices about maternity and the confidence to expect those choices to be respected.

Choice, independence, agency, self—the lived keywords of bad girls' individuality—were repeatedly denied and translated into childishness and dependency. Sexually rebellious girls, like Annie Jackson, became innocent victims of male passion and perfidy. Girls who controlled their own reproduction, like Olive Stokes, became innocent victims of quack medicine. So too did girls who chose to enter sexual commerce become innocent victims in the pages of the *Tribune*'s narrative and in reformers' attempts to protect and rescue them.

Madeleine Blair chose abortion for a subsequent pregnancy, but as an unwed seventeen- year-old unwilling to marry or enter a home, she chose prostitution for the moral and financial support it offered. Prostitution was illegal, but the laws were rarely enforced. Women under eighteen were restricted from entering brothels, but about 15 percent of Chicago's self-identified prostitutes claimed to be under this age. They shared Madeleine's belief that sex work was a legitimate choice for girls without money or family ties. They saw this decision as temporary, consistent with the new sexual ethic, and consonant with, not preclusive of, an eventual loving and comfortable marriage.[25]

Throughout the nineteenth century, prostitutes worked in all kinds of settings and in every section of the city. In private rooms, alleyways, saloons, and parks, girls serviced men in the neighborhoods. They hustled in theaters, dance halls, and other recreation venues. They prowled the railroad stations and, when boats came in, worked the docks. In the aftermath of the Fire, a specialized sex district began to emerge south of the downtown business district. The "Levee" stretched south on Clark and State streets between Van Buren and Twelfth. It was, according to the *Tribune*, "given over to dissipation and licentiousness of the lowest character." The paper, with some exaggeration, counted five hundred saloons, six burlesque theaters, one hundred concert halls, sixty pool rooms, five hundred brothels, and three thousand prostitutes. An indeterminate number of streetwalkers clustered in stairwells and doorways competing for men. The Levee also attracted young girls who strolled the nighttime streets with an "aimless free-and-easy style."[26]

At ease in the Levee, many girls found work in the sex district. Dora was a waitress in a concert saloon. Working five hours a night, she earned $18.25 a week, far in excess of what the average working girl made for six and a half eleven-hour days in a factory. Dora realized that her uniform, a short tunic and tights, contributed to her income, but she did not mind. She claimed she had "good legs" and it was a "pity" to keep them covered. Comfortable with her sexuality, Dora was unapologetic about her deviance from Victorian standards. Proudly, she declared, "I am a bad girl. . . . I don't make any pretensions to purity." Concert saloons excluded boys under eighteen, but allowed girls as young as fourteen or fifteen to solicit wine and ice cream from male patrons. It was not uncommon for such girls to drift into some form of sex work.[27]

Girls who prostituted made this choice for a variety of compelling reasons. Many immigrant and African American girls grew up in the

Levee. They witnessed commercial sex on a daily basis and saw it as an acceptable way to earn money. All girls grew up in a culture that valorized making large sums of money with little physical labor. The veneer of luxury that surrounded brothel life seemed to offer females the only way to realize this American Dream. Other girls found in the Levee an escape from physically or sexually abusive situations. The emerging culture of recreation also played a role in girl prostitution. For girls who grew up bartering their sexuality for access to amusement, actual prostitution was not unthinkable. Peer pressure, which encouraged revealing fashions, flirting, and sex play as a means to popularity, also made sex work seem like a lucrative, easy, and legitimate choice for girls.[28]

Whatever drew them into prostitution, girls often had difficulty finding secure, profitable employment in the industry. Brothels had a small but lucrative demand for adolescents due, in part, to the mistaken belief that sex with a virgin cured venereal disease. A clever girl might pass herself off as a virgin for several years. However, madams did not like to hire young girls. Those under eighteen brought unwanted police attention. In addition, older women tended to be more responsible about the hard work of prostitution. As a result, most child prostitutes were streetwalkers, especially prone to police harassment. Once arrested, girls had fewer alternatives to paying off their fines and spent more time in jail. There they learned new crimes and conditioned themselves to a lifetime of confrontations with the police.[29]

The career of Sallie Tierney—Chicago's best-known child prostitute—testifies to the grim life that some endured. The daughter of alcoholics, she was raised in saloons. "A considerable beauty," Sallie began to prostitute at thirteen. Over the next five years, she was arrested at least eight times. She learned to fight, began to carry a twelve-inch knife, and sometimes threatened prizefighters. Because of her fearsome personality, the girl frightened off potential customers. By the time she was twenty, Sallie was a homeless alcoholic. Her story was well known in Chicago in the late 1870s. Nonetheless, girls clung to the idea that through prostitution they could have good times, sexual adventure, money, and a happy future.[30]

This image was so strong—and Chicago's location as a railroad hub so convenient—that girls came from all over to prostitute. The city's reputation for sexual freedom and adventure beckoned them. When her parents refused to allow a Cincinnati girl to marry her lover, Lillian Salomon (sixteen) ran away to Chicago. She had done her research and showed up at a very exclusive Clark Street brothel and announced that she "fully intended" to prostitute. Much to Lillian's fury, the madam refused to employ the girl and sent for her father to remove his daughter. The Morris sisters from Springfield, Illinois, had better luck. The three girls, ages thirteen to seventeen, came to Chicago one Christmas to make money through prostitution. They were so successful that they eluded arrest for six months. When finally apprehended, the sisters were returned to their family. Still, it was acknowledged that a dozen girls each week found their way to Chicago under similar circumstances and commenced to prostitute.[31]

Given the low wages paid to girls, the opportunity to make money off their sexuality was also attractive. May Duigan, an Irish immigrant, recognized her value as a young, healthy, good-looking girl without family ties and saw no reason not to make money off her personal attributes. According to May's biographer, "selling herself at least kept some agency in her own hands." Maud Lewis (nineteen) and Nettie Shepherd (seventeen) had the same idea. They were taken into police custody as they tried to leave the city for Wyoming. Tired of the low pay, lack of personal freedom, and sexual harassment in their jobs as sewing girls, they intended to go west and prostitute for a few years. The girls planned to return to Chicago with so much money they would never have to work again. Maud and Nettie insisted they "understood perfectly well what sort of life was in store for them," but they preferred it to the "drudgery" of sewing.[32]

Not only did girls actively seek out opportunities to work in sexual commerce; they did not often rue their choices. The work was hard and the customers could be unappealing. New prostitutes, "tidbits," did not make much money. Moreover girls risked venereal infection, rape, violence, and pregnancy. But these were factors in the lives of all sexually active girls. Even jailed prostitutes did not usually express regret or shame about their choices. On April 22, 1875, Josephine Carnes (seventeen) and Nettie Dishrow (sixteen) were arrested for prostitution. They did not cry and "told no heartrending or sympathetic stories" about themselves. Rather, they calmly made bail and returned to the Levee.[33]

Ostracized by most Chicagoans, prostitutes found a true community in the sex district. Girls turned to each other for love and support, and these relationships made sexual commerce bearable. Those who came into the business from broken or abusive homes looked for an identity in the alternate families of the Levee. The prostitution business was still largely run by women, and female values predominated. Brothel girls referred to the madam as "mother." Coworkers who became like sisters blunted the harshness of prostitution. Asked if a sense of sisterhood existed among the girls at Mother Herrick's place, Betsy Clark replied, "you bet your life there is." Girls lent money to each other, shared clothes, cared for each other during illness, and paid for each other's funerals. They organized interventions to help friends through addictions and destructive love affairs. They empathized with their sisters' sufferings and shared the joys of a new romance or a windfall of cash. Girls in prostitution learned to trust and rely on each other as there was no one else who really understood their lives or cared about their fates.[34]

The life of a child prostitute in late-nineteenth-century Chicago was tough, but in their actions and words girls conveyed their belief that this life was no worse than other options available to them. It also offered many attractions. Sex work paid better than other jobs. It celebrated youth, beauty, and sexual liberation. It replaced birth families that were abusive. It allowed girls a measure of control over their sexual relations with boys and men. Sex work also offered a supportive community of other girls and women who looked out for one another. For the most part, girls expressed few regrets with their choice to prostitute.

Nonetheless, after 1880, the *Tribune* was increasingly committed to a narrative in which child prostitutes were victims of sinister forces. They argued this point, even as the facts in their own stories argued otherwise. Frances Payne (thirteen) was a white girl from a "very decent" family. She made regular visits to a Clark Street brothel that serviced black men. Her brother testified that she was a "willing participant," and Frances admitted having sex with multiple men, getting drunk, and never wanting to leave. The newspaper concluded that she was an "utterly helpless victim." In the fall of 1882, two teen girls "went willingly" and with their parents' permission to waitress at a mining camp near Green Bay, Wisconsin. After they arrived, the girls changed their minds and were immediately returned to Chicago. But, two weeks later, the man who accompanied the girls was arrested for "abducting" the "children" for prostitution. From then on, when the *Tribune* wrote about younger prostitutes, they often described the girls as "enticed," "induced," "forced," or "abducted."[35]

The paper warned parents that procurers were everywhere, waiting to trap pretty girls. Men who had previously been depicted as annoying mashers were now something much more sinister. But, as the sex business was still mostly managed by women, most alleged procurers were women. They offered "little ones" fruit or candy and then lured them into prostitution. These women were said to derive large profits by selling these "innocents" to men. Parents, the *Tribune* warned, needed to keep their daughters under "close and constant espionage."[36]

After issuing the alarm about procuresses, however, the paper was hard pressed to find one. For years, they reported on alleged abductions for prostitution in other cities before they could identify a potential procuress in Chicago. On October 30, 1887, Maud Cassidy was arrested for procuring fifteen-year-old Blanche Bonville for prostitution in the Wisconsin lumber camps. However, Blanche testified under oath that she prostituted in Chicago for a year before she ever met Maud, that she knew what was expected of her in the camps, and that she never wanted to get away. The defense concluded that Blanche "knew the life thoroughly and chose it of her own free will." Maud was acquitted. However, as the *Tribune* related the story, the girl was a "child" from a "respectable family" and "unquestionably of good character." The newspaper proudly boasted that the "vigilance of the public press" brought Maud Cassidy to justice and ended the "procuress business in this city."[37]

The enduring legacy of the procuress hysteria was the way girls began to use the myth to evade the negative consequences of their sexual choices. Bertha Lehmans (sixteen) left home with her married lover. They moved into Annie Baker's assignation house where, for three weeks, Bertha had sex with other men at her boyfriend's urging and also of her own volition. She freely came and went from the house and moved about the red light district in search of men and good times. At her family's request, the Illinois Humane Society investigated. When agents found the girl she refused to be "rescued." However, when her sisters threatened to have Bertha committed to the House of the Good Shepherd, she quickly recast her story as one of abduction and forced prostitution. In the new version of her tale, she was an innocent "child," "trapped and ruined" by a "very bad man." Annie Baker and Bertha's boyfriend went to jail. The girl suffered no negative repercussions for her dalliance with prostitution.[38]

As Bertha's story shows, adolescent prostitutes—just like sexually rebellious girls and those seeking abortions—learned that they had the power to manipulate the media and foil the laws and societies that aimed to control or protect them. During the Gilded Age, no less than seven major agencies and institutions began to concern themselves with preserving or reclaiming the virtue of adolescent Chicago girls. In the first decade of the twentieth century, two more institutions arose to meet the specific needs of Black girls. Their immorality was not greater than that of White girls, but due to the historic and persistent sexual abuse of Black women by White men, they were judged to be in special need of protection. All of these societies rested on a belief that bad girls were "helpless ones," driven to do wrong by poor parenting or poverty. In the words of one agency, adolescent girls were "too young to choose intelligently between virtue and vice." They were still children in need of protection from sexual temptations.[39]

These reformers believed that the state had the power and responsibility to act as a parent for all citizens who could not take care of themselves. This was validated by a new Illinois law that allowed any "responsible person" to file a petition looking into the welfare of any female under eighteen years of age who was "dependent." This included girls who were begging, homeless, who lacked "proper" parental care, wandered the streets or alleys, or consorted with "vicious persons." After a hearing in open court, girls could be committed to an industrial school until age eighteen. The ultimate expression of this ethos of *parens patriae* was the Cook County Juvenile Court, which opened in 1899. It was the nation's first court specifically for children. In addition to adult crimes, they could be charged with truancy, incorrigibility, and sexual delinquency. For girls, sex quickly became the principle issue, accounting for 80 percent of the charges against them. Thus, even though individual girls could manipulate the law and the presumption that they were helpless innocents, by the end of the century bad girl behavior was subject to a host of repressive laws and restrictions.[40]

Nonetheless, this subculture of sexually active Gilded Age girls has lasting historical significance. Whether challenging Victorian morality, seeking abortions, or participating in sexual commerce, girls espoused a new ethic that placed free sexual expression at the center of life and allowed girls to seek and enjoy sexual pleasure. They had agency and made choices—not always wise choices—that gave them control of their lives and bodies, even as outside agencies sought to restrict their independence. In so doing, they were the vanguard of a sexual revolution that came to fruition in the early twentieth century.

NOTES

1. Jane Addams, *The Spirit of Youth and City Streets* (New York: Macmillan, 1909), 5–8.
2. Horowitz, *Rereading Sex*, 356.
3. *Madeleine: An Autobiography* (New York: Knopf, 1919), 5.
4. *Chicago Tribune*, October 25, 1879.
5. Richard Lee Strout, ed., *Maud* (New York: Macmillan, 1939), 327–32.
6. *Chicago Tribune*, December 15, 16, 17, and 29, 1882; January 17 and 27 and February 9, 1883.
7. General Assembly of the State of Illinois, *Laws of the State of Illinois* (Springfield: Rokker, 1887), 170–71; Stephen Robertson, "Age of Consent Law and the Making of Modern Childhood in New York City, 1886–1921," *Journal of Social History* 35 (Summer 2002): 781–98; David Tanenhaus, "Between Dependency and Liberty: The Conundrum of Children's Rights in the Gilded Age," *Law and History Review* 23 (Summer 2005): 351–85.
8. *Chicago Tribune*, February 21, 22, 24, 25, and 26, 1888.
9. *Chicago Tribune*, June 16, 1883; Faderman, *Odd Girls and Twilight Lovers*, 41–45; Rupp, *A Desired Past*, 79–85.
10. *Chicago Tribune*, March 25, 1885.
11. Faderman, *Odd Girls*, 15, 38, 55–56; Rupp, *A Desired Past*, 86–94.
12. *Chicago Tribune*, July 12, 1896.
13. *Chicago Tribune*, April 22, 1877; Chicago Erring Women's Refuge for Reform, *Annual Report 1875* (Chicago: Chicago Erring Women's Refuge for Reform, 1875), 7–8; Chicago Erring Women's Refuge for Reform, *Annual Report 1876* (Chicago: Chicago Erring Women's Refuge for Reform, 1876), 9.
14. *Madeleine*, 32, 39, 81, 164.
15. *Chicago Tribune*, June 18, 19, 20, 21, and 24, July 27 and 29, August 1, and September 15, 1874.
16. *Chicago Tribune*, January 12 and 13, 1870; June 21, 1874; March 3, 1877; October 21, 1877; January 29, 1889; January 1, 1890; January 27, 1892; Reagan, *When Abortion Was a Crime*, 57.
17. *Chicago Tribune*, July 13, 1865; January 12, 1870; March 10, 1874; March 4, 1877.
18. Reagan, *When Abortion Was a Crime*, 47, 54–55.
19. *Chicago Tribune*, April 17 and July 13, 1874; March 25, 1876; August 23, 1877; October 21, 1879; August 27, 1880; November 29, 1881. Reagan, *When Abortion Was a Crime*, 19, 21, 30.

20. *Chicago Tribune*, November 29, 1887; Reagan, *When Abortion Was a Crime*, 31.
21. *Chicago Tribune*, August 23, 1877.
22. *Chicago Tribune*, April 11, 1873; June 9, 1874; March 4 and August 23, 1877; November 11, 1879; August 22 and 28 and November 16, 1880; May 6 and June 26, 1881; May 14, 1882; July 4, 1884; December 11, 1887.
23. *Chicago Tribune*, June 18 and 20 and July 30, 1874; April 29, 1877; May 19 and August 24, 1880; April 12, 1881.
24. *Chicago Tribune*, April 17, 21, and 22, 1875; April 7, 1878; August 29, 1880; July 21 and September 13, 1881; July 13, 1884.
25. *Madeleine*, 36, 115, 165; Blair, *I've Got to Make My Livin'*, 35.
26. *Chicago Tribune*, January 16, 1880; January 15, 1882; March 30 and April 1, 1883.
27. *Chicago Tribune*, January 29, 1874; November 23, 1879.
28. *Madeleine*, 8–13; (Chicago) *Broad-Ax*, June 22, 1911; Peiss, *Cheap Amusements*, 5, 10, 58–60.
29. Chicago Erring Women's Refuge, *Annual Report, 1877* (Chicago: Chicago Erring Women's Refuge for Reform, 1877), 14; *Sporting Life*, November 25, 1882; *Madeleine*, 72, 109; Benjamin Reitman, *The Second Oldest Profession* (New York: Vanguard, 1931), 229.
30. *Chicago Tribune*, March 9, 1875; March 10 and May 4, 1875; April 1, 1877; January 6, 1878; April 24 and May 18, 1879; February 29, 1880.
31. *Chicago Tribune*, January 6, 1878: May 28 and September 26, 1879.
32. *Chicago Tribune*, May 28, 1879; Nuala O'Faolain, *The Story of Chicago May* (New York: Riverhead, 2006), 38.
33. *Chicago Tribune*, April 22, 1875.
34. *Chicago Daily Journal*, July 19, 1853; *Chicago Tribune*, May 29, 1857; *Chicago Times*, December 16 and November 27, 1870; (Chicago) *Street Gazette*, September 15, 1877; *Sporting Life*, November 25, 1882; *Madeleine*, 55, 65, 113, 165.
35. *Chicago Tribune*, September 15, 1880; September 26 and October 9, 1882; February 9, December 4, 5, and 14, 1883; August 13, 1885; January 6, 1887; July 26, 1888; October 12, 1890.
36. *Chicago Tribune*, February 9, 1883.
37. *Chicago Tribune*, October 13, 1885; November 4, 1886; February 2, April 4, October 30, and December 28, 1887; January 8, March 2, and March 4, 1888.
38. *Chicago Tribune*, August 7, 8, and 13, 1885.
39. *Chicago Tribune*, October 1, 1879; March 27, 1886; (Chicago) *Broad-Ax*, November 4, 1899, and February 3, 1900; T. H. MacQueary, "Schools for Delinquent and Truant Children in Illinois," *American Journal of Sociology* 9 (July 1903): 1–23; Knupfer, *Towards a Tenderer Humanity and a Nobler Womanhood*; Flanagan, *Seeing with Their Hearts*; Hoy, *Good Hearts*.
40. Tanenhaus, "Between Dependency and Liberty," 372–74; Knupfer, *Reform and Resistance*.

9

Ohio Departures

George as Progressive Youth in Sherwood Anderson's Winesburg, Ohio

JOHN JAMES AND TOM UE

Sherwood Anderson opens *Winesburg, Ohio: A Group of Tales of Ohio Small Town Life* (1919) with a short story titled "The Book of the Grotesque," from which his central protagonist, George Willard, is noticeably absent. In it, Anderson describes an "old man with a white mustache," a solitary writer who wants to raise his bed off the ground "so that it would be level with the window," enabling him "to look at the trees when he awoke in the morning." The writer hires a carpenter to raise the bed. At first glance, the two characters share some similarities. Both men sport white mustaches and smoke cigars, and they are advanced in years. However, the writer is depicted as youthful and imaginative in outlook, and his capacity for creation positions him as savvy and forward-thinking. The carpenter, by contrast, cannot overcome his traumatic experiences as a prisoner in Andersonville and his loss of a brother to starvation. The story of this old man and his brother was inspired by Anderson's own experiences, although the precise occasion on which this vignette took place is unclear: "I remember in particular an old man, one Jim Lane. He had been in Andersonville prison. He had seen his brother die of hunger there. He was a tall old man and his lean face stood up above the heads of weeping women. He also wept. I saw the tears running down his gaunt old cheeks." The carpenter's and his brother's harrowing experiences in the prison camp, in Georgia, where twelve thousand of thirty thousand Union prisoners died, resonate closely with those of many of its prisoners. Fifteen-year-old William Smith, a soldier in the 14th Illinois Infantry, described the prisoners as a "great mass of gaunt, unnatural-looking beings, soot-begrimed, and clad in filthy trousers"; thirteen-year-old Ranson J. Powell, a drummer for the Union Army's 10th Virginia Regiment, had a daily ration consisting of a teaspoon of salt, three tablespoon of beans, a half-pint of unsifted cornmeal, and water from a nearby creek that also served as the camp's sewer; and fifteen-year-old Billy Bates weighed only sixty pounds when he escaped from the prison. Anderson's allusion to this specific prison justifies the carpenter's emotional response and, to an unknowing audience, his "ludicrous" expression: "when he cried he puckered up his lips and the mustache bobbed up and down."[1] This historical reference forcefully demonstrates how the carpenter continues to be haunted by his traumatic past, to the extent that it impedes his ability to complete the writer's plan for raising the bed.

"The Book of the Grotesque" articulates a central conflict in *Winesburg*, one that finds expression throughout the short story cycle in the grotesque motif, from the gaunt and "ghostly figure" of Elizabeth Willard to the hateful and isolated Wash Williams. Anderson understands the carpenter as a "grotesque" because he clings to the past, allowing it to stifle his work capacity in the present. The writer, though he seems particularly reflective, retains the youthful spirit of innovation that readers will identify in George Willard. Anderson describes the writer: "You can see for yourself how the old man, who had spent all of his life writing and was filled with words, would write hundreds of pages on this matter. The subject would become so big in his mind that he himself would be in danger of becoming a grotesque." He avoids this fate by keeping alive the "young thing inside him," which, because it eschews affixed "truths," enables him to adjust his perspective to cope with his contemporaneous social and economic changes. But, as the narrator tells us, "The grotesques were not all horrible. Some were amusing, some almost beautiful, and one, a woman all drawn out of shape, hurt the old man by her grotesqueness." By referring to the "progression of figures" who will come to occupy the book variously as "grotesque," "amusing," "beautiful," and even "loveable,"[2] Anderson demonstrates sympathy for these characters, many of whom struggle to adapt to the social changes gradually enveloping the Midwest in this period.

George Willard's narrative, that of an artist in transition, positions him as witness and experiencer of an ideological conflict between a Gilded Age generation and a younger, Progressive one, and finally as one who avoids becoming a grotesque. David I. Macleod traces the progression in values, in the period from 1890 to 1920, from the "family economy" model, wherein "children were integrated as rapidly as possible into family activities and socialized to be helpful and economically productive while still young," to the model of "sheltered childhood," in which "children were set apart, protected from adult concerns, their activities carefully graded." As Macleod shows, this change was provoked by a number of factors and it demanded both resources and commitment: "By the early 1900s commitment to this ideal of [the sheltered] childhood was well established among the urban middle class and increasingly among the upper tier of the working class." Macleod attributes the popularization of the sheltered childhood model to "[u]rbanization, declining ratios of children to adults, better living conditions, [and the] belief that children needed to develop at a measured pace through different stages." However, as Macleod reveals, "[E]ven in towns and cities it was still contested. And reformers had only limited resources to force the pace of change."[3] *Winesburg, Ohio* dramatizes the challenges inherent in the historical progression of a family economy model to one of sheltered childhood, particularly as it pertains to a small midwestern community. George's maturation narrates the ideological concerns that he inherits from his parents and his gradual subversion of them. Ultimately, his story foregrounds the centrality of adaptation to an evolving idea of childhood in the Gilded Age and Progressive Era.

George's Narrative and the Formation of Character

George Willard belongs to a generation that experiences the transition from the Gilded Age to the Progressive Era. He is the product, unlike his parents, of a generation of children who, owing to smaller families, are promised more compassion and understanding and an educational background that places more weight on imagination and individualism. As he becomes more observant and more critical of his environment, George recognizes the flaws and the limits that circumscribe Winesburg's development. He is particularly receptive to the plights of his townspeople. Anderson suggests, through George's departure, that the young reporter rejects the values of his parents and their generation in favor of greater artistic freedom. George displays compassion and understanding, qualities essential to the transition from the Gilded Age to the Progressive Era.

One of our first impressions of George comes from Wing Biddlebaum. Wing understands himself to be a teacher to George and "made a picture" for him: "In the picture men lived again in a kind of pastoral golden age. Across a green open country came clean-limbed young men, some afoot, some mounted upon horses. In crowds the young men came to gather about the feet of an old man who sat beneath a tree in a tiny garden and who talked to them." In an analogue to this role, and somewhat ironically, Wing criticizes the young reporter for his tendency to be influenced by others: "You are destroying yourself. . . . You have the inclination to be alone and to dream and you are afraid of dreams. You want to be like others in town here. You hear them talk and you try to imitate them." To some extent, this perception of George as impressionable is corroborated by Elmer Cowley, who views him as "belong[ing] to the town, typif[ying] the town, represent[ing] in his person the spirit of the town," and so, in the process of challenging the young reporter, he could "challeng[e] all of Winesburg through him." The weekly *Winesburg Eagle* affords George opportunities for many kinds of personal and professional developments. "The paper on which George worked had one policy," we learn: "It strove to mention by name in each issue, as many as possible of the inhabitants of the village. Like an excited dog, George Willard ran here and there, noting on his pad of paper who had gone on business to the county seat or had returned from a visit to a neighboring village."[4] The attention to details and personal curiosity that his occupation necessitates and, in consequence, nurtures in George prepare him for a literary project like *Winesburg, Ohio*. However, when we first meet George, these potentials are as yet unrealized, and he is not even particularly good at his job.

Seth Richmond, George's eighteen-year-old friend and sometime romantic rival, acts as a foil to him. George is older than Seth, but only insofar as "it was [George] who was forever courting and the younger boy who was being courted." They are near contemporaries in age and, indeed, maturity. The two characters swap romantic advice. George explains to Seth, "I've been trying to write a love story. . . . I know what I'm going to do. I'm going to fall in love." Using this as a pretext and a cover for his shyness toward Helen, the banker's daughter, with whom "he had been for a long time half in love," George confides to Seth his desire to fall in love with Helen because "she is the only girl in town with any 'get-up' to her" and asks Seth to convey his affections. The gaucheness with which George approaches this romantic prospect and his obliviousness to Seth's own feelings for Helen reveal George's inexperience in matters of the heart. Seth too yearns to leave Winesburg, as he confides to Helen, "I've got to strike out. I've got to get work. It's what I'm good for." However, his aspirations contrast strongly with George's. As the narrator reveals, "The idea that George Willard would some day become a writer had given him a place of distinction in Winesburg." While each boy's goal is Progressive in its own right, George's creative capacity, combined with the documentation and representation that he may someday offer the people of Winesburg, have the greater potential to impact the social reforms characteristic of the Progressive Era. Seth's wish to leave Winesburg in order to "work and keep quiet" is, by contrast, less ambitious. Aside from his desire to become a mechanic, which perhaps indicates his embracing of technological change, Seth's outlook differs little from the conservative viewpoint held by Winesburg's Gilded Age generation. It is unsurprising then that Helen ultimately understands Seth's wish to "strike out" as a boyish one. Though upon first hearing it, she thinks, "This boy is not a boy at all, but a strong, purposeful man," she finally dismisses him, once her favorite: "'I think I'd better get going along,' she said, letting her hand fall heavily to her side. A thought came to her. 'Don't you go with me; I want to be alone,' she said. 'You go and talk to your mother. You'd better do that now.'" Seth immaturely responds to Helen's rejection in a whisper to himself: "She'll be embarrassed and feel strange when I'm around. . . . That's how it'll be. That's how everything'll turn out. When it comes to loving some one, it won't never be me. It'll be some one else, some fool, some one who talks a lot, some one like that George Willard." Seth challenges George's adaptability, which is essential to his identity. At one point, a solitary Seth passes by but says nothing to their mutual acquaintance Turk Smollet. He thinks to himself, "If George were here, he'd have something to say."[5] George *is* open to the people of Winesburg, including outcasts like Elmer Cowley and Wing Biddlebaum—both of whom, like Seth, take him for a participant in Winesburg's social hegemony.

And yet, George is not at all like his fellow townspeople. George's romance with Helen reveals his personal growth. When the drunken Tom Foster talks of making love with Helen, George's "own heart flamed up and he became angry," and he asks Tom to quit. George feels even more angry when his mother's death prevents him from meeting with Helen. In the story "Sophistication," he no longer wants to boast before her, but instead to show her how much he has evolved. Helen returns home from college in Cleveland for a day at the fair. She spends it mostly with one of her instructors, a young man, but finds him lacking:

> Helen White was thinking of George Willard even as he wandered gloomily through the crowds thinking of her. She remembered the summer evening when they had walked together and wanted to walk with him again. She thought that the months she had spent in the city, the going to theatres and the seeing of great crowds wandering in lighted thoroughfares, had changed her profoundly. She wanted him to feel and be conscious of the change in her nature.

Helen recognizes something in George that is not in the young instructor, despite his "put[ting] on the airs of the city" and his attempt to appear cosmopolitan in spite of his having been raised in an Ohio town. Anderson hints at a difference between the sham, the artist who tries to appear city-like, and the real thing. George, we learn, wishes for something different from a partner: "If he prefers that the other be a woman, that is because he believes that a woman will be gentle, that she will understand. He wants, most of all, understanding." George's desire for a companionate relationship suggests a move away from the other kinds of romances he has had, and yet he continues to struggle to articulate his feelings for Helen:

They [George and Helen] stopped kissing and stood a little apart. Mutual respect grew big in them. They were both embarrassed and to relieve their embarrassment dropped into the animalism of youth. They laughed and began to pull and haul at each other. In some way chastened and purified by the mood they had been in they became, not man and woman, not boy and girl, but excited little animals.... For some reason they could not have explained they had both got from their silent evening together the thing needed. Man or boy, woman or girl, they had for a moment taken hold of the thing that makes the mature life of men and women in the modern world possible.

Although both Seth and George ultimately choose departure over Helen, the contrast in their respective treatments of Helen reveals a great deal about their maturity. George and Helen develop a greater understanding of one another, and we no longer observe the awkwardness George had exhibited in his first interactions with Helen. When they last appear, "she [takes] his arm and walk[s] beside him in dignified silence." Their silence contrasts with the quiet that Seth reportedly seeks, but never finds. Indeed, Seth prevents himself from achieving this goal—he is the one, at the story's end, who continues to speak—and never develops a mutual understanding with the opposite gender. The equality observed between George and Helen is due principally to their maturation, as Anderson suggests: "In youth there are always two forces fighting in people. The warm unthinking little animal struggles against the thing that reflects and remembers." Thus, at the end of "Sophistication," we learn, "the more sophisticated thing"—the one that reflects and remembers—"had possession of George Willard." He no longer responds strictly to his animal desires in the present, but considers the ways in which those actions have in the past affected (and may in the future affect) his fellow human beings. George and Helen view one another as equals, demonstrating genuine maturity, but also a more Progressive outlook than the sheltered-childhood models selected by their not always happy parents. Helen's father is largely absent except for references to his acquisitions, and her mother operates in separate circles: she organizes a women's club for poetry and she snobbishly thinks that "[t]here is no one here fit to associate with a girl of Helen's

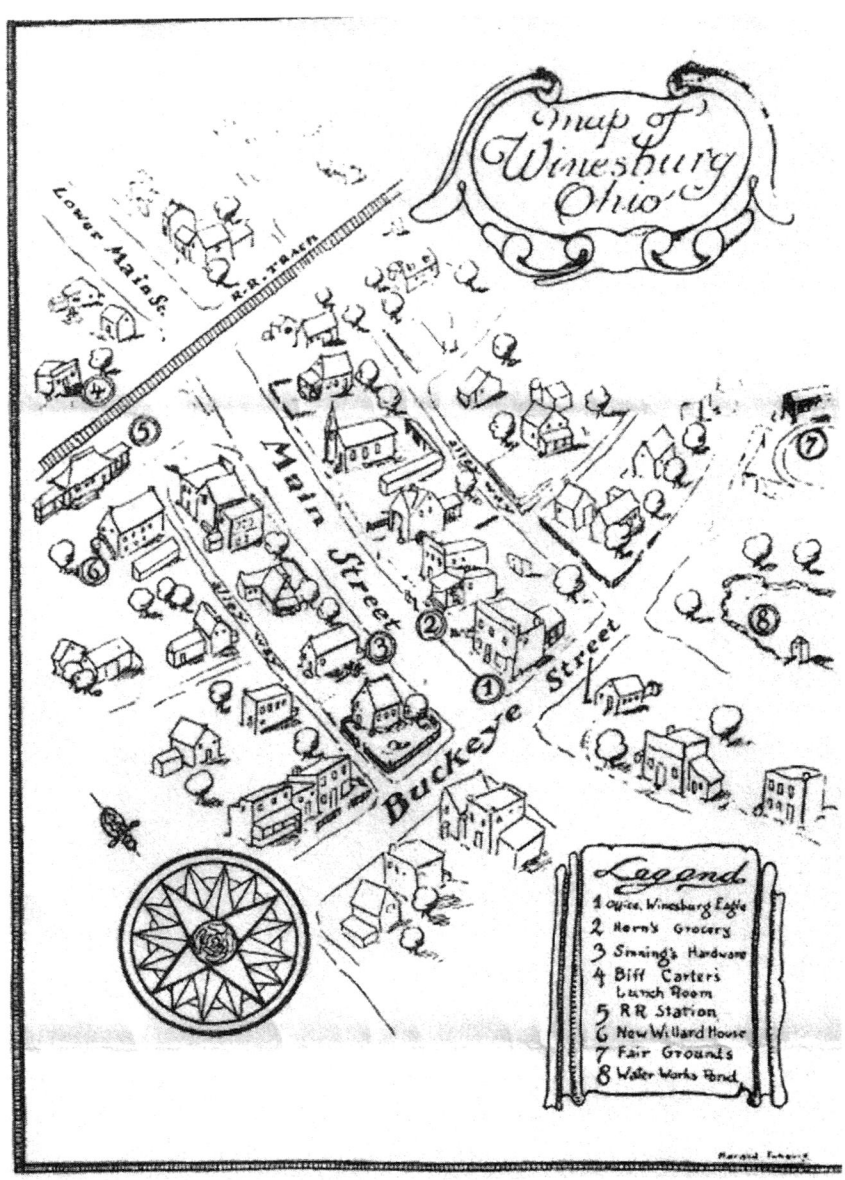

Harald Toksvig's map of Winesburg reveals the proximity of George's home to the railway, and foreshadows the book's narrative goal of George leaving the town. (Sherwood Anderson, *Winesburg, Ohio: A Group of Tales of Ohio Small Town Life*. New York: Huebsch, 1919)

breeding," despite the Winesburg money that her husband transacts on a daily basis.[6]

George's relationship with his parents also provides insight into the many ways in which he differs from his fellow townspeople and, furthermore, exhibits the abovementioned qualities endemic to a Progressive youth. Early on, he expresses his discontent to his mother, and repeatedly communicates to his friends his goal of leaving Winesburg. However, George's impetus seems rooted less in an intrinsic desire for success than in a reaction against the physical and emotional decay observed in his surroundings. George's home, the New Willard House, is anything but new. The guests who make it their temporary homes are "transient" and, in July, "had become scarce." "The hotel," we learn, "was continually losing patronage because of its shabbiness." Despite the fact that he has inherited a hotel, Tom Willard is utterly unable to update the business and attract new clientele. Elizabeth remembers a time when he was a clerk in her father's hotel: "Tom was painting and repapering rooms in the hotel. . . . There was always paint on his hands and face during those days and he smelled of paint. He was trying to fix up the old hotel, make it new and smart." With the modifying phrase "during those days," Elizabeth situates Tom's efforts in the past, suggesting that these earnest attempts have long been abandoned. Anderson describes the New Willard Hotel as it is now as a "disorderly old" one, with its "faded wallpaper" and "ragged carpets": "The hotel was unprofitable and forever on the edge of failure and he wished himself out of it. [Tom] thought of the old house and the woman who lived there with him as things defeated and done for. The hotel in which he had begun life so hopefully was now a mere ghost of what a hotel should be." Tom feels trapped in this environment—economically, because of his investment in it, and socially, because of the image of defeat that it inevitably evokes. Elizabeth internalizes this decay, and conveys it in her appearance: "Although she was but forty-five, some obscure disease had taken the fire out of her figure." Tall, gaunt, and with a face marked with smallpox scars, this "ghostly figure" is aged before her time.[7]

While families of the time were, by historical standards, small, George might enjoy what Macleod describes as the privilege of having "the nurture that came with being an only child or one of two or even three . . . of a minority." A family-economy model might help alleviate some of the expenses associated with running the hotel, though it might, as in Anderson's own case, further distribute the family's already meager resources. More importantly, and more specifically, Anderson's decision foregrounds the challenges faced by sheltered childhood when the parental figures are not particularly effective. The material resources that are available to George through his being an only child and the future heir of a hotel and that are unavailable to Anderson find no correlation in George's parents' care and attention, and he too fails to attain much of a sheltered childhood. Tom Willard, his father, reprimands him: "Will Henderson [the paper owner and editor] has spoken to me three times concerning the matter. He says you go along for hours not hearing when you are spoken to and acting like a gawky girl." Tom's belittling of George reveals his misogyny: "You're not a fool and you're not a woman. You're Tom Willard's son and you'll wake up." The narrator undermines our impression of Tom by revealing, first, his unrealized political ambitions, and, secondly, his general lack of accomplishments: "He had always thought of himself as a successful man, although nothing he had ever done had turned out successfully. When he was out of sight of the New Willard House and had no fear of coming upon his wife, he swaggered and began to dramatize himself as one of the chief men of the town." It is only away from the visualized failure of both Tom's shabby home and his wife that he can fantasize about his importance. Despite his demonstrated lack of accomplishments, Tom's assertion reveals the kinds of pressure that he and others in Winesburg continue to exert on George. Tom's understanding of male supremacy is in keeping with that of child welfare advocates of his time; moreover, it is a comparatively new model of the family that found its roots in the 1830s and that gained currency with the expansion of the British-stock middle class.[8] His conception of gender is moved by his desire to show off his status as a member of the property-owning middle class, one to which he ascends only through marriage. Ironically, however, Tom fails to realize that his inability to make the hotel profitable belies the notion of a patriarch single-handedly supporting his family, the image promoted by the rhetoric of child welfare.

Elizabeth and George share, in her view, "a deep unexpressed bond of sympathy, based on a girlhood dream that had long ago died." We, as readers, are led to suspect that the depth of their understanding exists purely in her imagination, for "[i]n the son's presence she was timid and reserved," and it is only sometimes, and always in private, that she utters "half a prayer, half a demand, addressed to the skies":

> Even though I die, I will in some way keep defeat from you. . . . If I am dead and see him becoming a meaningless drab figure like myself, I will come back. . . . I ask God now to give me that privilege. I demand it. I will pay for it. God may beat me with his fists. I will take any blow that may befall if but this my boy be allowed to express something for us both.

Elizabeth utilizes George to vicariously express her suppressed emotion, keeping her son stunted: "And do not let him become smart and successful either. . . . "

Our suspicions are confirmed by the narrator, who reveals, "The communion between George Willard and his mother was outwardly a formal thing without meaning." The narrator elaborates on the uncomfortable silence that infuses their conversations: "In the evening when the son sat in the room with his mother, the silence made them both feel awkward." Elizabeth's faulty assumptions, as well as each party's respective reserve, render communication impossible. The disparity between their understandings is revealed to us most clearly when, after George reveals to his mother his desire to leave Winesburg, she asserts, "I suppose you had better wake up. . . . You think that? You will go to the city and make money, eh? It will be better for you, you think, to be a business man, to be brisk and smart and alive?" George, who cannot know that he is following the young Elizabeth's unrealized ambitions to leave Winesburg nor that, in so doing, he is "express[ing] something for [them] both," understands only her spoken criticism and its close resemblance to his father's: "I suppose I can't make you understand, but oh, I wish I could. . . . I can't even talk to father about it. I don't try. There isn't any use. I don't know what I shall do. I just want to go away and look at people and think." Tom and Elizabeth exemplify ineffective adult and parental figures who fail to offer their children real and constructive guidance; and yet they seek, in George, a vehicle for the realization of their own unlived lives. Gertrude Wilmot, a character who "had never paid any attention to George" previously, turns up at his departure to "voic[e] what everyone felt" when she says, "Good luck." Winesburg turns to George, by turns, for recognition, identification, and representation.⁹

Winesburg in Context

Winesburg draws much from Anderson's experiences in his hometown, Clyde, Ohio, as well as the various small Ohio towns that he inhabited in his youth, and it offers a historical impression of the period. Anderson began writing his *Memoirs* in 1933 and continued working on it until his death in 1941. He draws comparisons between this project and his writing of *Winesburg*: "The idea is really . . . to do an autobiography in a new way, not in the life of the teller but in the lives that touch his life . . . much as I used the figure of George Willard in *Winesburg* but carrying the idea into more mature years." Ray Lewis White emphasizes this connection when he argues that Anderson's *Memoirs* differ from his other autobiographical writings because of his "return to a more conventional narrative line and the *Winesburg* form." Anderson elaborates on this autobiographical connection in his discussion of the book's origins:

> I tried to write of my own boyhood but couldn't do it so I invented a figure I called George Willard and about his figure I built a series of stories and sketches called *Winesburg, Ohio*.
> Later I found that there was an actual Winesburg, Ohio, but, when I gave the title to the book, I didn't know that.
> I looked in a book that gave a list of Ohio towns but found no Winesburg. Perhaps the book only gave the names of towns on railroads. I am told no railroad goes to the real Winesburg.
> The point is that I firmly believe that anyone reading that book is bound to have a rather sharp impression of my own youth, of what I saw and felt in the people about me.

Rex Burbank writes, "Clyde was committed to the idea of progress, and it competed with the nearby towns for such commercial assets as railroad sidings and industrial plants." According to Kim Townsend, "When the Andersons arrived [in 1884], Clyde was a town of about

2,500, destined, it seemed, to become another Columbus or Toledo." Clyde consisted of "a few stores, William McPherson's blacksmith shop, a church, a cemetery, and two taverns." By Anderson's adolescence, the town had a population of approximately four thousand. However, Clyde's promises of modernization and urban expansion remain unrealized. Burbank states, "[L]ike thousands of other Midwestern hamlets, it lost the race for progress to towns that were more favorably located and more adept in attracting industry." He continues, "[P]ost–Civil War Clyde, Ohio, was an agricultural village which, long since settled, lay stagnant between an exhausted agrarian era and a nascent industrial age." By 1960, the three railroad systems and fourteen trains a day that ran through the town in the 1880s had been reduced to a small freight business, and no passenger trains had run through Clyde in twenty-two years.[10]

In contrast, Winesburg houses a population of eighteen hundred, and what was once a tiny "village of twelve or fifteen houses clustered about a general store on Trunion Pike" has grown, over the space of fifty years, into "a thriving town." Anderson remembers a time, much different from George's and, in fact, his own:

> In the last fifty years a vast change has taken place in the lives of our people. A revolution has in fact taken place. The coming of industrialism, attended by all the roar and rattle of affairs, the shrill cries of millions of new voices that have come among us from over seas, the going and coming of trains, the growth of cities, the building of the interurban car lines that weave in and out of towns and past farmhouses, and now in these later days the coming of the automobiles has worked a tremendous change in the lives and in the habits of thought of our people of Mid-America. Books, badly imagined and written though they may be in the hurry of our times, are in every household, magazines circulate by the millions of copies, newspapers are everywhere. In our day a farmer standing by the stove in the store in his village has his mind filled to overflowing with the words of other men. The newspapers and the magazines have pumped him full. Much of the old brutal ignorance that had in it also a kind of beautiful childhood innocence is gone forever. The farmer by the stove is brother to the men of the cities, and if you listen you will find him talking as glibly and as senselessly as the best man of us all.

The improved travel networks that Anderson describes pave the way for the dissemination of ideas, and they contribute significantly to the dawning of modernity and to the increasingly globalized community of which Winesburg is very much a part. The proximity of George's home in the New Willard House to the railway, as demonstrated in Harald Toksvig's map drawn for *Winesburg, Ohio*'s first edition, accentuates its profound impact on the hotel, local businesses, and the wider community. More specifically for George, his room in the hotel's second floor enables him to look out at the railway and the limitless possibilities of the world outside of Winesburg that it evokes. Anderson paints Jesse Bentley's time, the period immediately following the Civil War, as a simpler one:

> Men laboured too hard and were too tired to read. In them was no desire for words printed upon paper. As they worked in the fields, vague, half-formed thoughts took possession of them. They believed in God and in God's power to control their lives. In the little Protestant churches they gathered on Sunday to hear of God and his works.[11]

Anderson's use of "too" as a refrain effectively emphasizes the hardships that people in the pre-industrial pioneer days suffered in America and the strains those hardships placed on human curiosity. If Anderson, like George Gissing in his 1891 novel *New Grub Street*, criticizes the lack of correlation between the unprecedented output of reading material, on the one hand, and a lack of good reading, on the other, Anderson also sees these workers as part of a machine that pays insufficient heed to human conditions.

Winesburg had seen better days than it does in George's time. A stagnant general store displays "three combs of honey" standing in the window that had "grown brown and dirty in their wooden frames." They have become that way, we are told, because the "honey had stood in the store window for six months" without being sold. The store sells little merchandise and yet maintains an overstock of inventory that inspires townspeople to jeer, "it sold everything and nothing." Belle Carpenter's house is "gloomy" and "old," and "[a] rusty tin eaves-trough had slipped from its fastenings at the back of the house and when the wind blew it beat against the roof of a small shed, making a dismal drumming noise that sometimes persisted all through the night." The young girl of "Tandy" inhabits an "old unpainted house on an unused road," with a father who largely ignores her in favor of promoting agnostic ideas among his fellow townspeople. The girl lives "half forgotten" on "the bounty of her dead mother's relatives." The town's decay, while predominant, is not universal: Jesse Bentley, the owner and overlord of a farm, "owned machinery for harvesting grain. He had built modern barns and most of his land was drained with carefully laid tile drain." Banker White owns a new stone house, and has the material wealth to send his daughter Helen to college.[12]

In addition to the regional changes in this period, Anderson's *Memoirs* offers insight into his own family's life, an important influence on his writing of George's. Anderson describes Clyde and his family life:

> The little house in Clyde was very small. How we all managed to live in it is, as I remember the house, still a mystery to me for other children would have been continually coming. More children coming and father without work. He had been brought to Clyde to work in a harness shop there but had lost his job.
>
> It may have been due to one of the periods of depression, the two men who owned the shop, the brothers Irvin, compelled to retrench, no work coming into the shop, no harness being sold, or it may have been father's fault, his work neglected, he perhaps running off to some meeting of Civil War veterans or perhaps even a period of drinking when he could not work, but at any rate there is a winter of hardship fixed in my mind, mother struggling to in some way take father's place as the family breadwinner.

Anderson portrays a community that faces repeated bouts of depression. Irwin Anderson, Anderson's father, resembles George's father, Tom Willard. Just as Tom walks the streets of Winesburg, "spruce and business-like" and "swagger[s] and . . . dramatize[s] himself as one of chief men of the town," so "Irwin never did quite live up to his vows. He was happier swapping tales about the Civil War or playing the alto horn than he was fulfilling the obligations of a husband and a father." Anderson reflects more self-consciously on his remembering of his father:

> [I]t was only after I had become a mature man, long after our mother's death, that I began to a little appreciate our father and to understand a

little his eternal boyishness, his lack of feeling of responsibility to others, his passion for always playing with life, qualities that I have no doubt our mother saw in him and that enabled her in spite of the long hardship of her life with him to remain always faithful and, for anything I ever heard her say, a devoted wife.

But as Burbank notes, and as Anderson well understood, "Irwin Anderson was at least partly the victim of economic cycles and historical changes. Like other harness makers of the late nineteenth century, he found the demand for his skill diminishing as industry moved into the Middle West." The family's destitution resulted in part from "Irwin's easy-going irresponsibility," but it was owing as well to "the encroachments of mass-production manufacturing and depressions."[13]

Anderson had fonder memories of his mother, Emma, to whom he dedicated *Winesburg*. In its first edition, published by B. W. Huebsch, Anderson described her as one "[w]hose keen observations on the life about her first awoke in [him] the hunger to see beneath the surface of lives." For Burbank, "Emma seemed to have all the desirable qualities that [Anderson's] father lacked," most notably "stoic endurance, self-sacrifice, and sympathetic curiosity." Emma "remained to Sherwood a symbol of broken dreams, of a life spent in a dreary routine of washing and cooking and childbearing, a life starved for affection from her husband and devoid of adventure and excitement." According to Townsend, "[T]here is no doubt that [Anderson's] mother deserves all the credit he gives her for keeping the family as much of a unit as it was." The challenges that Emma faced during a terrible winter are poignantly described by Anderson in his *Memoirs*. Emma's pregnancy prevented her from taking in washing, so that

> we had become objects of charity, neighbors bringing food to our door, we children half unaware of the terror of actual hunger and yet, as children are, vaguely aware of our mother's fight and sadness, tears coming suddenly to her eyes, so that we all began to cry loudly in sympathy with her, the strange long periods of silence in the house, myself, with the two other children, Karl and Stella, going along the railroad tracks that ran along the rear of our house, picking up pieces of coal dropped from trains to keep our stove in our house going, we all in the winter evenings

huddled about our one stove in the little kitchen, no lamp lighted because there would have been no oil for the lamp, the crawling into bed in the darkness, all of us children in the one bed huddled close to keep warm.[14]

During this time, Anderson's father was absent from home: "He had painted the sign announcing mother's willingness to become a sewing woman and that may have set off the artist in him. It may have been at that time that he threw up the trade of harness making to become a sign writer and he had gone off somewhere seeking signs to paint." The distribution of the family's meager resources owing to the constantly growing family moved Anderson to write,

> Is the feeling that comes thus to a small child, seeing the sudden new shapelessness of a mother, sensing without quite knowing of the causing event, is it jealous of a mother's love to be again more widely distributed? I only know that I remember as a part of the experience that particular winter, along with resentment, that other children of the neighbourhood could be more warmly clad, that they could have new shoes when the soles of mine had become loose and that my toes stuck out at holes in the toes, that they lived in warmer houses, that their fathers seemed to have a kind of substantial dignity my own father could not achieve, that along with these resentments was this other and sharper one so that when the child was born I hated it also and that, after I had been called into a room to see it, lying so small and red in the bed beside mother, I crept away into a little shed at the back of the house and had a good long lonely cry.

Anderson's description is in keeping with the challenges to the family-economy childhood model that Macleod describes: Irwin cannot support his growing family. Emma's courage is reflected, to some extent, in Elizabeth Willard, who, when she is well, "do[es] the work of a chambermaid among beds soiled by the slumbers of fat traveling men." Indeed, Anderson suggests this parallel in his *Memoirs*: "I had myself written, in my *Winesburg* tales, the story of a woman who seemed to me a rather fine mother. It happened that she had been with two or three other men before she took one in marriage. I called my story 'Mother.' . . . " The importance of maternal relationships in *Winesburg* cannot be understated, and as David Stouck observes, "Almost all of the men in the stories live alone with their mothers in Winesburg, or with some maternal figure (a grandmother, an aunt)."[15]

Ironically, the world outside of Winesburg that Elizabeth and George aspire toward is not necessarily more promising. For all of their aspirations and bickering, their lens on the world outside of Winesburg is incredibly narrow. Years before George's time, members of theatrical companies had confided to Elizabeth when they came to Winesburg and stopped at what is now New Willard House, "It's not like that. . . . It's as dull and uninteresting as this here. Nothing comes of it." Here, Anderson foregrounds how physical displacement alone is not Progressive. John S. Lawry writes of George's departure, "It should probably be added that Willard's colorless, almost anonymous departure from Winesburg . . . does not prophesy a future of liberation or joy in the city." Raymond Wilson argues that "Departure" does not resolve George's maturity theme and that "the inherent sensitivity, nurtured by his mother, must dominate the philistine worldliness urged by Tom Willard." George's character development and his artistic formation require him to strike a balance between the prosaic qualities exemplified by his father and the metaphorical and poetic ones exemplified by his mother, and this remains very much in process by the end of *Winesburg*. Meanwhile, Jacobson makes the case that *Winesburg* leaves ambivalent whether or not George has sufficiently matured, and there is nothing to suggest that George changed enough to be *Winesburg*'s narrator: "*Winesburg* not only provides no hint of how George will emerge as a writer, but in fact suggests that the odds are against his doing so. The book includes several failed artists, men who at one time may well have looked as promising to their companions as George does to his." In fact, as Jacobson observes, there is no mention of George's aspiration to be a writer in the cycle's last story, "Departure," or in the last third of the book: "*Winesburg* concludes with the narrator receding into a still adolescent boy who faces an undefined future."[16] Anderson's ending of *Winesburg* at the level of question makes both George's narrative and *Winesburg* not works of "grotesque": they are neither distorted nor absurd but rather works that are in production. This theme and its expression are central to Anderson's understanding of Progressivism: by circumventing and withholding one's creation and one's adoption of a set of values, Anderson reminds us that the individual, like his project as a whole, is always in process and needs always to be adaptable.[17]

NOTES

1. Sherwood Anderson, *Winesburg, Ohio*, edited by Charles E. Modlin and Ray Lewis White (New York: Norton, 1996), 5; Sherwood Anderson, *Sherwood Anderson's Memoirs: A Critical Edition*, edited by Ray Lewis White (Chapel Hill: University of North Carolina Press, 1969), 166–67; Mintz, *Huck's Raft*, 121, 124–25. Anderson, *Winesburg, Ohio*, 5. All references to *Winesburg, Ohio*, unless indicated otherwise, are to the Norton edition.

2. Ibid., 16. Anderson puns on meanings of the term "grotesque" as "[c]haracterized by distortion or unnatural combinations; fantastically extravagant; bizarre, quaint," and as "[l]udicrous from incongruity; fantastically absurd." "Grotesque, adj.," *Oxford English Dictionary Online*, July 2012, Oxford University Press, http://www.oed.com.libproxy.ucl.ac.uk/view/Entry/81794?rskey=PBig5l&result=1&isAdvanced=false (accessed July 8, 2012). In their footnote, Charles E. Modlin and Ray Lewis White demonstrate how these meanings are intertwined and emphasize the importance of time to changes in social and moral values when they observe, "*Grotesque* derives from grotto, because on the walls of grottos (or caves) ancient artists sometimes drew human figures that were distorted, exaggerated, or ugly, at least by later standards of beauty." Anderson, *Winesburg, Ohio*, 6. See also the senses of the noun "grotesque" as they pertain to our understandings of style and of character: "[a] kind of decorative painting or sculpture, consisting of representations of portions of human and animal forms, fantastically combined and interwoven with foliage and flowers," "[a] work of art in this style," and "[a] clown, buffoon, or merry-andrew." "Grotesque, n.," *Oxford English Dictionary Online*, July 2012, Oxford University Press, http://www.oed.com.libproxy.ucl.ac.uk/view/Entry/81794?rskey=PBig5l&result=1&isAdvanced=false (accessed July 8, 2012). Anderson, *Winesburg, Ohio*, 7, 7, 6, 6–7. Marcia Jacobson further distinguishes the narrator from *Winesburg*'s characters:
   > It is worth noting that the narrator does not say that he becomes a convert to the writer's ideas, simply that he learns from them. That is his stance throughout the book: He is not dogmatic, but is interested in what people have to teach him and is eager to do them justice. He is, in fact, a rather likeable character, whereas George [the book's central protagonist] is not always so appealing.

   Marcia Jacobson, "*Winesburg, Ohio* and the Autobiographical Moment," *New Essays on Winesburg, Ohio*, edited by John W. Crowley (Cambridge: Cambridge University Press, 1990), 59.

3. Macleod, *The Age of the Child*, xi–xii, 31, 31, 31.
4. Anderson, *Winesburg, Ohio*, 11, 11, 107, 111, 72. Jacobson distinguishes George from the much more knowledgeable narrator:

    Most of the characters in *Winesburg* approach George at some point, desperately trying to tell him their stories. They look to him as one who will listen—he is a reporter, after all—and one skilled with words who might be able to translate their inchoate feelings into something that makes sense. But, typically, they are unable to make themselves clear to him. The failure is often theirs, for George is a willing enough listener. But George, too, is often unable to respond. Sometimes he lacks the intuition or the courage to understand. . . . Sometimes he is too sure of himself. . . . But most often George simply does not know enough.

    Jacobson, "Autobiographical Moment," 60–61. See Tom Ue and John James, "Progressive Youth and the Gilded Age: Sherwood Anderson's *Winesburg, Ohio*," unpublished paper, Children in Text, Person, and Theory: An Interactive and Collaborative Research Methodology Workshop, Ontario Institute for Studies in Education, University of Toronto, April 19, 2012, for an analysis of George's romantic relationships and how they chart his personal growth.
5. Anderson, *Winesburg, Ohio*, 72, 73, 87, 73, 76, 72, 77, 76, 77, 77, 74.
6. Ibid., 121, 132, 133, 131, 136, 136, 134, 134. In this, George refuses to follow Ned Currie's example. A former writer for the *Winesburg Eagle*, Ned abandons his lover, Alice, despite his promise that they must now "stick to each other." Ibid., 60. See Raymond Wilson's analysis of the "hand" rhythm in "Sophistication." Wilson convincingly demonstrates how "Anderson sustains the rhythm as George expresses, through hands, his new mature attitude of 'reverence for all the people of the town.'" Raymond Wilson, "Rhythm in *Winesburg, Ohio*," *Great Lakes Review* 8, no. 1 (Spring 1982): 36, http://www.jstor.org/stable/20172622 (accessed June 15, 2012).
7. Anderson, *Winesburg, Ohio*, 18, 18, 126, 16, 16, 16.
8. Macleod, *Child*, 14; Anderson, *Winesburg, Ohio*, 19, 19, 19. Macleod, *Child*, 8.
9. Anderson, *Winesburg, Ohio*, 17, 17, 17, 17, 17, 17, 21, 21, 137, 137.
10. Ray Lewis White, "Introduction," in *Sherwood Anderson's Memoirs: A Critical Edition* (Chapel Hill: University of North Carolina Press, 1969), xxiv, xxviii; *Sherwood Anderson's Memoirs*, 22; Rex Burbank, *Sherwood Anderson* (New York: Twayne, 1964), 22; Kim Townsend, *Sherwood Anderson* (Boston: Houghton Mifflin, 1987), 4, 4–5; John H. Sullivan, "Winesburg Revisited," *Antioch Review* 20 (Summer 1960): 215; Burbank, *Sherwood Anderson*, 22, 23; Sullivan, "Winesburg Revisited," 216.
11. Anderson, *Winesburg, Ohio*, 87, 116–17, 34, 34.
12. Ibid., 105, 105, 105, 98, 78, 30.
13. Anderson, *Sherwood Anderson's Memoirs*, 37–38; Anderson, *Winesburg, Ohio*, 16, 19. Townsend, *Sherwood Anderson*, 9. Anderson, *Memoirs*, 44; Burbank, *Sherwood Anderson*, 24.

14. Sherwood Anderson, *Winesburg, Ohio: A Group of Tales of Ohio Small Town Life* (New York: Huebsch, 1919), n.p.; Burbank, *Sherwood Anderson*, 26–27, 27; Townsend, *Sherwood Anderson*, 12; Anderson, *Memoirs*, 38.
15. Ibid., 38, 39–40; Anderson, *Winesburg, Ohio*, 16; Anderson, *Memoirs*, 409; David Stouck, "*Winesburg, Ohio* and the Failure of Art," *Twentieth-Century Literature* 15 (October 1969): 148.
16. Anderson, *Winesburg, Ohio*, 20; John S. Lawry, "The Arts of Winesburg and Bidwell, Ohio," Sherwood Anderson Issue, edited by Jack Salzman, *Twentieth-Century Literature* 23 (February 1977): 57; Wilson, "Rhythm," 38; Jacobson, "Autobiographical Moment," 62–63, 69.
17. John James and Tom Ue would like to thank Philip Horne, exemplary editor, model historian, and exceptional teacher; Patrick A. Morris from the Newberry Library for his considerable help; Dejana Nikitovic, Vasuki Shanmuganathan, and audience members at Children in Text, Person, and Theory: An Interactive and Collaborative Research Methodology Workshop for their many helpful suggestions; and Tyler Shores for his insightful reading. James thanks the W.L. Lyons Brown Library at Bellarmine University, the Butler Library at Columbia University, and the School of Arts and Sciences at Bellarmine University. Ue thanks the Social Sciences and Humanities Council of Canada, the Canadian Centennial Scholarship Fund, and University College London.

10

Fit Body, Fit Mind

Scandinavian Youth and the Value of Work, Education, and Physical Fitness in Progressive-Era Chicago

ERIKA K. JACKSON

On May 1, 1915, on the grounds of North Park College and Theological Seminary, an air of jubilance permeated the bucolic campus perched on the outskirts of Chicago. At the Christian college established by Scandinavians, the school's student body assembled on North Park's grounds not only to acknowledge the customary festivities surrounding the celebration of May Day but also to participate in a make-shift protest revealing a divide among students, faculty, college administrators, and the larger community. The conflict centered on the construction of a new building, which the majority of those at North Park College believed was vital to the success of the student body as well as to the future of the college itself. However, the campus community did not intend the desired building to be predominantly used for academic purposes. Instead, they wanted to build a gymnasium—a desire that members of the Swedish Evangelical Mission Covenant, who were responsible for the college's founding, viewed as a vain measure and incompatible with a Christian way of life. At the May Day festivities, many of the students were seen holding signs that the community's elders viewed as offensive and in direct conflict with their beliefs, like one placard reading, "The alumni have pledged $5,000 toward the building of an auditorium. This summer we intend to build a gymnasium." Within the context of Progressive-Era Chicago, when other recent immigrant youth had much bigger problems like finding work and a safe place to live, one might have deemed this conflict to be unnecessary and somewhat selfish. Yet, for Scandinavian youth who experienced remarkable intellectual success within Chicago as an immigrant group, this conflict would establish notable agency for the community's youth, giving them the power to decide where they wanted their lives to take them.[1]

The founding members of the covenant first established the school as an institution for Scandinavians, as a forum for their religious beliefs, and to institutionalize the importance of higher education. In this exchange, their youth would come forward to exert their own agency by molding the discourse away from the traditional notion of what it meant to be Scandinavian, to instead formulate their own identities as Scandinavian Americans. The conflict surrounding the erection of a gymnasium would intensify over the summer of 1915 into a war of ideologies, marking a significant division between two generations: an older generation of Scandinavians who years before had come to Chicago to begin a new chapter for their church and families; and a younger group of first- and second-generation Scandinavian Americans whose intent was to build their lives as Americans first, and Scandinavians second. To the students of North Park College, the building of the gymnasium illustrated the vital connection of physical and intellectual fitness—a connective relationship emphasized in popular Scandinavian culture. Yet the foundation of this relationship was one that was more popular in youth culture in the early 1900s; to the older and more traditionally devout generation of Scandinavians, the focus of the community's youth on physical and intellectual fitness went against their evangelical doctrine to build themselves according to God's plan. North Park student Hilmer Gustafson presented the former argument in the student yearbook, *The Cupola*, arguing that "a thorough education consists in the harmonious development of all bodily, mental, and moral faculties. Physical education is therefore of utmost consequence and is the only way to preserve the balance of the physical forces of mankind." The faculty agreed with this assertion; for example, a Professor Risberg spoke out on his beliefs that the purpose of the new building would align with "true Christianity and serve Christian ends." On the other side, a series of articles in the Swedish American church community newspaper, *Missions-Vännen*, condemned sport as incompatible with Christian life. To the older community leaders, athletics bred competition, and the church did not recognize competition as a suitable endeavor for its younger generation. The utmost goal of the community was to produce a new league of evangelical ministers, parishioners, and missionaries through the work of the church and through studies at North Park College. Some covenant members even threatened to discontinue all other educational departments at the college besides the Theological Seminary, in hopes of shifting the purpose of North Park College to align more with the curriculum of Moody Bible Institute. The ensuing battle between the two sides—the united front of students and faculty versus the church leadership—reflected a thoroughly modern conflict of old and new ideals. Finally, at the annual conference of the Swedish Evangelical Mission Covenant that June, the covenant allowed President Nyvall to give a brief explanation in support of the issue of authorizing the trustees to take out a loan of fifteen thousand dollars in order to build the proposed gymnasium. The final decision regarding the fate of physical education at North Park would come down to a vote of the conference delegates—eighty-nine approved of the gymnasium plan and twenty-four dissented. In a concluding measure, the delegates expressed their disdain over the public battle spread across the pages of *Missions-Vännen* and adopted a telling resolution that "confidence in the president of the school and faculty be expressly given and that a protest be entered against the ungracious criticism directed against them." Despite such strong feelings, all parties would reach a tenuous resolution by April 30, 1916, expressed at the official dedication exercises for the gymnasium. In a fitting dedication speech that noted the compromise, the president of the Swedish Evangelical Mission Covenant stated that the dedicated structure would be known as the gymnasium-auditorium building. As an athletic center, it would "minister to the development of healthy bodies and sound minds," and as an auditorium, it would be "a place for vital sermons and great lectures" and contribute to the "artistic and aesthetic development of students."[2]

Outside of the historical context of the Progressive Era, this seemingly harmless confrontation might appear to be merely a conflict typical of college and preparatory-school culture—the older generation of adults chiding the younger generation for their juvenile wants and ways. However, when one considers that this was a college that Chicagoans viewed as a respected institution of higher learning, established by Scandinavian immigrants for their youth, a much different conflict comes into focus—one that illustrates young immigrants speaking out about the value of their education and what *they* wanted out of it, rather than standing by as their parents dictated their lives for them. As this essay illustrates, in Progressive-Era Chicago, Scandinavian youth exhibited a strong work ethic and sense of agency in their lives, emphasizing the attainment of education first, and employment second. While many of Chicago's newest groups of immigrant youth toiled in factories and other positions involving manual labor, most yearned for the day when they could work to fulfill their greater ambitions in the professional world of labor. Numerous Scandinavian youth also found themselves at work and looking forward to futures in business, the church, and education; however, an exponential number were able to realize their goals through further educational opportunities provided to them by community-led institutions. In 1900, when Illinois made it illegal for children under fourteen to work for wages, a vast majority of immigrant children would leave school the day they turned fourteen so they could contribute to the family wage. This was not the case for Scandinavian youth, regardless of sex, who often graduated from high school. Many would sacrifice in whatever way necessary so they could receive the postsecondary education so vital to their goals.

Because of their earlier migration patterns, Scandinavian youth and children from the 1880s on were in a position to achieve great success in Chicago. Their parents instilled in them the notion of getting ahead in American life, while still insisting that they focus on the customs and traditions of home. Chicago's Scandinavian children and youth embodied the progressive ideals celebrated within America between the 1880s and 1920, and because of this embodiment, they achieved notable opportunities not available to many other immigrant youth. An analysis of their living patterns and personal decisions illustrates that Scandinavian youth longed to be "American," yet displayed pride in their ethnic identities as Scandinavian Americans. Their Chicago neighbors viewed them as upstanding young citizens due to their focus on educational success, physical fitness, and Christian faith. Even as many young immigrants did not have access to education and toiled in adult jobs, Scandinavian youth achieved great levels of success by embodying what Americans desired of "good" immigrants—they were of the "right" faith and displayed adult behaviors and goals within society, even when many of them were still considered children. In recent years, scholars of Scandinavian Studies have built a notable historiography on the experiences of Scandinavians within Chicago; however, the voices of their children remain largely unheard. The goal of this study is to uncover those voices, as illustrations of the efforts of an immigrant group destined to succeed in America by way of their personal drive and commitment to their expressed intellectual, physical, and spiritual goals.[3]

Children and Youth in Progressive-Era Chicago

In the birthplace of progressive reform, Chicago witnessed severe issues of child labor and endangerment, as uncovered by reformers like Jane Addams and residents of Hull House, who sought to assist the massive population of European immigrants and their children within their city. The residents of Hull House collaborated in 1895 to report on the climate of Chicago's immigrant neighborhoods. In *Hull-House Maps and Papers*, the authors emphasized that, unlike many of the well-known progressives from the Chicago school of sociology who documented the problems of urban sprawl, they intended their work to be constructive and to offer direct solutions to the problems of urban degradation, especially for the city's youngest inhabitants. Their study focused on the neighborhood where Hull House was built, on the west side of Chicago near Halsted and Twelfth streets, a neighborhood where the most recent immigrants to the city resided. The main thoroughfare of the neighborhood appeared to give one the impression of a "well-to-do" neighborhood, according to the authors, with its collection of tobacco stands, saloons, factories, and occasional small dwelling houses, "tucked in like babies under the arms of industry." Altogether, the inhabitants of this west side neighborhood represented eighteen different nations. The majority came from Italy, Russia, Poland, and Bohemia. Scandinavians represented "a mere handful" of the occupants of this neighborhood;

they would move to the northwest once they became acclimated to the city. From the perspective of the Hull House authors, it is clear that Scandinavians did not fall into a category of people with whom they should concern themselves in regard to social success or problems of child endangerment.[4]

Instead, by the 1880s, progressives focused their energies on the children of southern and eastern Europe, the "new" immigrant class, rather than on Scandinavians, who were already acclimated to the city and its customs. Life was not pleasant for the youngest of these "new" immigrants, who often worked as part of the family wage system with their parents and siblings. For instance, young Italian boys of the Ewing Street Italian "colony" would leave their homes every morning at 2:30 a.m. to secure the first stacks of the morning newspaper. After they sold their last papers during the morning rush, they filled the rest of their days shining the shoes of the city's businessmen. The neighborhood's young immigrant girls could be found in clothing stores and sweatshops, working thirteen hours a day throughout the week—fifteen hours on Saturdays—despite the "efforts of the clothing-clerks to shorten the working-time by trade-union methods." While this was the picture that also best represented the early lives of numerous Scandinavian youth in Chicago, for most, it was only a temporary arrangement that they would have to endure.[5]

The experiences of one young Swedish American girl who lived in the same west side neighborhood near Hull House can attest to the comparative ease many Scandinavians experienced during the 1880s. Pauline Nelson Hegborn was born in 1882 in Chicago to John and Betty Nelson, Swedish immigrants who moved to Chicago in the late 1870s after their marriage. In her memoirs, Pauline painted a picture of an idyllic childhood in the notably diverse neighborhood described by the Hull House residents; her memoirs detailed her encounters with a variety of Irish, Scandinavian, German, and other European immigrant families near her house on Hunt Avenue. Her parents still relied on services provided by Swedish businesses and remained part of the Swedish-speaking community, whereas Pauline expressed her desire from a very young age to be an "American girl." To this young Swedish American, the city provided constant excitement, from the endless drone of fire engines, which caused the neighborhood children to "go blocks to see [the] fire," to the simple pleasures of purchasing a "dab of colored ice cream on a piece of paper" for a penny. On Thursday and Sunday evenings, when young Scandinavian servants and others who "worked for the rich people" received the weekly reprieve from their jobs, Pauline recalled that they would come to her house for dancing, leisure, and a good smörgåsbord of foods from home. She described her youthful excitement while watching her father play the violin, while the "happy young folks" would dance the "old folk dances." Her parents, who were still comparatively young themselves, could relate to the young people they entertained and found comfort in keeping up the traditions of home within Chicago. In comparison to the harsh demands that shop girls and newsboys faced, according to the residents of Hull House, Pauline portrayed her childhood as altogether carefree, with parents invested in her well-being. "Not a care in the world," she chirped in her memoirs, as she described how her father would come home from work and "would have to start out to find us; sometimes he would meet us half way. I was not alone; plenty of company." Pauline acknowledged that she was aware that neither her family nor her neighbors were prosperous by any means, and many people, especially recent immigrants, had to get by with seasonal work or by taking in boarders. Yet, when Pauline was ten years old, her family acquired the means to move into a new home further west from their first one; at this time she exclaimed that "these [are] sure the happy days of my childhood which I'll never forget."[6]

One reason Scandinavians were in a much more favorable position within Chicago society by the 1880s had to do with patterns of immigration. Scandinavians were among the founding immigrant groups of Chicago, with the earliest known settler arriving in 1838, while the largest wave of immigration occurred during the famine years from 1868 to 1870. By the dawning of the Progressive Era in Chicago, earlier Scandinavian migrants like Pauline Nelson's family had already acclimated to the city and had begun to build their own enclaves within the western and northwestern regions of the city. Another reason Scandinavians witnessed far less hardship during the Progressive Era pointed to a growing notion of social preference among Americans, who began to favor immigrants from northern and western Europe altogether in comparison to those who began to arrive in droves from southern and eastern Europe during the 1880s. Generally, Americans viewed Scandinavian immigrants predominantly because of their perceived intellectual aptitude, their faith-based Protestant values, and their stereotypical physicality—blonde-haired, blue-eyed. One American author interested in Swedish life and culture in particular wrote that rural Swedish girls were "very often" beautiful, fair-faced and fair-haired, were "particularly charming," and would seek out their own church community within a foreign city or space. However, quite possibly the most important element that contributed to Scandinavians' favorable social position within Chicago was their progressive behaviors. Most Scandinavians embraced the notion of using personal action to combat the problems of urban industrialism, while the theoretical basis of pragmatism and the progressive emphasis on efficiency and expertise were integral components of especially Norwegian and Swedish cultures. Because of the favorable social position they cultivated within Chicago, Scandinavians and their children were able to experience a varied way of life, above and beyond the struggles that many other immigrant groups endured within the city.[7]

The Establishment of North Park College: A Progressive Ideal

In February 1885, when delegates from sixty-three covenant churches in America met in Chicago to form the Swedish Evangelical Mission Covenant, the endeavor was part of a larger goal to provide Scandinavian and Scandinavian American youth with a dual education in academics and religion. J. O. Lindgren, an early covenant member, reflected upon the progressive spirit of many Scandinavians to help build places of schooling and worship for youth. Prior to immigrating to the United States, Lindgren recalled stumbling upon a group of "miserable, ragged children engaged in all sorts of mischief" while walking the back streets of Stockholm one evening. He would go on to rent a former dance hall "of the most disreputable variety" and turn it into a school for children and youth who had no opportunities for education. After founding the "Rag School" in Hornskroken, Lindgren watched as his educational experiment doubled in size from fourteen to thirty students, despite the fact that he funded the school out of his own pocket, with the occasional small gift from someone who had heard about the school. On the basis of this ideal, Lindgren and his fellow covenant members would go on to later negotiate a deal with the Swedish University Land Association to build what would become North Park College on eight and one-half acres of land in the North Park community—a college that would provide general education courses as well as seminary courses to prepare students for the ministry, all following the tenets of Protestant ideology.[8]

Prior to the first academic year at North Park, while builders erected the first building on campus (Old Main), the administration released the first academic catalog, advertising the direction that the new school would take with its four departments: theological, academy and primary, commercial, and music. The diversity of the departments showed the intention of the administration and faculty to provide educational opportunities to all deserving Scandinavian youth, regardless of skill level, in order to ensure their success in America. For instance, the school established the primary and academy department for those who had previously been denied the "privileges of a good common school education," or those who might have had some schooling in "the old country," but who, "having come to this country, . . . find themselves in need of knowledge of the English language." Successful studies within the primary department were a prerequisite for acceptance into the academy department—the equivalent of a contemporary preparatory school—to study basic college-level courses for two years. Despite its emphasis on college-level courses equivalent to American college or university courses, the curriculum of the academy department required that all students complete study of a Swedish language course. The reason for this requirement, however, was not grounded in the notion of cultural persistence. Rather, faculty of the academy department argued that Swedish was an important study because of its "noble literature" and because studying the language was an aid in the study of other languages. Nevertheless, "it also has its practical value as there will in the future, as in the past, be a demand for Swedish-speaking men in all trades and professions." As the faculty saw it, Swedish acquisition would be vital to success in business within the Swedish community in the United States and back in Sweden. But as Swedish American youth became more assimilated, they came to believe that English was more valuable for future success than Swedish. However, the faculty continued to believe that the student who intended to continue his or her studies at an American college or university would not "lose anything by studying this language, as it is getting to be recognized more and more by our leading Universities." Even for the many Norwegian, Danish, and Finnish students who would attend North Park, the notion of Swedish national dominance is made quite clear through this example alone.[9]

From its beginning, North Park College marketed itself as a coeducational institution that strove to give its students the necessary learning and character to compete in the business world and aimed to "develop the intellect, strengthen the will, and improve the understanding of the student." North Park also stressed the importance of an affordable education for deserving young Scandinavians and Scandinavian Americans—one that even the newest arrivals could afford, or could have a relative or reputable sponsor pay in tribute. Students had many choices in terms of living and schooling arrangements. North Park required certain fees for tuition, but students could elect to take a ten-week term or half a term, or could pay a discounted price up front for an entire school year's tuition. Students could also choose to pay for board and lodging; however, many commuted to the North Park community from other areas of the city. Altogether, as the college promised in its catalog, students could attend for a whole school year and their total expenses, including tuition, board, lodging, and incidentals need not exceed $150, which today would amount to $3,878.09. Based on that promise, as well as the will of would-be students of North Park, the relatively small first class flocked to the community in the fall of 1894. An analysis of the registration ledger for fall 1894 shows that fifty new students registered for classes at the new college, categorized in the ledger according to their place of birth, as well as the location from which they came to the college. The majority of incoming students for the 1894-95 school year were born either in Sweden (thirty) or in the midwestern states of Illinois, Iowa, or Michigan. Only one student came directly from Sweden, while the incoming class originated mostly from Chicago, rural Illinois, Minnesota, and Michigan, showing that those who first came to North Park were largely immigrants who had lived in the United States for a certain period of time (not specified within the registration ledger).[10]

As the new student body of North Park College descended upon campus, their excitement for the upcoming school year was palpable. One young student remembered his perceptions of the "Smoky Babylon" of Chicago, which soon shifted as he traveled north by electric railway to encounter the "beautiful, new born little school village" of North Park. "Our hearts were overflowing with great expectations," he remembered of his first weeks at North Park, where he soon encountered a unique college spirit where the entire campus community came to resemble a family unit, much like the families that most of its young coeds had left behind. Also like many other students at North Park, the author arranged to live with "father and mother Leaf," one of the families within the community. Several of North Park's students were only in their mid- to late teens when they elected to study apart from their families, who made arrangements for their children to stay with other families within the Swedish Evangelical Mission Covenant while in Chicago. Persistence in the face of adversity, a goal expressed in the motto of the school—*ad estra per aspera* ("to the stars through difficulties")—illustrated the dedication of North Park's students to their work ethic in school. Their tenure at North Park was an experience to be taken as seriously as their dedication to a Christian way of life. "Our college at North Park is a *Christian Institution*," the young author wrote in praise of the young school, pointing out the level of respect its students had for their professors as "true Christians, whose words and theories in the school room were great, but whose lives and characters as illustrated by their practical career were greater." He would go on to complete his reminiscence of North Park with a hearty endorsement of athleticism, an idea that was "one of the most conspicuous paragraphs in the new college rules," and would become a topic of intense scrutiny into the new century.[11]

In the fall of 1895, the introduction of physical education to North Park's curriculum also marked the beginnings of a cross-generational conflict that would, over time, embroil the otherwise disciplined campus community in frenzied debate. The program, headed by Axel Werelius, a student of the commercial department, emphasized the Ling system of gymnastics, a physical fitness regimen made popular in Sweden by Per Henrik Ling, who embraced connections between intellectual and physical fitness. Werelius and his team of twelve male students would garner considerable recognition within Chicago. In an article in the *Daily Inter Ocean* in March 1896, a reporter took particular note of the "wildest leap" said to have ever been performed on American soil: "This 'tiger's leap' as the Swedes themselves have named it, is certainly a treat that is well worth seeing, especially when performed as it was at the North Park College last night." The new college was beginning to gain attention within Chicago as an institution that rigorously trained its youth to become upstanding members of the spiritual community. However, some of the community's elders worried that the college would gain notoriety for its emphasis on physical education. This conflict would come to a head in the midst of great tension arising from the conflict overseas; however, at this point, the faculty and students agreed that the goals of physical education and intellectual development would set North Park apart from other institutions of higher learning, especially one led by a community of former immigrants.[12]

Turn of the Twentieth Century

Between the late-nineteenth and early-twentieth centuries, a new wave of immigrants coming from the Scandinavian countries began to shape the context of the experiences of youth in Chicago. This group differed from previous waves of western and northern European immigrants in that a large segment of them were young, single, and motivated to migrate for the purpose of work opportunities within the midwestern city. Many young immigrants were drawn to Chicago's North Shore, where the palatial homes of the city's elite provided abundant jobs, especially for Scandinavians, whom the rich employed because of their revered work ethic, their pleasant demeanor, and their physicality. Scandinavian youth were fully aware that acquiring the English language was a key to success in American society. They viewed domestic service as a gateway to learning the skills necessary to acceptance into places of higher education like North Park, which was the goal of many young immigrants. Scandinavian domestic servants, typically referred to as "Swedish maids" regardless of their country of origin, already came to America with vast work experience and were usually in their teens or very early twenties. Swedish maids quickly gained a reputation for their honesty and hard work, as Stina Hirsch explained in her master's thesis on her family's experiences as Swedish domestics, and in turn the experience of work influenced their values, habits, styles, and behaviors. Young *pigor* (Swedish for domestic servants) became commonplace to Chicagoans riding the trains on Thursday afternoons—the citywide "maid's day off" —as many would ride north to places like North Park and south to Lakeview to experience the joys of the homes they missed. In all, as Hirsch explained, the young Scandinavian men and women who came to America during the early twentieth century for work, many of them still boys and girls, each had his or her private hope to aspire to something much more than being a worker in somebody else's home, shop, or factory.[13]

Many other Scandinavian and Scandinavian American youth did not have the opportunity to experience the collegiate life of North Park, and instead had to work to achieve the independence and success they sought. In 1898, at the age of sixteen, Pauline Nelson graduated high school, and within a few months applied for and received a position working downtown at Montgomery Ward as a shopgirl—a position that many young women, American or foreign born, would have coveted early in the century. Nelson did not take the job for its pay (As she explained, "[W]e did not make big wages those days; I started at [$4.50] a week.") but instead viewed the position as a chance to move up the social ladder personally and professionally. Regularly during their lunch breaks and on the weekends, Nelson and her coworkers would pool together their earnings to spend their leisure time taking in the city—shopping, going to restaurants, and going to movies, but also prioritizing the intellectual benefits the city had to offer through its museums and the Art Institute of Chicago. In the summer, Montgomery Ward would hold an eagerly awaited employee picnic to congratulate their workers for their dedication and hard work, and as Nelson recalled, it was "all everyone talked about and could not wait till the day." It was on a boat ride at one of those picnics that she met her future husband, Ben Hegborn, another young Swedish American. While Nelson would resign from her position at Montgomery Ward in the summer of 1904 prior to her marriage that November, her experiences differed greatly from those of other American-born children of European immigrants. Not only did Pauline and Ben decide upon a period of courting so that she could continue to work at Montgomery Ward but also Pauline waited until she was twenty-two years old to marry, rather than marrying at sixteen, when she met Ben, and resigning from her position just months into work, as many other young women would have done. This was actually a quite commonplace practice for young Scandinavians. As author Margareta Matovic explained, Scandinavian women most often delayed marriage until their midtwenties to ensure economic stability for both parties going into the marriage. Nelson did not use her experience of work to find a husband, but rather she used her time at Montgomery Ward to savor the joys of youth, while also prioritizing her role as a worker within Chicago.[14]

Comparatively, many of the young coeds who would attend North Park College were only able to do so because they took positions as workers in various trades in order to support themselves and their educational endeavors. Many of North Park's young students worked as railway workers on the Chicago Elevated Railway, which allowed them to remain dedicated to their studies by day, while simultaneously earning the pay to afford them at night. A writer for *The Cupola*, Joseph Anderson, wrote that because of their reputable work ethic, these young Scandinavian Americans, "with very few exceptions," would get work when they sought it. For young students whose main priority focused on their academic careers, work on the rails was favored because of its "very simple" requirements. According to Anderson, "one must go through a mental and physical examination to determine whether one is able to read, write, and speak English and to distinguish colors, and whether one has a fairly good physique." All of the aforementioned requirements would most definitely be out of the realm of possibility for the most recent immigrants to the city, as well as those who were not as attuned to their physical fitness as Scandinavian American youth. Furthermore, as Anderson explained, the railway company was quite accommodating to "student guards" within the context of labor. Trains would be purposely assigned to student guards that would bring them back up to North Park's campus in time not to "interfere with [their] morning classes and evening studying." Also keeping in mind the devotion of the student guards to their spiritual life, the railway company assigned them no work on Sundays, which was also commonplace for "Swedish maids," who were given their Sundays off to travel to their respective places of worship. On average, student guards could expect to receive fifteen dollars a week, and their employers gave them astonishing flexibility to work anywhere from two to five hours a day. This was enough, Anderson concluded, "to pay our school expenses and leaves us enough money over to take us and our best friends to a concert occasionally." In a humorous aside that illustrates the dedication student guards put into even their part-time jobs, Anderson noted that one of the most difficult elements of the job was not to become self-conscious about the riders "taking your measure" of job performance but instead to "look out the car window and pretend you see something interesting out there." It is clear from Anderson's assessment of student employment, as well as the labor of other young Scandinavians and Scandinavian Americans, that the value of hard work was crucial to their identity and personal self-worth.[15]

North Park College into the Twentieth Century

At the turn of the new century, it was clear that North Park College was beginning to identify itself as a significant institution of higher learning destined for great things in the future, and its students could expect the value of their education to be immeasurable. "The time has come when we are recognized in educational circles," the administration wrote in North Park's 1901–1902 course catalog, which assured prospective students that the college's courses were well planned, comprehensive, and thorough. The curriculum of the Business Department was comparable to that of the "very best schools of its kind," while its alumni boasted of good and efficient training and, ultimately, success in their careers, where many held "profitable and responsible positions." Since its creation in 1894, the Academy Department garnered a reputation as a first-rate private high school in Chicago, and its diploma would admit the holder to any of the colleges of the University of Illinois. "To the young man and woman who yearns for an education," the catalog boasted, "you can invest your time and money in no better way than in securing a good and practical education." The school began to market itself as an institution with small class sizes and individualized attention and zeal for Christian mission, all within a beautiful locale in one of "Chicago's prettiest suburbs." The school was far enough from the city's "allurements and annoyances" to protect the students from temptation, yet close enough for students to enjoy the intellectual pleasures of Chicago's public libraries and museums. Most important, however, was North Park's mission to become each student's home away from home, where he or she could mature into a serious academic while taking in the pleasures of Scandinavian culture and heritage. "Come to North Park College," the catalog exclaimed. "[W]e shall gladly help you in your noble work—the making of yourself."[16]

The catalog made a point of speaking first to prospective students and, second, to their parents, which further illustrates the notion that the school's faculty expected young Scandinavian Americans to act responsibly in their own educational endeavors, while also recognizing the role of their parents in their decisions. The catalog stated, "[W]e earnestly urge upon our young people to consider all these advantages offered to them by North Park College," while also calling the attention of "Christian parents, who love the Gospel of Christ" to send their children to North Park, where they would continue to be taught in the Christian ways of home "by communion with warmhearted teachers and comrades." For parents who were nervous about the prospect of sending their children away to college or private high school, the administration of North Park assured them that their young sons and daughters would graduate North Park driven by a mission to succeed in expressing their Christian zeal and fulfilling their intellectual capabilities. North Park, they advised, was "a very spiritual atmosphere" that trained its students for leadership as preachers, missionaries, and religious workers in general, while every department was charged with the spirit of Christianity. This call for students would result in a continuing increase in North Park College's enrollment in subsequent years; between 1899 and 1920, the student body would increase from 64 to 167 students, while its demographics would begin to change as periods of immigration shifted. According to the registration ledger for the 1903–1904 school year, the majority of students reported that they were born in Sweden, Finland, or Norway, with a scattering of students born in the Midwest. These demographics would change significantly within a matter of just over ten years, as the onset of World War I slowed immigration. Furthermore, the notion of ethnic preservation would become a topic of discussion into the 1910s as the administration of North Park continued to refine its marketing strategies: was the college to go down in history as a Scandinavian American institution of higher learning, or as a state-of-the-art American college that would compete with the likes of comparable colleges? The answer to this question would be answered by North Park's students, who would grow into a group of articulate and passionate youth into the 1910s.[17]

By the 1910s, the Scandinavian people of Chicago and their children were beginning to experience significant generational differences; while many Scandinavian immigrants hoped to instill their cultural heritage as a major element in their children's lives, their children instead sought to be viewed as average American youth, and not as hyphenated identities. One of the major conflicts that arose between immigrant parents and their children during the 1910s was over ethnic preservation through the teaching of foreign languages within the public schools. Historian Anita Olson Gustafson documented a particular struggle by the Swedish population of Chicago over the teaching of the Swedish language in the public schools; while the Swedish community desired to succeed in America, it also did not want to lose grasp of its ethnic identity and began a campaign for language preservation within the Board of Education of the City of Chicago. Yet, as the case study concluded, despite the efforts of leaders within the Swedish community, the majority of Swedish American high school students still could not be persuaded that they would have a need for the Swedish language in their future careers within America. The same notion would also prevail at North Park College during the 1910s. While the Swedish Evangelical Mission Covenant originally established the college in order to train predominantly Swedish youth for theological careers, the mission of the school would change over time to reflect this generational shift. English would replace Swedish as the primary language used in the seminary by 1913, although Swedish language courses remained in the curriculum for the seminary's young students, as well as for those who chose to take Swedish as an elective language course. Over time, the administration made a deliberate decision to teach all of the college's courses in English. By the 1910s, second-generation Scandinavian Americans who attended North Park College outnumbered immigrant students, while the majority continued to take part in the cultural heritage of their parents, which included campus and community festivities. It was also a decision that took into account marketing strategies for the college; the change in language from Swedish to English enabled the school to broaden its appeal in attracting non-Swedish and non-covenant youth to attend in greater numbers, thereby helping the school to grow over time.[18]

By 1916, the work ethic, the dedication, and the personal desires of North Park's students would culminate in the very public struggle over the building of the gymnasium-auditorium building. While the student body of North Park identified themselves as Scandinavian Americans proud of their heritage and respectful of community leaders, they also knew that they could not bear to go without, in their student lives, a means to exert physical energy through gymnastics. The campus facilities of North Park provided them ample accommodations conducive to their hard intellectual work, but North Park's students expressed that physical fitness was a necessity just as important as their academic studies. This debate between students and community elders was made apparent in the pages of the 1916 issues of *The Cupola*, where one student author argued,

> When Galileo Galilei supported the doctrine that the earth revolves about the sun, and gave his reasons . . . his contemporaries did not accept his doctrine; but later generations have adopted it because his doctrine was valid. Thus it is with people of today with regard to physical education. Strange though it may seem, there are those who inquire dubiously and hesitatingly: "What is the use of physical culture?"

To this young author, and the majority of his student peers, this interaction seemed to be the norm when addressing the discussion to their parents, to community elders, and especially to those within the covenant. Yet, he went on to explain that, despite the ignorance of the older generation, North Park's youth needed to be prompt and unwavering in their answer to such a query, that "the aim of physical culture is to promote, by means of exercise, the development of the body and to retain a normal health," which in turn would bring balance to the powers of both body and mind and "enable us to enjoy life." Many high school and college students overburdened themselves with their studies, the author explained, and if attention to physical fitness was not paid, those intelligent youth would be doubly burdened with "dark hollows under their eyes, and a miserably dwarfed constitution." The argument of North Park's students, as well as its faculty, that a gymnasium would not be used for purposes of vanity was a persuasive one and, in the end, would win them a new multipurpose state-of-the-art building. This debate would not be the last at North Park over the role of physical fitness. For instance, North Park's women's athletic teams, which were highly popular over the course of the 1920s, would be disbanded and replaced by intramural activities in 1929 due to the covenant deeming it to be "unladylike" for women to compete against other teams athletically. However, the student body had won a decisive battle in shaping their future at North Park College—a future that involved a great amount of intellectual vigor, but also strength in both numbers and opinion.[19]

Conclusion

In 1922, North Park College was entering its thirtieth year in Chicago. The school, its student body, and its city saw immense transformations during those three decades. During that same year, North Park's students began to run their first monthly newspaper, *North Park College News*, to document the accolades received by its students, as well as to publish their viewpoints more regularly than did *The Cupola*, which only ran annually. In its first editions, which focused on campus activities such as dances and athletics events, as well as on current topics of debate, the young authors published a reflective piece, which asked, "Why Maintain North Park College?" The author emphasized the role North Park College played within Chicago as a Christian school, established by Scandinavians in order to ensure the professional success of their youth in America. However, the article also marked a significant move North Park's students made in the school's thirty years to make the institution their own, focused on their expressed goals that tied physical exertion to intellectual growth. The author wrote that from the perspective of its faculty and administration, the school stood for "good scholarship and for good citizenship" and sought to "serve all of our people" by training the city's future leaders. From the perspective of its students, while the school was vital to achieving the noted endeavors of its elder generation, the author pointed out that first and foremost, "a college education develops the mind and enlarges the mental capacity as physical activity promotes physical growth," thereby increasing "mental power and sharpen[ing] the intellect more keenly to discern the truth." Interestingly, the author was then able to tie the goals of the students back to those of their community; while many within the community did not agree with the younger generation's emphasis on physical exertion as key to intellectual development, the author wrote that, in turn, physical fitness enlarges one's personality, "increas[es] his earning power, and fits him for leadership or makes him follow more effectively the leadership of others." The students of North Park were carving out a path of great success within America and knew that the path they intended to take could only be paved by way of a sound education. Yet, the agency they illustrated within the first thirty years at North Park, as well as within the city, is quite remarkable when one considers the context of the immigrant experience for children and youth in Chicago and throughout America during the late nineteenth and early twentieth centuries.[20]

NOTES
1. Leland H. Carlson, *A History of North Park College: Commemorating the Fiftieth Anniversary, 1891–1941* (Chicago, 1941), 240–53.
2. Ibid., 247–49. North Park College and Theological Seminary, *The Cupola* (Chicago: North Park College, 1916), 30; *Missions-Vännen*, January 12, 1915; January 26, 1915; and February 9, 1915. The series was reprinted in the mission youth league's newsletter, *Missionsförbundets Ungdomstidning*.
3. The historiography of Scandinavians in Chicago and the Midwest continues to be driven largely by recently published anthologies, rather than monographs, while the documented experiences of youth and children within the community are also in need of further analysis. For a brief selection of the most recent works on the Scandinavian American experience, see Philip J. Anderson and Dag Blanck, *Swedish-American Life in Chicago: Cultural and Urban Aspects of an Immigrant People, 1850–1930* (Chicago: University of Illinois Press, 1992); Philip J. Anderson, Dag Blanck, and Peter Kivisto, eds., *Scandinavian Immigrants and Education in North America* (Chicago: Swedish-American Historical Society, 1995); Margareta Matovic, "Embracing a Middle-Class Life: Swedish-American Women in Lakeview," in *Peasant Maids–City Women: From the European Countryside to Urban America*, eds. Christiane Harzig et al. (Ithaca, NY: Cornell University Press, 1997), 261–97; Joy Lintelman, *I Go to America: Swedish American Women and the Life of Mina Anderson* (Minneapolis: Minnesota Historical Society Press, 2009); Betty A. Bergland and Lori Ann Lahlum, eds., *Norwegian American Women: Migration, Communities, and Identities* (Minneapolis:

Minnesota Historical Society Press, 2011); Philip J. Anderson and Dag Blanck, eds., *Norwegians and Swedes in the United States: Friends and Neighbors* (Minneapolis: Minnesota Historical Society Press, 2012).

4. *Hull-House Maps and Papers: A Presentation of Nationalities and Wages in a Congested District of Chicago* (Chicago: Crowell, 1895), vii, 4, 17. See also Flanagan, *Seeing with Their Hearts.*
5. *Hull-House Maps and Papers*, 54.
6. Pauline Nelson Hegborn Personal Papers, Hegborn-Nelson Family Collection, 1870–1984, Folder 2, Manuscript Collection 39, North Park University Special Collections and Archives.
7. Ulf Beijbom, "Olof Gottfrid Lange–Chicago's First Swede," in *Swedish-American Life in Chicago*, 19–38; *Historisk Statistik för Sverige, Befolkning 1720 –1967* (Stockholm, 1969), table 49, 129; Mrs. Woods Baker, *Pictures of Swedish Life; or, Svea and Her Children* (New York: Anson D.F. Randolph, 1894), 89.
8. Early Covenant History Collection, Box 5, Folder 14: Historical material: Chicago 1st Covenant, Record Series 10/0, North Park University Covenant Archives and Historical Library; John E. Peterson, *The Campus History Series: North Park University* (Charleston, SC: Arcadia, 2009), 8–9.
9. North Park College Catalog, Box 1, Folder 2: North Park College Catalog (1893–1894), pp. 22–24, Record Series 9/1a, North Park University Covenant Archives and Historical Library. While this essay focuses on Scandinavians and the larger Nordic culture, it was quite clear that Swedish immigrants dominated in both population and cultural hegemony in comparison to Danes, Norwegians, or Finns (who were not recognized as such at the time).
10. North Park College and Theological Seminary Catalog (1896–97), 3, 5; computation based on the historical rate of inflation as compared to 2012; Registration Ledger, North Park College, 1894, North Park University Archives.
11. Verner (no last name given), "School Life at North Park as I Remember It," *Linnea: Tidskrift För Hemmet Och Ungdomen* (Minneapolis, MN: Skoog, December 1897), 12–13.
12. Carlson, *A History of North Park College*, 117–18; *Daily Inter Ocean*, March 21, 1896, 4.
13. Joy Lintelman, "On My Own: Single, Swedish, and Female in Turn-of-the-Century Chicago," in *Swedish-American Life in Chicago*, 89–99; Stina Hirsch, "The Swedish Maid, 1900–1915" (M.A. thesis, DePaul University, 1985), 5.
14. Pauline Nelson (Hegborn) memoirs; Matovic, "Embracing a Middle-Class Life," in *Peasant Maids–City Women*, 270.
15. Joseph N. Anderson, "Students' Employment," *Cupola* (1920), 82.
16. North Park College and Theological Seminary Course Catalog (1901–1902), 9–13.
17. Ibid.; Peterson, *North Park University*, 11; Registration Ledger, North Park College and Theological Seminary (1903–1904).

18. Anita Olson Gustafson, "Ethnic Preservation and Americanization: The Issue of Swedish Language Instruction in Chicago's Public Schools," in *Scandinavian Immigrants and Education in North America*, 62, 71; Peterson, *North Park University*, 9, 11.
19. *Cupola* (1916), 29; Peterson, *North Park University*, 11, 31.
20. "Why Maintain North Park College?" *North Park College News* (March 1922): 8.

11

Duty and Destiny

A Progressive Reformer's Coming of Age in the Gilded Age

ANYA JABOUR

In 1902, Confederate veteran, former Democratic congressman, distinguished lawyer, and *Lexington Herald* newspaper editor W.C.P. Breckinridge published a lengthy editorial on "The Problem of the Daughter." In this piece, Breckinridge sensitively detailed the challenges confronting the "New Woman" in turn-of-the-century America. He pondered the difficulties confronting that "rare girl," dissatisfied with "her allotted place in that 'sphere' of life (which someone else has assigned her to)," who yearned to use her talents and apply her intellect to "all the realities of life."[1]

W.C.P. Breckinridge's oldest unmarried daughter personified the educated and ambitious "New Woman." Ultimately, Sophonisba Preston Breckinridge (1866–1948) would become one of the most renowned reformers of the Progressive Era. However, the path from Gilded Age daughter to Progressive Era reformer was a long one beset with obstacles. At the time her father penned this piece, Sophonisba Breckinridge was thirty-six years old and still struggling to find her calling. Like other pioneering women of her generation, Breckinridge found it difficult to reconcile the "family claim"—a daughter's responsibility to her family—with "family culture"—a family's expectations for high achievement.²

Although combining duty and destiny complicated Sophonisba Breckinridge's coming of age and delayed her professional career, it also prompted her to chart her own course not as a benevolent patrician but as a progressive reformer. Both by modeling herself on and by differentiating herself from other family members, Breckinridge fulfilled her duties and defined her destiny. Duty and destiny defined both Breckinridge's Gilded Age girlhood and her adult career as a progressive reformer.³

From the beginning, it was clear that Breckinridge's life would be defined by duty and destiny. In the Bluegrass State, the Breckinridge name was synonymous with public service and political leadership. Like similar prominent families both north and south, the Breckinridges selected one daughter as a "designated daughter," in whom they invested their highest hopes for public service. Sophonisba Preston Breckinridge, born on Easter Sunday, 1866, named for her paternal grandmother, and nicknamed "Nisba," was the obvious choice for this role.⁴

Although Nisba was the second child, her relationship with W.C.P. was more typical of first-born children, and in particular, of first-born daughters in privileged nineteenth-century families. Especially in families with only younger sons, as was the case with the Breckinridges, fathers often encouraged their oldest daughters' ambitions, supervised their educations, and tolerated unconventional behavior. Issa Desha and W.C.P. Breckinridge's first child, Ella, was born shortly before the Civil War. After missing his first child's first four years while he served in the Confederate Army, W.C.P. claimed his "Peace Baby," as he called Nisba, as his own. While Issa suffered through repeated pregnancies (seven in all) and nursed sickly children (two of whom died as infants), W.C.P. took charge of Nisba's upbringing, even teaching her the alphabet by pointing the letters out in his law books. Nisba idolized her father and identified with him to such an extent that when, late in life, she attempted to write her own autobiography, she confessed, "I cannot speak of myself without speaking at length of him."⁵

Serious, studious, and "anxious to please" her father, who valued education highly, Nisba excelled in her studies from a young age. Her earliest preserved school report, evidently from a local day school, is a weekly report dated January 24, 1873. Six-year-old Nisba earned perfect scores in every category: attendance, deportment, neatness, spelling, reading, writing, geography, arithmetic, mental arithmetic, composition, and poetry. Since her older sister, Ella, was more interested in boys than books, and her younger sister Curry's dyslexia hindered her studies, Nisba, as her mother once remarked, was her father's "only hope for an educated daughter."[6]

As the Breckinridges' designated daughter, it was Nisba's duty to perpetuate the Breckinridge dynasty's reputation. "The [Breckinridge] name has been connected with good intellectual work for some generations—for over a century," W.C.P. counseled. "You must preserve this connection for the next generation." Nisba's mother, Issa, also expected Nisba to live up to the family name—to fulfill her destiny—by doing "noble things."[7]

Nisba's parents both encouraged her to seek alternatives to marriage and motherhood. Observing her mother's nonstop childbearing and chronic health problems may well have led Nisba to reject marriage and motherhood at an early age. Moreover, Issa frequently denigrated her own limited education and narrow horizons and repeatedly urged Nisba to make the most of her keen intellect and her greater opportunities. W.C.P. also encouraged Nisba to seek alternatives to the "aimless life" of the southern belle. Like many elite but indebted whites in the uncertain economy of the postbellum South, he hoped that higher education and "honest toil" would enable his daughter to support herself rather than depend on either her father or a husband.[8]

At the same time that they regarded their daughter as capable of exceptional achievements and urged her to take advantage of her opportunities, however, the Breckinridges also expected her to adhere to traditional expectations. Most significantly, they, like other nineteenth-century parents, expected their daughter to fulfill not only her parents' highest hopes for individual achievement but also their every demand for family service. In the same letters in which they urged Nisba to strive for public recognition, they also reminded her to tend to private duties. Repeatedly, the Breckinridges praised their "dutiful" daughter for her loyalty to her family and her willingness to subordinate her own wishes to their demands. Nisba understood that just as being selfless and dutiful was the *sine qua non* of being a good daughter, so being "selfish and inconsiderate" was undesirable, even "hateful."⁹

The Breckinridges insisted that a daughter's duty was consistent with a noble destiny. In a typical missive, W.C.P. admonished her that "duty is the noblest pursuit & compatible with the highest attainments." Similarly, Issa responded to news of her daughter's superior classroom performance that she was "glad of every recognition of your ability & dutifulness," suggesting that part of Nisba's duty was to demonstrate her ability and thereby uphold her family's reputation. Duty and destiny were, the Breckinridges suggested, not only entirely compatible but also closely intertwined.¹⁰

For Sophonisba Breckinridge, coming of age meant a prolonged quest for a way to reconcile destiny and duty. Fulfilling her father's expectations for intellectual achievement offered a way to balance these seemingly contradictory objectives. Determined to grant his daughter's mind "a fair chance to show its power," W.C.P. convinced the trustees of Kentucky Agricultural and Mechanical College (now the University of Kentucky) to admit women, and in 1880, fourteen-year-old Nisba became a member of the school's first entering class to include women. Both Nisba's youth—most girls her age were just beginning secondary education—and her gender set her apart from her fellow classmates. Indeed, men students outnumbered women by a ratio of five to one. Although A&M allowed women to attend classes, it by no means treated them as equals. Female students could only earn certificates, not diplomas, and there was significant resistance to their presence on campus.¹¹

Nonetheless, while at A&M, Nisba discovered one way to reconcile duty with destiny: by using her own achievements to enhance her family's reputation. "I cared about grades because it pleased my Father to have me make good grades and justified his position with reference to the treatment of women," she later explained in her never-completed draft autobiography. However, her recollection of her competition with the men in her class for top grades, and even more, her account of an altercation with an instructor "who did not like girls in his class," indicated that Nisba also had something to prove. In her memoirs, she related, with relish, an occasion on which she turned the tables on the sexist instructor. The math professor attempted to "humiliate" his lone female student by giving her particularly difficult problems to solve.

One day he succeeded in stumping her in front of the class, but she figured out the solution in the middle of the night. The next day, she said nothing to him, suspecting that "he would try again to humiliate me" and also knowing that "that was a day when the trustees were likely to drop in." When she was able to solve the problem for the visiting trustees, she was "maliciously complacent" at her "triumphant" performance.[12]

While Nisba was demonstrating women's intellectual capacity, feminists were demanding political equality. Kentucky had an active suffrage movement throughout Nisba's childhood. Suffrage pioneer Susan B. Anthony spoke in Kentucky in 1879; two years later, when Nisba was fifteen years old, the American Woman Suffrage Association met in Louisville. In the 1880s, Kentucky women held office in the national association and founded their own organization, the Kentucky Equal Rights Association.[13]

A souvenir in her personal papers indicates that Nisba was both aware and supportive of the women's rights movement from an early age. Among her papers is a picture of the Smith sisters of Glastonbury, Connecticut, dated 1877. A handwritten notation on the reverse identifies them as refusing to pay "tax without representation." Because the notation also references the *History of Woman Suffrage*, a six-volume work published by women's rights pioneers beginning in 1881, Nisba's earliest knowledge of the suffrage movement can be dated to her teens with reasonable certainty.[14]

Nisba's nearly simultaneous introduction to the suffrage movement and to institutionalized sexism inspired a lifelong commitment to women's rights. As an adult, she would become one of the most well-known feminists of the early twentieth century. She served as vice-president of the National American Woman Suffrage Association; promoted the nation's first "mothers' pensions" for poor single mothers; and conducted pioneering studies of women's wage work, political activity, and social reform.[15]

Although neither of Nisba's parents supported the suffrage movement, both influenced her in her commitment to women's rights, broadly defined. Issa's frequent pregnancies and related health problems probably inspired Breckinridge's later concern with women's control over their own bodies. In addition, the deaths of two younger siblings—one in 1870 and a second in 1872—made a profound impression on Nisba. Breckinridge later became an ardent advocate of family planning, birth control, and pre- and postnatal care for both mothers and infants. W.C.P.'s insistence on giving his daughter educational opportunities both increased Nisba's awareness of gender discrimination and gave her the tools with which to challenge it.[16]

Like other southern girls of her generation, Nisba grew up with the expectation that she might need to support herself, rather than rely on either inherited wealth or a husband's income. As a college graduate, Nisba also was part of a cohort of "new women" in turn-of-the-century America who dedicated themselves to higher education and social reform. And, of course, as a Breckinridge, Nisba knew that she was destined to do "noble things." Reflecting both family traditions of public service and shifting expectations for "new" women, several of Nisba's contemporary kinswomen pursued careers as teachers and reformers.[17]

Nisba's own leanings in the direction of public service were apparent at a young age. As she detailed in her autobiography, her father offered Nisba and her older sister, Ella, their choice of either a dollar or a party as a reward for good marks. While fashionable and popular Ella chose the party, intellectual and serious Nisba chose the dollar. But she did not use the money for herself. Nisba had "quite a little sum saved" when a female visitor, a missionary to China, gave such a stirring account of Chinese children's dire poverty that Nisba promptly donated all her savings to alleviate their suffering. Breckinridge doubtless included this story in her autobiography because it so succinctly established her early interest in assisting the poor, and perhaps also because it hinted at both her devotion to the welfare of American immigrants and her participation in international welfare movements as an adult.[18]

When she was "quite a big girl," Nisba had another lesson in helping the less fortunate—and avoiding snap judgments. While walking with her father in Lexington's business district, she watched "a forlorn looking man" approach her father and was surprised when her father handed a five dollar bill to "the beggar, as I thought the stranger to be." When she asked for an explanation, her father said that "this apparently down-and-out man was an ex-confederate soldier," an intelligent man from a respected family, who had become addicted to morphine after being wounded in battle. Nisba learned from this experience to consider each individual's circumstances, rather than blaming the poor for their plight. The encounter also opened her eyes to the negative consequences of there being "no psychiatric treatment" and no "occupational provision" for physically or mentally incapacitated people. Both of these insights would inform her later work on behalf of the poor and the disabled.[19]

Nisba grew up hearing stories about her ancestors' public service, political leadership, and distinguished bloodlines. Many of these stories revolved around the secession crisis and "the bitter cleavages of opinion characteristic of many families of the border states." On her mother's side, both the Currys and the Deshas were "ardent advocate[s] of the Confederate Cause," but the Civil War had divided the Breckinridge clan. Nisba's grandfather, Robert Jefferson Breckinridge (1800–1871), was a Presbyterian minister and an outspoken antislavery advocate. Two of his sons served in the Union Army; two others, including Nisba's father, joined the Confederate Army. "It is difficult to imagine the family strains in the face of such varied and difficult problems," Nisba reflected in her autobiography.[20]

Perhaps it was this intimate knowledge of war's destructiveness that inspired a Confederate officer's "Peace Baby" to become a committed pacifist. A founding member of the Woman's Peace Party, which later became the U.S. chapter of the Women's International League for Peace and Freedom, Breckinridge was an official delegate to the International Congress of Women at The Hague in 1915, at which women from both belligerent and neutral nations demanded peaceable solutions to international differences. Breckinridge never wavered in her pacifism, remaining an outspoken opponent of militarism throughout both world wars.[21]

Nisba's pacifism also shaped her adult understanding of her father's military service. While many children of Confederate veterans grew up learning to revere the Lost Cause and its fallen soldiers, in her autobiography, Nisba chose to interpret the Civil War differently. According to her, at the end of the war, her father gracefully conceded the Confederacy's defeat and committed himself to "a new union which the arbitrament [sic] of war had determined was 'one and indissoluble.' Being both brave and honest," she concluded her account of her father's military service, "he accepted the verdict of the Confederate failure and made his contribution to the building of a new nation."[22]

Other evidence suggests that Nisba's parents were more enthusiastic supporters of the Confederacy than she chose to record for posterity. Her mother was an officer of the local chapter of the United Daughters of the Confederacy; her father held periodic reunions of his old military unit. Like other Confederate parents, the Breckinridges upheld white supremacy at the same time that they revered the Lost Cause. In the early 1870s, W.C.P orchestrated an early citywide election before the Fifteenth Amendment went into effect to preempt blacks from voting; he also defended local officials who enforced a "capitation tax" (Kentucky's version of the notorious "poll tax" that robbed newly enfranchised blacks of their potential political power). W.C.P.'s record on race helped win him election to Congress in 1885, a position he held for ten years, in large part due to the support of white-supremacist southern Democrats.[23]

W.C.P.'s tenure in office coincided with a particularly bloody period in southern history. Although white Kentuckians had been divided during the secession crisis, they were unanimous in their determination to maintain white supremacy in the postwar era. White vigilantes terrorized black citizens in their own homes, and white mobs turned lynchings into public spectacles. Lexington was one of the key sites of racial violence, and W.C.P. provided legal defense for suspected Klansmen accused of brutalizing local blacks.[24]

Since she did not address these issues in her autobiography, it is impossible to know how much young Nisba knew about these events at the time. Nisba's older sister, Ella, later claimed of her childhood, "There was no race problem in Lexington in the days of which I write." Although white children in the postwar South were often witnesses to—and sometimes participants in—mob lynchings, there is no direct evidence that the Breckinridge children ever observed racial violence. However, politics and violence were only one part of a complex combination of factors that enforced African American subordination and reinforced white supremacy in the postwar South. For southern children, a much more pervasive force was racial socialization.[25]

If the Breckinridge children were sheltered from the most brutal aspects of blacks' subordination, they nonetheless enacted white supremacy on a daily basis in their own home. To support her remarkable statement about the lack of a "race problem" in postwar Lexington, Ella detailed the "pleasant relations" between the Breckinridge family and their African American servants, including Clacy, the children's nurse, who, Ella explained, had been awarded to Issa "as a first present to the hour-old baby" and subsequently "nursed my Mother through every illness, received every one of her children into her arms, loved, scolded, and disciplined every one of us . . . and would gladly have died for any one of us." Throughout Ella's reminiscences, African Americans appear only in subservient roles.[26]

Ella's memoirs make it clear that the Breckinridge family abided by a code of conduct intended to reinforce white supremacy. In the Jim Crow South, white and black children alike learned "racial etiquette" from their elders, with blacks learning to defer to whites with whom they came into contact, and whites learning to be polite while maintaining social distance. White parents trained their offspring to display their own racial superiority and reinforce blacks' servility by referring to adult African Americans by their given names, rather than by a title and surname, while at the same time requiring blacks to use titles when referring or speaking to whites of any age. This pattern is clear in Ella's reminiscences; Nisba also displayed this linguistic hierarchy in fragmentary, handwritten autobiographical notes (not included in later drafts of her autobiography), in which she referred to the younger African American women who worked in her household by their first names and called the elderly household manager "Aunt Polly"—"Aunt" and "Uncle" being the most honorable terms that a southern white could bestow on a black person.[27]

When in 1884, Nisba, dissatisfied with her experience at A&M, enrolled at Wellesley College, which admitted African American students, her parents made it clear that they expected her to use racial etiquette to maintain white supremacy. "I hope there will be no necessity for you to come in contact with them," Issa pronounced. But, indicating Nisba's thorough training in racial etiquette, she added, "I have such faith in your good breeding—good sense & true lady hood," that "I have no fear of your contamination or of your not doing what is becoming a lady." What was required of a "lady," of course, was to exhibit her "good breeding" by treating her social inferiors with polite distance. Likewise, while W.C.P. opined that it would impossible to regard African Americans as equals, he also reassured himself—and perhaps reminded his daughter—that "to a gentleman or lady there need be no personal embarrassment."[28]

Nisba's cultural conditioning was evident in her early letters home from college, in which she expressed discomfort at being in close quarters with African Americans. In one letter home, Nisba noted that she had been assigned a train compartment with "two colored youths." Anticipating her parents' reaction—and revealing her own prejudices—she wrote, "Pleasant? But the conductor was pleasant and changed it for me so that Clair and I were together, and we had a very nice trip." Clearly, despite a lifetime of daily interaction with black domestic servants, Nisba did not think that it was at all "pleasant" to associate with African Americans as equals, and she was relieved that the conductor complied with her request to change her seat so that she did not have to share space with them.[29]

Although Nisba carefully avoided contact with African Americans en route to school, she confronted a greater challenge once she arrived on campus. "There are three negro girls here," she informed her mother, one of them a "Greek scholar." She added, "I have only seen one, a 'Miss' Smith, and she is very nice looking." Despite her praise of the black student's appearance and intelligence, Nisba's racial socialization was evident in her uncomfortable use of the title "Miss," which she enclosed in quotation marks to indicate her skepticism about the applicability of an honorific to an African American.[30]

Initially, Nisba's childhood socialization held fast; Issa was relieved to learn that her daughter saw "nothing of the colored girls." Ultimately, however, attending college would become the key to unlocking the chains of cultural conditioning forged in Nisba's childhood. While at Wellesley, Nisba became very close to Alice Freeman, the young and progressive college president. Nisba's admiration for Freeman, together with what her father called the college president's "fanaticism" on the issue of racial equality, forced her to reexamine her racial conditioning. Perhaps anticipating her parents' likely response, Nisba did not include information in her letters home about her increasingly frequent contact with blacks or her growing commitment to racial equality. In her autobiography, however, she related several incidents that challenged her racial socialization and changed her views on racial equality.[31]

Both the effectiveness of her childhood training and the ways that college challenged familiar beliefs are suggested by Breckinridge's later account of the first time she shared a meal with African Americans. When President Freeman invited an African American choir from Fisk University to dine with the students and faculty, Nisba was in a quandary. Wellesley protocol called for students to serve each other—and guests—at the dinner table. For Nisba, who was accustomed to being served by African American servants, this was a reversal of familiar racial dynamics. Moreover, sharing a meal symbolized social equality. Although white family members necessarily shared household space with black domestic workers, white southern parents taught their children to maintain physical separation and social superiority by dining separately from (and prior to) African Americans. Caught between her childhood training and her desire to please the college president, Nisba served the black women seated at her table, but was unable to eat her own meal.[32]

Visiting speakers, as well as students, challenged Nisba's racial upbringing—and her parents' Confederate loyalty. On one occasion, escaped slave and former abolitionist Frederick Douglass spoke at Wellesley about his experiences in slavery, his acquisition of literacy, and his escape to freedom. To her parents, Nisba confessed that it made her uncomfortable to hear her northern classmates discuss slavery, but she also commented that she found Douglass's account "a pitiful story."[33]

Although she did not mention it in her letters home, in spring 1887, a debate surrounding the Junior Promenade revealed how much Nisba's attitudes about racial equality had changed. In three years at Wellesley, Nisba had become friendly with fellow classics student Ella Smith, the "Miss" Smith she had mentioned when she first arrived on campus. Smith wanted to invite guests to attend the Junior Promenade, which Nisba described as "our chief event of college life." Several white students objected, arguing that educational equality did not necessitate social equality. Nisba, who had been elected class president her freshman year, used her influence to convince her classmates to admit Smith's guests to the event. In her autobiography, Breckinridge indicated that the Junior Promenade was a decisive turning point; it was, she said, "the occasion of my working through the problem of racial relationships."³⁴

Nisba became a lifelong advocate for African American social welfare and civil rights. In later years, she helped found the Chicago Urban League, a civil rights organization, as well as a chapter of the National Association for the Advancement of Colored People. She insisted on extending social services to African Americans and helped ensure their inclusion in public-welfare legislation. And she used her Kentucky connection to promote a federal antilynching bill, both by writing to Kentucky elected officials and by planting pro–civil rights editorials in the newspaper her brother Desha edited, the *Lexington Herald*.³⁵

Attending Wellesley changed Nisba's views on race; it also reinforced her commitment to public service. As a group, the college's all-female faculty prepared their students for professional careers and public service. Several faculty members—including those Nisba especially admired—were active in social reform movements, ranging from the suffrage movement to the labor movement. Public lecture series addressed a broad range of topics, devoting special attention to "important social problems." Student activities also addressed social and political issues. Indeed, Nisba's class at Wellesley ushered in a "Social Science craze." One of the most popular series of lectures, which Nisba attended, addressed women's citizenship status and common law, providing students with "thorough and interesting instruction" in the legal framework of the "covered woman," whereby a married woman's legal identity was subsumed by her husband's and she became incapable of holding property or making contracts. As an adult, Nisba would pay special attention to women's legal equality, demonstrating particular concern with establishing women's independent citizenship.³⁶

Nisba was profoundly affected by all this focus on social responsibility. One winter, she told her father, she was unable to enjoy the heavy snowfall because President Freeman's prayers for the "poor and needy" rang in her ears. "Do you suppose someday I will be called to do something for them?" she pondered. The sense of mission common to first-generation collegiate women reinforced Nisba's desire to carry on the family tradition of public service.³⁷

While at Wellesley, Nisba distinguished herself not only as "the most brilliant student in the class" but also as a natural leader, an "all-around girl" who participated in sports, social activities, and student government as well as excelling in her schoolwork. By the time she graduated in 1888, Nisba not only had established a reputation as "the most popular girl at Wellesley," but she also had impressed her classmates as a future reformer. The class prophecy, presented in the form of an imaginary women's convention held twenty years in the future, described the illustrious careers of the Class of 1888; the class sibyl predicted that Breckinridge would found a settlement house, become a legal advocate for women, and build a reputation as "the great friend of the people." As it turned out, this was a remarkably accurate prediction; Nisba would indeed live and work at a settlement house for many years; she went on to earn a law degree; and she devoted her career to serving women, the poor, immigrants, African Americans, and other disenfranchised and dispossessed members of society.[38]

Immediately after college, however, Nisba returned to her parents' house in Lexington. Like many other first-generation college graduates, she faced a severe crisis after graduation, characterized by a conflict between the "family claim" and the "social claim." Initially, she attempted to reconcile duty and destiny by accompanying her parents to Washington, D.C., where she taught mathematics and her father attended Congress. Maintaining a home in Lexington, the family lived in Washington boardinghouses while Congress was in session. At one point, they stayed at Riggs House, where prominent suffragist Susan B. Anthony also was a guest. A later *New York Times* article indicated that the suffrage leader encouraged Nisba in her "penchant for a professional career" and attempted to "indoctrinate" her in "woman's rights principles." Anthony found a receptive audience. In later years, Nisba would become a prominent feminist activist as well as a pioneering professional woman in the fields of law and social work.[39]

Although they expected her to live at home and serve her family, Nisba's parents also encouraged her in her career aspirations, if not in her commitment to women's rights. W.C.P. helped her gain her first teaching post; he also allowed her to study law in his office and helped her to take the state bar exam, although he did not invite her, as she had hoped, to work with him in his own law practice. In 1891, after a bout of influenza terminated her first teaching job, the Breckinridges sent Nisba with her younger sister, Curry, to Europe to study.

Disappointed with their sons' performance—Robert, the younger, literally ran away to sea and was presumed dead, while Desha, the older, struggled to find a professional identity—the Breckinridges encouraged their unmarried daughters to continue their educations with the intention of pursuing professional careers. (Ella had married in 1889.) "If God gave our girls more purpose than our boys," pronounced Issa, "He intended they should do more." Curry studied languages, while Nisba studied law. Nisba also tutored Curry, who was dyslexic; her sister's learning difficulties further sensitized Nisba to the challenges facing people living with disabilities. However, both girls' studies were abruptly interrupted in late June 1892, when Issa contracted dysentery and W.C.P. sent money to permit the Breckinridge girls to return home immediately. Hastily boarding a ship for America, Nisba and Curry arrived home only to find that their mother had already expired.[40]

The next few years were difficult ones for Nisba, in which she repeatedly put her own goals on hold in order to fulfill family obligations. As the oldest unmarried daughter living at home, Nisba assumed responsibility for running the household and educating her younger sister. Previously, Nisba's older sister, Ella, had filled the role of a "daughter at home," or "domestic daughter," allowing Nisba to be the designated daughter. Now, however, Ella had begun her own family, and the remaining Breckinridge daughter, Curry, was only seventeen years old when Issa passed away. The family claim bound Nisba to domestic duties for the next several years. Although events following her mother's death postponed Nisba's career, they also further defined the form it would eventually take.[41]

Less than a year after Issa's death, W.C.P. secretly remarried. Almost immediately, another woman filed suit for breach of promise. Claiming that W.C.P. had reneged on his promise to marry her, Madeline Pollard provided incontrovertible evidence that she and the defendant had engaged in a lengthy extramarital affair, beginning in 1884, when she was seventeen years old and W.C.P. was forty-seven, and continuing into 1893, during and after Issa's final illness. Although W.C.P. and his legal counsel attempted to portray Pollard as an experienced seductress rather than an innocent victim, he lost the lawsuit; the following year, in 1894, he also lost his bid for reelection.[42]

Although "dazed" by the revelations, Nisba continued to offer her father unstinting affection. "Believe me always, Papa, your loving daughter Sophonisba," she closed one letter to her beleaguered father. In her autobiography, Breckinridge struggled to make sense of her father's infidelity. "As I look back, now, I see how complicated and difficult a burden he carried," she mused. She hastily brushed aside her father's relationship with Pollard (never mentioning her by name), writing, "It is not necessary to give the details of the scandal." Instead, she focused on her father's evident devotion to his wife: "My mother's health was frail and she was entirely unaware of any deviation on his part. He was devoted, he was endlessly kind, and there could not be in our minds any question of his fidelity." At least in her written recollections, Breckinridge accepted her father's version of events, in which the real culprits were his political enemies, who exploited a good man's one weakness "to send in his place to Washington a mediocre representative of certain special interests."[43]

Nisba was "an infinite comfort" to her father during and after the scandal, first by packing his belongings in Lexington in preparation for his return to the capitol for the trial, and then by relocating to Washington for several months during and after the trial to care for his new wife, whose preexisting emotional problems escalated into a nervous breakdown under the pressure of the highly publicized trial. "Of course, you know how faithfully I want you to succeed," she assured him, "& how I will help you in every possible way." Indeed, Nisba assisted her father both by assisting in his legal defense by taking statements from witnesses about the Pollard affair and by copying his campaign speeches, in which he attempted to defend his reputation while admitting his infidelity.[44]

By the mid-1890s, it appeared that Nisba's duties outweighed her destiny. Turning down a sociology fellowship at the University of Wisconsin and giving up her plans to attend law school at the University of Michigan, she devoted herself to "home matters" and became, in her father's words, "the mainstay—the cement of the family." Like so many other dutiful daughters of her generation, Nisba, it appeared, would give the "family claim" precedence over what she called a "false desire for independence."[45]

Although on the surface Nisba appeared to be a devoted and dutiful daughter, she became subtly more independent and more critical of her father after the scandal. Indeed, several of the reforms she undertook in later years may have been fueled, at least in part, by her disappointment with her beloved, but flawed, father. Just as she formed her own views on race rather than accepting those of her family, so she also embraced political stances that differed from those of her father.[46]

As an adult, Breckinridge engaged in multiple reform movements that ran counter to her own father's political record. In her autobiography, she discussed her father's position on the Pullman Strike of 1894. W.C.P. had supported President Grover Cleveland's use of the militia to arrest and imprison socialist labor leader Eugene Debs on the grounds that the strike interfered with U.S. mail delivery. Looking back, Breckinridge characterized the president's actions as "an unfair use of the [executive] authority" and defended Debs's effort "to secure better working conditions and fairer treatment for the Pullman employees." After relocating to Chicago the following year, Breckinridge would become friends with labor activists and social reformers who supported unionized labor and criticized both the Illinois-based Pullman company for cutting workers' wages during the economic downturn of 1893 and the U.S. marshals and soldiers whose clash with striking workers resulted in the deaths of thirteen strikers and injury to fifty-seven others. Given the timing of the strike, which coincided with her father's trial, it seems likely that for his daughter, his politics had been tainted by his personal life. Certainly Breckinridge consistently supported organized labor in later life, becoming a well-known advocate of protective legislation and the minimum wage as well as a member of the Women's Trade Union League.[47]

It is also plausible to speculate that Breckinridge's later commitment to civil service reform stemmed from her father's difficulties. In W.C.P. Breckinridge's papers, his letters about the Pollard case are interspersed with letters from constituents seeking favors, particularly asking W.C.P. to use his position to obtain government appointments for them. In addition, W.C.P. had used his political influence to obtain a government position for his long-time mistress. Finally, in assembling his defense, W.C.P. may well have bribed informants with promises of political appointments in return for exculpatory statements. Both because Nisba was involved in her father's defense and because she organized his papers before donating them to the Library of Congress, it is certain that she was aware of her father's use of political patronage. Along with Jane

Addams, Julia Lathrop, and other Hull House reformers, Breckinridge would later become a fierce critic of political corruption and cronyism. For decades, she served on a civil service committee that selected public officials on the basis of education and experience, subjected applicants to both written examinations and extensive interviews, and held itself strictly apart from the political corruption of the Second City.[48]

The Pollard case also may have influenced Breckinridge's later position on sexuality. Decades after defending her father in the Pollard case, Breckinridge defended suspected prostitutes in Chicago's courts, spearheading a successful campaign to eliminate the involuntary internal examinations of suspected prostitutes. Such practices, Breckinridge asserted, were unacceptable "based upon the two fundamental principles of an equal moral standard for men and women, and of the equal treatment of men and women by the law of the land." Unlike many of her contemporaries, Breckinridge saw sexually active women as victims of a sexual double standard, not as shameless seductresses or fallen women. Given that W.C.P.'s defense had rested on impugning Pollard's character—that is, on the sexual double standard—this is a particularly intriguing viewpoint. While she did not reject her father, Breckinridge did reject the sexual double standard, insisting that where extramarital sex was concerned, men were equally culpable. Although she avoided criticizing her own father in her memoirs, W.C.P.'s adultery affected her deeply. Possibly disappointment with her father led her to denounce the sexual double standard and defend sexually active women.[49]

Perhaps most importantly, however, it was following the Pollard case that Nisba left home for good. By the mid-1890s, she later recalled, "the question of my health and my future became acute." Her severe depression and failing health finally prompted her father to allow his "self-sacrificing" daughter to prioritize her destiny over her duty. "I do trust, my precious child, that you may find the door open to the life you desire," he wrote in 1897. Nisba seized the opportunity to pursue advanced degrees and professional possibilities in Chicago. Although she maintained a close relationship with her Kentucky kin and returned to Lexington for frequent visits, after 1895 she never left Chicago, she later said, without a return ticket in her possession.[50]

Nisba's advanced age—she was twenty-nine when she left home for the University of Chicago—highlights the prolonged coming-of-age experience that was typical of college-educated women in the late nineteenth century, many of whom did not leave the family home or establish an independent identity until their mid- to late twenties. As Hull House founder Jane Addams observed, the conflict between the "family claim" and the "social claim" was acute. It was not at all uncommon for future reformers and professionals to struggle with depression and poor health, search in vain for acceptable outlets for their ambitions and abilities, and care for other family members before they made the shift from "dutiful daughters" to "new women." This difficult period often lasted for a decade or even longer. Like her contemporaries, Breckinridge hesitated for several years before finally striking out on her own to, as one friend expressed it, "take care of [her]self . . . and take life with the open hand!"[51]

Even in Chicago, and well into her thirties, Nisba continued to seek ways to reconcile her duty with her destiny. As she had done previously, she sought her father's approval by doing well in school, and she chose topics that reflected his career as a lawyer and politician. After earning her M.A. in political science in 1897 and her Ph.D. in political economy in 1901, she both followed in her father's footsteps and blazed new trails by becoming the first female graduate of the University of Chicago's new law school in 1904.[52]

In the meantime, W.C.P. had come to terms with his daughter's ambitions. As he wrote in his 1902 editorial, eventually, "after a season of irresolute and uncomfortable protest" on the part of the daughter and "reflections and awakenings" on the part of the father, "he begins to comprehend that some of the strange new demands made by women are but the outcome of an unrepressed individuality" and "are but a part of the development of the new social conscience in which women, as well as men . . . have become the heirs."[53]

Unfortunately, W.C.P.'s sudden death in 1904 prevented father and daughter from celebrating her achievement and his acceptance. However, her father's death finally freed Nisba from the "family claim." Released from the responsibilities of family duty, Nisba embraced the possibilities of family culture. Fulfilling her destiny, this daughter of the Gilded Age claimed her birthright as a member of an illustrious family and carried on the Breckinridge legacy as a progressive reformer.[54]

NOTES

1. Quoted in James C. Klotter, *The Breckinridges of Kentucky* (Lexington: University Press of Kentucky, 1986), 194–95.
2. Patricia A. Palmieri, "Patterns of Achievement of Single Academic Women at Wellesley College, 1880–1920," *Frontiers: A Journal of Women's Studies* 5.1 (Spring 1980): 63–67, quotations p. 64.
3. For other treatments of Breckinridge's childhood, education, and early career, see Fitzpatrick, *Endless Crusade*; Melanie Beals Goan, "Establishing Their Place in the Dynasty: Sophonisba and Mary Breckinridge's Paths to Public Service," *Register of the Kentucky Historical Society* 101.1 and 2 (Winter/Spring 2003): 45–73; Johnson, *Southern Women at the Seven Sister Colleges*; and Klotter, *Breckinridges*, chap. 14.
4. Palmieri, "Patterns of Achievement," 64; Klotter, *Breckinridges*, chap. 14.
5. WCPB to SPB, March 30, 1885, Sophonisba Preston Breckinridge Papers, Library of Congress (hereafter SPB Papers); and Sophonisba Preston Breckinridge Autobiography, Sophonisba Preston Breckinridge Papers, Special Collections Research Center, University of Chicago (hereafter SPB Autobiography). On female reformers' relationships with their fathers, see especially Brown, *The Education of Jane Addams*, 13–15; Sklar, *Florence Kelley and the Nation's Work*, 29–30; Conrad, *Perish the Thought*, 12, 51–54, 187, 191, 195, 238; and Welter, *Dimity Convictions*, 6.
6. SPB Autobiography; Report of Nisba P. Breckinridge, January 24, 1873, in Miscellany, 1873–1917; and IDB to SPB, April 6, 1885, SPB Papers.
7. Klotter, *Breckinridges*, 317; IDB to SPB, January 22, 1885, SPB Papers.
8. IDB to SPB, October 7, 14, and 19, 1884; and WCPB to SPB, March 30, 1885, SPB Papers; and IDB to SPB, June 26, October 25, 1891, W. C. P. Breckinridge Papers, Breckinridge Family Papers, Library of Congress (hereafter WCPB Papers).
9. WCP to SPB, March 30, 1885, SPB Papers; SPB to IDB, Sunday Aft., n.d. [Spring 1885], Issa Desha Breckinridge Papers, Breckinridge Family Papers, Library of Congress, (hereafter IDB Papers).
10. WCPB to SPB, May 10, 1885; and IDB to SPB, January 19, 1885, SPB Papers.
11. WCPB to SPB, March 30, 1885, WCPB Papers; *Annual Register of the State College of Kentucky* (Lexington: Transylvania Printing, 1881), 8, 12; and State of Kentucky Matriculators Book (1869–1889), 106, 122, 136, 156, all in University Archives and Special Collections, Margaret King Library, University of Kentucky, Lexington, Kentucky (hereafter University of Kentucky).
12. SPB Autobiography.
13. Hay, *Madeline McDowell Breckinridge and the Battle for a New South*, 79–80; Paul E. Fuller, *Laura Clay and the Woman's Rights Movement* (Lexington: University Press of Kentucky, 1975), 24–26.
14. Miscellany, 1873–1917, SPB Papers; Ida Husted Harper et al., *History of Woman Suffrage* (New York: National American Woman Suffrage Association, 1881–1922).

15. S. P. Breckinridge, "Neglected Widowhood in the Juvenile Court," *American Journal of Sociology* 16.1 (July 1910): 53–87; Sophonisba P. Breckinridge, *Women in the Twentieth Century* (New York: McGraw-Hill, 1933); and Jane Addams to SPB, March 21, May 7, and August 11, 1912; SPB to Jane Addams, April 17, 1912; Anna Howard Shaw to Jane Addams, August 16, 1912, all in Jane Adams Papers Project (microfilm).
16. SPB to Jane Chandler, April 7, 1930; and SPB to Marguerite Owen, January 13, 1932, SPB Papers.
17. Censer, *The Reconstruction of Southern White Womanhood, 1865–1895*; Jabour, *Scarlett's Sisters*, chap. 6; Frankfort, *College Women*; Goan, *Mary Breckinridge*; and Hay, *Madeline McDowell Breckinridge*.
18. SPB Autobiography; Martha Branscombe, "A Friend of International Welfare," *Social Service Review* 22.4 (December 1948): 436–41.
19. SPB Autobiography; Breckinridge and Marion Hathway, *The Young Cripple and His Job* (Chicago: University of Chicago Press, 1928); "Hope to Parole Many Insane after Tests," *Chicago Daily Tribune*, Nov. 2, 1929, p. 1.
20. SPB Autobiography; Amy Murrell Taylor, *The Divided Family in Civil War America* (Chapel Hill: University of North Carolina Press, 2005), 25, 28.
21. Alonso, *Peace as a Women's Issue*, 58–69; Lela B. Costin, "Feminism, Pacifism, Internationalism, and the 1915 International Congress of Woman," *Women's Studies International Forum* 5.3–4 (1983): 300–315; "People's Peace Group Formed," *Chicago Daily Tribune*, October 12, 1939, p. 8; and S. P. Breckinridge, Review of Mary Louise Degen, *The History of the Woman's Peace Party*, *Social Service Review* 14.2 (June 1940): 383.
22. SPB Autobiography.
23. WCPB to SPB, May 10, 1885, June 1, September 4, 1891; *Lexington Daily Press*, July 8, 1871; *Lexington Dollar Weekly*, July 22, 1871; *Kentucky Gazette*, February 15, 1873; *Courier Journal*, February 17, 1873; and Council Proceedings, January 14, 1870, January 4, 1872, and June 6, 1872, Miscellany: Speeches and Articles by and about Breckinridge Family, SPB Papers; Jabour, *Topsy-Turvy*, chap. 6.
24. Jabour, *Topsy-Turvy*, chap. 6; Marshall, *Creating a Confederate Kentucky*.
25. Eleanor Breckinridge Chalkley, "Magic Casements," University of Kentucky; DuRocher, *Raising Racists*.
26. Ibid.
27. Autobiographical Notes, Miscellany: Speeches and Articles by and about Breckinridge Family, SPB Papers; Ritterhouse, *Growing Up Jim Crow*, chaps. 1 and 2.
28. IDB to SPB, September 19, 1884; and WCPB to SPB, October 3, 1884, SPB Papers.
29. SPB to WCPB, January 9, 1887, WCPB Papers.
30. SPB to IDB, n.d., IDB Papers.
31. IDB to SPB, September 26, 1884; WCPB to SPB, October 3, 1884, SPB Papers. See also Bordin, *Alice Freeman Palmer*.
32. SPB Autobiography.

33. SPB to IDB, May 27, n.d., IDB Papers.
34. SPB to WCPB, March 13, 1887, IDB Papers; SPB Autobiography.
35. Fitzpatrick, *Endless Crusade*, 180–82; Sandra M. Stehno, "Public Responsibility for Dependent Black Children: The Advocacy of Edith Abbott and Sophonisba Breckinridge," *Social Service Review* 62.3 (September 1988): 485–503; and Thomas R. Underwood Papers, Box 1, University of Kentucky.
36. SPB to WCPB, January 31, 1887, WCPB Papers; SPB to IDB, Sunday, n.d.; SPB to IDB, Thursday night, n.d.; and SPB to IDB, January 27, 1886, IDB Papers; Wellesley Annals, "Wellesley in 1884–5," p. 3; and Wellesley Annals, "Wellesley in 1886–7," pp. 5 and 13, Wellesley College Archives (hereafter WCA), Wellesley, Massachusetts; and Palmieri, *In Adamless Eden*; and Sophonisba P. Breckinridge, *Marriage and the Civic Rights of Women: Separate Domicile and Independent Citizenship* (Chicago: University of Chicago Press, 1931).
37. SPB to WCPB, n.d., WCPB Papers.
38. May Estelle Cook, "Sophonisba Preston Breckinridge, 1866–1948," *Wellesley Magazine*, October 1948, p. 35; Marion Angelina Ely, "Class Prophecy," Class of 1888 Records, WCA; IDB to SPB, February 18, 1885, SPB Papers; and Horowitz, *Alma Mater*, 156–59.
39. Joyce Antler, "After College, What? New Graduates and the Family Claim," *American Quarterly* 32 (Fall 1980): 409–34; SPB Autobiography; "Ready for the Bar," *New York Times*, November 29, 1892, p. 1; Anya Jabour, "Relationship and Leadership: Sophonisba Breckinridge and Women in Social Work," *Affilia: Journal of Women and Social Work* 27. 1 (February 2012): 1–16; and Robyn Muncy, "Gender and Professionalization in the Origins of the U.S. Welfare State: The Careers of Sophonisba Breckinridge and Edith Abbott, 1890–1935," *Journal of Policy History* 2.3 (1990): 290–315.
40. IDB to SPB, May 11, 1892; and WCPB to SPB, June 27, 1892, SPB Papers; Klotter, *Breckinridges*, 163.
41. Palmieri, "Patterns of Achievement."
42. Klotter, *Breckinridges*, 161–69.
43. SPB to WCPB, August 28, September 25, 1893; SPB to WCPB, January 27, 1894, WCPB Papers; SPB to WCPB, December 30, 1893, SPB Papers; and SPB Autobiography.
44. WCPB to Mr. Mitchell, May 10, 1894; SPB to WCPB, January 8, 1894; SPB to WCPB, May 4, 5, 7, [July 20], July 21, 1894; and WCPB to DB, July 11, 1894, WCPB Papers.
45. WCPB to Curry Breckinridge, December 15, 1896; and WCPB to SPB, December 28, 1896, SPB Papers; and SPB to WCPB, November 20, 1894, WCPB Papers.
46. This was also the case for Florence Kelley. See Sklar, *Florence Kelley*, 109–12.
47. SPB Autobiography; Louise W. Knight, "Biography's Window on Social Change: Benevolence and Justice in Jane Addams's 'A Modern Lear,'" *Journal of Women's History* 9.1 (Spring 1997): 111–38; Sklar, *Florence Kelley*, 268–74; Sophonisba Preston Breckinridge, "Legislative Control of Women's Work," *Journal of Political*

Economy 14.2 (February 1906): 107–9; Breckinridge, "The Illinois Ten-Hour Law," *Journal of Political Economy* 18.6 (June 1910): 465–70; "Will Ask Parties for Living Wage," *Chicago Daily Tribune*, June 14, 1912, p. 7; "University Girl Upholds Toilers," *Chicago Daily Tribune*, October 17, 1906, p. 5.
48. "Merit System Put in Effect in Social Courts," *Chicago Daily News*, March 2, 1931, clipping in Miscellany, 1928–1931, SPB Papers; and Muncy, *Creating a Female Dominion in American Reform, 1890–1935*, 31–33.
49. Sophonisba P. Breckinridge, *Social Work and the Courts* (Chicago: University of Chicago Press, 1934), 479; Anya Jabour, "Prostitution Politics and Feminist Activism in Modern America: Sophonisba Breckinridge and the Morals Court in Prohibition-Era Chicago," *Journal of Women's History* 25 (Fall 2013): 141–64.
50. WCPB to SPB, November 21, 1897, SPB Papers; and SPB Autobiography.
51. Josephine to SPB, December 30, [filed ca. 1892], SPB Papers; Joyce Antler, *Lucy Sprague Mitchell: The Making of a Modern Woman* (New Haven, CT: Yale University Press, 1987); Bordin, *Alice Freeman Palmer*; Brown, *Education of Jane Addams*; Frankfort, *College Women*; Horowitz, *The Passion and Power of M. Carey Thomas*; and Sklar, *Florence Kelley*.
52. See note 3.
53. Klotter, *Breckinridges*, 194–95.
54. Ibid., 184; Anya Jabour, "Homegrown Heroine," in Tom Appleton and Melissa McEuen, eds., *Kentucky Women* (Athens: University of Georgia Press, forthcoming).

DOCUMENTS

Thinking with Their Heads

Perhaps the most intrusive "reform" of the Gilded Age and Progressive Era was the establishment of boarding schools for Native Americans who, often against their and their parents' wills, were wrenched from homes and families and forced to attend schools where they were stripped of their clothes, hair, and cultures. They were also Christianized and trained in useful skills, at least by European American standards. By the early 1900s, thirty thousand Native American students were attending 150 boarding schools in any given year.

One of those students, Don Talayesva, a Hopi Indian born in 1890, entered the Keams Canyon School in 1901. On his first day at the school, he reported in his autobiography, the matron "took me into the building and gave me a bath, clipped my hair, and dressed me in clean clothes." During the next few months, he struggled with a new language, with new cultural assumptions, with strange food and new demands for personal hygiene. By the end of the school year, he

> had learned many English words and could recite part of the Ten Commandments. I knew how to sleep on a bed, pray to Jesus, comb my hair, eat with a knife and fork, and use a toilet. I had learned that the world is round instead of flat, that it is indecent to go naked in the presence of girls, and to eat the testes of sheep or goats. I had also learned that a person thinks with his head instead of his heart.[1]

The generally positive experiences of the first year would be followed by more complicated interactions with the personalities and assumptions of white teachers and administrators, who ultimately failed to stamp out completely his traditional values and point of view.

Talayesva later attended a different school in California, but would eventually return to Arizona to live out his long life on the Hopi reservation. His experiences with the reformers who intervened in his life were far more dramatic than those of most American youth—although the determined efforts to erase native culture in many ways mirrored Progressive efforts to shape the values and behavior of immigrant children during the same period—but the mixture of acceptance and resistance displayed in his memoirs is similar to the fusion of adaptation to reformers' goals and insistence on exerting their own agency that emerged in white children's encounters with reform efforts.

The documents in this section show children and youth dealing with the best and the worst that the Gilded Age and Progressive Era could offer them. Their words, or paraphrases of their words, come from court proceedings, surveys of newsboys, high school newspapers, and sociological studies. Like Don Talayesva—although in less extreme ways—they all dealt with the issues that every boy and girl faces when growing up, although that process was complicated by the particular issues and concerns of their lifetimes.

NOTE

1. Don C. Talayesva, *Sun Chief: The Autobiography of a Hopi Indian,* edited by Leo W. Simmons (New Haven, CT: Yale University Press, 1942), 94–96.

Many Little Boys at Work: Casualties of Child Labor

In the era before governments regulated workspace safety, scores of thousands of factory and railroad workers, miners, mechanics, and others were killed and maimed at work every year. There was no such thing as workman's compensation, and virtually no insurance coverage was provided for anyone, let alone the working poor. As a result, when injuries occurred, workers, including the hundreds of children hurt or killed in a typical year, had no choice but to go to court to sue for damages or wrongful death. The courtroom became a place for everyone involved in child labor—the workers, their parents, and their employers—to state their cases. The testimony of two seriously injured boys, one white, one black, both under the age of thirteen, tells the story of child labor from the point of view of the youth performing it. Twelve-year-old Fitz Stanley lost an arm working in a cotton mill, while eleven-year-old Richard lost a leg after an accident at a race track. Their experiences highlight the dangers and lack of accountability on the part of employers highlighted by anti-child labor activists. At the same time, they both show the informal nature of many children's relationships with the workplace and the interaction between other family members and child workers. Finally, they also reveal the fragility of working-class families at the turn of the century, when death and economics broke up family units with distressing regularity.

The first transcript includes lawyers—denoted by "Q"—asking questions of Fitz and, at the end, one of his fellow workers, who explains the boyish hijinks that led to Fitz's injuries.

Testimony of Fitzhugh Stanley, Lynchburg Cotton Mills, Virginia[1]

Q: Do you know how long you have been twelve?
A: No, sir.
Q: Are your mother and father living?
A: No, sir.
Q: Do you know how long they have been dead?
A: No, sir.
Q: Who do you live with?
A: I live with Mrs. Johnson.

Q: Who is Mrs. Johnson?
A: Aunt Alice.
Q: What kin is she to you?
A: Half-kin.
Q: Half-kin what—sister, or not?
A: Sister.
Q: She is your half sister?
A: Yes, sir.
Q: Can you read or write?
A: No, sir.
Q: Have you ever been to school any?
A: Yes sir, I have been some.

. . . .

Q: Who is Gus?
A: My brother.
Q: Is he a grown up man?
A: Yes, sir.
Q: Did you get a job at the cotton mills when you first went there?
A: No sir.
Q: What did you do when you went over there first?
A: Helped Gus.
Q: Did anyone pay you anything for that?
A: No sir, he would give me some money on Saturdays.

. . . .

Q: How did you happen to get a job at the cotton mills?
A: I had been upstairs sweeping.
Q: What room were you sweeping in?
A: I had been sweeping upstairs and downstairs too.
Q: Upstairs, is that where Gus worked?
A: Yes, sir.
Q: How did you happen to get a job there?
A: Harry Watts came after me first, and he got me a job downstairs; he came up there first after me.

. . . .

Q: What did you do after that?
A: They put me in the bagging room.
Q: What did you do in the bagging room?

A: Doffed. [Changing the bobbins that collect spun yarn.]
Q: Who put you in the bagging room—who told you to go work in the bagging room?
A: I don't know who was the fellow, I don't know him.
Q: Was he one of the men who worked down there?
A: Yes sir, he works down in the room there. Harry Watts told me to go in there.
Q: Go in where?
A: In the bagging room.
Q: Who did you work under in there?
A: I don't know who the man is.
Q: Is it the same man you were talking about a minute ago?
A: Yes, sir.

. . . .

Q: How long does it take for one of those bobbins to get full?
A: I think an hour.
Q: And you have to watch them there and change them—take off the full ones and put on empty ones?
A: Yes, sir.
Q: How many frames did you have to attend to?
A: Two, me and another boy.
Q: How many bobbins are on those frames?
A: I don't know.
Q: A good many?
A: No sir, I don't know; I never did count them.
Q: What time did you have to go to work at the cotton mills in the morning?
A: Six.
Q: Was it as early as that? Was it half past six or six?
A: Half past six.

. . . .

Q: What made you stop at that machine and not go on?
A: I don't know.
Q: Go on and tell the jury how it happened—tell the truth.
A: Some little boys were there.
Q: What little boys?
A: The Duncan boys.

Q: What are their names, do you know?
A: Their names are Walter and Lee, and Willie Grubbs.
....
Q: What were those boys doing when you came up?
A: Throwing the belt off and putting it on.
....
Q: What made you do that?
A: I seen them boys there doing it.
Q: And is that the reason you did it too?
A: Yes, sir.
Q: Had you ever seen boys play with the belt before?
A: Yes, sir.
....
Q: Did you know it was any harm to play with it?
A: No, sir.
Q: Had anyone ever warned you?
A: No, sir.
....
Q: Did you cry?
A: No sir.
....
Q: What happened to you then?
A: They took it off.
....
Q: But what did they [other little boys] do at the time this thing happened?
A: They run.
Q: They left as soon as you got hurt and ran away?
A: Yes, sir.
....
Q: What did they do to you at the hospital?
A: Took my arm off.
Q: Now take off your coat and let the jury see where they took your arm off.
....
Q: Do they have many little boys at work at that mill?
A: Not in the bag room, there ain't but four.
Q: I mean at the cotton mills?
A: Yes, sir.

Q: Have they many little girls too?
A: Yes sir.
Q: Some no bigger than you?
A: Yes, sir.
Q: Some still smaller?
A: Yes sir.

Cross-examination by counsel for defendant:

Q: You were employed just for two or three days were you not?
A: For two days.
. . . .
Q: Who was it told you and some of the little boys they would whip you if you didn't keep your hands off the machine?
A: Nobody didn't.
Q: You say when you first got hurt Charlie Gallion came to you?
A: Yes sir, I called him.
Q: And you told Charlie—you said, "Charlie, I was playing with the machines; don't tell my brother."—didn't you?
A: Yes, sir.
Q: You were afraid your brother would get after you for playing with the machines?
A: Yes, sir.

Testimony of Willie Grubbs, Coworker, Age Fifteen

Q: Did you see him when he got hurt?
A: Yes, sir.
Q: Tell us all about it.
A: Me and Walter Duncan went to the water closet and was coming back, and Lee Duncan and Fitzhugh were standing there fooling with the belt. Fitz pulled the belt off and threw it back on—Lee pulled it off first and put it back on, and then Fitz pulled it off and put it back on, and then I said, "Fitz, come on, let us go on back," and he said nothing, but pulled the belt off again and started to throw it back and got his arm caught and that is all I know.

Q: This wheel here is No. 1 and this wheel is No. 2 (indicates on photograph)—is that the belt from 1 to 2?
A: Yes, sir.
Q: Now show the jury how he did it?
A: He throwed it off that wheel.
Q: That is No. 2?
A: Then he put it back on and pulled it off again, and then got the belt twisted.

Testimony of Richard Hunter[2]

Richard Hunter—or Hite (even the boy seemed unsure of his name) was injured as an untrained, occasional worker at a Kentucky racetrack.

Q: What is your name?
A: Richard Hite—Richard Hunter.
Q: Are you called—What are you called by the boys in the neighborhood, what name?
A: Richard Hite.
Q: How old are you?
A: Ten years old.
Q: How old?
A: Ten—I mean to say eleven.
. . . .
Q: Did you go to the race track?
A: Yes, sir.
Q: Who did you go with?
A: Mr. Joe Drake. [A neighbor]
Q: How did you happen to go out there with him?
A: He asked me. He asked me a long time before though, and I would not go. One day my mother told me to go to school—
. . . .
Q: Who did you see when you got there?
A: I seen a crowd of boys and the trainer.
. . . .
Q: What did you do while you were out there?

A: I told you I brought water for the horses, and rode two horses, old horses.

. . . .

Q: How did you happen to get hurt?
A: June Collins [a trainer] put me on a horse.
Q: Talk slow, I cannot hear you.
A: June Collins put me on a horse, and it hadn't been long when it throwed a white boy, out there, and the white boy brought him in.

. . . .

Q: Where were you put on him?
A: I was put on him when he brought him in the stable, carried him to the stable, around through the stable to put him in the stall.

. . . .

Q: What happened?
A: A fellow was cleaning out the stall, and he throwed something—some hay out of the stall on a sack, and the horse seen it coming out and he tore out running right up the pass-way.
Q: Up the pass-way?
A: Yes, sir; and he stumbled and fell.
Q: Were you trying to stop the horse?
A: Yes, sir.
Q: Could you do it?
A: No, sir; I could not.
Q: What happened to you when the horse fell?
A: I fell to the ground.
Q: Then what happened?
A: When he went to get up, he got up on me.
Q: How were you hurt?
A: On the foot, down below my ankle.
Q: Then what happened?
A: Two boys come in and two men, one name Grease and one named Slick, and carried me into where we stayed at, and put me—laid me across the bed, and this white boy that was around there, he got a hot brick and put to my feet.
Q: Where did they take you?
A: To the hospital.
Q: How long did you stay in the hospital?

A: I don't know, sir. . . .
Q: What did they do to you while you were there? Perform an operation on you?
A: Yes, sir.
Q: Cut off your leg?
A: Yes, sir.
Q: Had you ever had any experience riding horses before you went out there to the race track?
A: No, sir.
Q: Had you ever ridden anything?
A: I rode a mule once or twice.

NOTES
1. *Lynchburg Cotton Mills v. Stanley*, 102 Va. 590, Case No. 3235, pp. 41-49, 70, Supreme Court of Virginia Archives, Library of Virginia, Richmond, Virginia.
2. 139 Ky. 315 (1909), Case No. 38886, pp. 22-24, 26-28, 77-78, 82, Supreme Court of Kentucky Archives, Kentucky Department of Libraries and Archives, Frankfort, Kentucky.

My People Never Knew Whether I Was Going to School or Not

For a number of decades, the juvenile court system was considered one of the greatest accomplishments of Progressive-Era reformers. The juvenile courts were seen by their supporters as a kinder, gentler way to usher young folks who ran afoul of the law, school authorities, or even social mores through the criminal justice system and toward more productive, responsible, and orderly lives. The accounts that follow appeared in a 1918 study of the juvenile court system in Cleveland, Ohio. Taken from interviews with young boys and girls who came into the court, the stories suggest some of the ways adolescents spent their time—going to movies, "hanging out," to use a term unknown at the time, playing games whose names modern youngsters would not recognize. But to reformers, the kids' testimony was intended to display the chaotic lives that led inevitably, in the minds of reformers, to immorality and criminality. In a large sense, of course, these tales of indifferent childrearing, of the failure or absence of schools and government institutions, and of youth trying to find their ways in a complicated world, represent many children growing up in the teeming cities of the era.

Delinquency and Spare Time [1]

No. 7 was a fifteen-year-old boy, of Austrian parentage, now [at] the State Industrial School at Lancaster for the second time. Both parents are living; the father is a laborer. There is one older sister and one younger. The family income for five was $18.00 a week; they lived in three clean rooms. The report of the field worker and the boy's own illiterate statement, given below, afford vivid illustrations of the relations between his delinquencies and his spare-time activities.

His daily time schedule before he went to Lancaster for the second time shows at least 11 hours a day spent in the streets, at the movies, in the railroad yards, and at the "athletic club." He is typical of other boys of the Haymarket district who have been sent to the State Industrial School for the second time. His first commitment was due to the fact that he was out nights, truant from school, and a general nuisance in the neighborhood. The second time he was up for being out nights and for breaking into cars; he had done both of these things at the time of his misdeeds, but his car-breaking offense was not then detected.

His recreation included many activities. He liked to go to the movies, and went to the burlesque theaters because of the "good" jokes and dancing to be found there. He played ball, but had never had an opportunity to join a regular team, because none had been formed in his neighborhood; there was no playground or park near. He, with a group of other boys, had gone to their councilman at one time and asked that a playground be given to their ward, but they had received no satisfaction. The Wheeling and Lake Erie railroad yards have always been a source of much enjoyment to them. Hopping "freights" and breaking into cars formed the chief features of their play. Much fruit is brought into the city over the Wheeling & Lake Erie road and unloaded near this district, and the boys have at different times stolen bananas, oranges, apples, and watermelons. Once they stole 10 cases of ginger ale, for which they had each to pay $3.00 damages.

Before he started to work, such small sums of money as he had to spend were got by gambling—mostly by shooting craps—until one day he and his friends found an easier and more profitable way. They held up a well-dressed man and took $20.00 from him, giving 50 cents back to him, so that he should have enough to get his supper and rent a bed for the night.

The boy liked to go to the P—— Athletic Club, in the Haymarket district, because the men allowed him to hang around, using him at different times to set up pins and clean the pool table. For this he was always accorded a welcome and at different times enjoyed playing the piano player, boxing, and playing pool. He and several other boys frequently stayed in the clubrooms, even after the members had gone home, sometimes until three o'clock in the morning. Once or twice they stayed all night, sleeping on the pool tables.

About six months before he was sent to Lancaster for the second time, he "got a girl." She lived in the flat below the one in which he lived. It was very easy to talk to her, because she ran around with his sister. He took her to the movies quite frequently and once or twice to a vaudeville. When asked why he did not take her to a burlesque theater, he said that he did not think it "the place for a lady to go." About this time he and two other boys conceived the idea of showing the girls an especially good time, and proceeded to carry out the suggestion of a man at the athletic club—namely, that they get a taxi and take the girls out for a long ride. They hired a taxi at $2.00 an hour, driving to Rocky

River, a suburb west of the city, where they stayed some six hours, walking around and showing the girls the "sights." They did this not because they liked the girls so much, but because they thought it would sound and feel "big" to entertain in this way.

When this boy was small he liked to go to the lake front to swim, but since he has become older he says that that is "only for kids." Instead of going to the lake he would rather go to Luna Park. He says that in all his life he has never held up a drunken person; he thinks that that would be taking advantage of a man. When asked what he read, he stated that he always read the *Cleveland News*, but was never interested in books.

"My people never knew, when I left home in the morning," he said with a laugh, "whether I was going to school or not." This boy wants to be entertained. He wants to have a good time; he wants to have things as other people have them, but owing to conditions in his home he could not entertain his comrades there and so, to have his fun, saw his friends outside of his home.

Since his return from the Industrial School he attends the regular dancing and gym classes at Central Friendly Inn, a settlement house in his district. Before he went to the school the last time, he worked in a machine-shop, but quit because he thought the ten-hour day too long. He then took a place with a food company, where he had to work only eight hours. His own description of a Sunday is:

> I go to church on Sunday and when I come home from church I play ball and go to Luna Park and when I come from the Park I go home and eat supper and then I go to a show, and when I come out of the show I play drop-three and then I go home and go to bed.

* * * *

The next few cases, to return now to the stories of individual delinquents, are those of the girls who live in the same central business district. The story of the first of these girls, No. 11, is an illustration of the dangers of the railroad freight yard as a place for young girls to spend spare time in. The home of this delinquent was on the other side of the central district, next to the tracks that follow the river. She was an eleven-year-old Austrian girl. Her offence was a sexual one, in which she was more a victim than a partner. She said that she could not attend the settlement classes because they came on washday and she had to help at home. She never drew books from the library, never used the playgrounds, and did not know what a park looked like. She was in the 5-A grade. Her written statement of her games shows what a child she was:

> When I played house we gave each one a name Anna or Mary and played aunts or cousins we would go to the store and buy a loaf of bread and then we would take about three pieces and make a party and then we would put the rest in the cupboard and when we would all be finished we would take the dolls and go to sleep with them.

The field worker says:

> The children in this neighborhood play in the gully beside the tracks and many of them gather coal from the tracks. It was there that they met the railway detective and switchman and it was in the shed, a temporary shelter-house, that the offenses were committed. These men gave the girls—six of them—candy, gum, roller skates, money, flower-trimmed hats, dresses, and shoes, and allowed them to take coal at any time. This had been going on for more than a year. The children told theirs parents that they told these men that they were poor and could not buy coal, so they gave them coal and also the clothing. The delinquent was not allowed to use the skates at home because her mother was afraid that she would get hurt. At school the teacher took them away because the child came late to school.
>
> I asked the delinquent whether she had ever picked wild flowers. She said "no," but she had seen some flowers in a downtown window the day she had been caught; the probation officer told her they were tulips. To my questions, "How often do you go to the woods?" she replied:
>
> "I don't know what a woods is."
>
> When I tried to picture it to her she said, "It must be like green grass, that grows along the fence in the gully. . . . Birds? Oh yes, some sparrows. Bluebirds? I don't know them."

NOTE

1. From Henry W. Thurston, *Delinquency and Spare Time: A Study of a Few Stories Written into the Court Records of the City of Cleveland* (New York, 1918), 25, 29-31, 38-39.

A Friendly Study of Boys

One of the most examined groups in the Progressive campaign to study child workers were the newsboys; tens of thousands of these ten- to twenty-year-old boys (and a few girls) hawked newspapers every morning and late afternoon in business and entertainment districts in every city and most towns in America. They were the child workers that everyone encountered, and scores of studies examined every aspect of their lives. The following extract from a study commissioned by the Civic Federation of Dallas, like the others, examined their work and school habits and their family lives. But in this section, the interviewers focused on the ways that this particular group of about 250 boys thought about their present and projected themselves into the future.

The Newsboys of Dallas [1]

READING AND MUSIC

As a study of *the boy* without special reference to his occupation, the field workers sought his inclinations in reading and music with the following interesting disclosures:

Like to Read:

Yes	191
No	45
No record	17

Reading Most Liked:

Adventure	89
Fairy Tales	28
Boy Scouts	27
History	18
War	11
Wild West	9
Hero Stories	7
Hunting and Animals	6

Love Stories	5
Travel	4
Biography	3
Mechanics	2
Athletics	1
Magazines	1
No record	52

Like to Sing:

Yes	117
No	100
No record	46

Like to Hear Others Sing:

Yes	158
No	53
No record	52

Music Liked:

Jazz	65
Band	27
Violin	19
Vocal	18
Piano	8
Classical	5
Victrola	5
Religious	3
No record	113

MOVING PICTURE SHOWS

Two hundred twenty-two (222) boys admitted attending moving picture shows a total of 475 times a week. We have a suspicion that this is a VERY conservative estimate. However, if the same average of attendance were maintained by the 132,000 adults and children of Dallas over *10 years of age* and the average admission were 20 cents, this one amusement bill would reach the enormous sum of $2,900,000.00 annually, or an amount reaching well toward the cost of the entire municipal government.

What Shows They Like Best

Inquiry was made as to what shows appealed to the boys most and first, second and third choices were given. The following needs no comment:

	1st ch.	2nd ch.	3rd ch.	Totals
Adventure	85	79	25	189
Wild West	66	52	37	155
War	41	39	37	117
Travel	11	15	48	74
Love Affairs	14	6	11	31
Feuds	10	3	8	21
Comedy	5	4	3	12
Vaudeville	2	1	0	3
Serials	1	1	1	3

GENERAL INCLINATIONS

The field workers discussed in a friendly way with the boys the following three questions:

"If he could do just as he wanted, where would he go?"

"What would he do?"

"If money [was] no object, what three things would he first buy?"

The answers are tabulated in the following tables:

Where Would He Go?

Stay in Dallas	44
All over the World	20
New York	15
California	14
Go to School or College	13
"Out West"	12
To the Country	8
Europe	7

Alaska	5
Galveston	5
Visit Relatives	5
Africa	3
Army or Navy	3
No Opinion	25
No Record	47

While two boys in each instance chose the following: South America; France; Florida; Denver; Italy; Mountains; Oklahoma.

And one boy in each instance chose the following: Mt. Vernon; Arizona; "North"; Enter the Movies; China; Detroit; Persia; Philippines; Kidd Springs; the "Zoo"; Chicago; Washington; San Marcos; El Paso; Houston; Waco; Yellowstone Park; White Rock; London; Clarksville.

It is perfectly logical that with the taste as expressed for motion pictures and reading of adventure and "Wild West" that the wander-lust should be in the heart of the boy.

Undoubtedly, the negligible home life of many of these boys contributes to their desire to get away. Then when you add the excitement of street life and the lure of the picture—there is a combination which breeds wander-lust.

Including the 20 who would travel "all over the world," 45 out of the 188 who expressed a preference or 24 per cent, would extend their travels beyond the United States while 56 (30%) would travel to other parts of the country outside Texas. Ten are satisfied to go somewhere else in Texas, while Kidd Springs, the Zoo and White Rock would fulfill the ambition of one boy in each case. It is significant that 13 would plan to go to school and college.

What Would He Do?

The boys were more at a loss as to just what they would do if they could "cut loose."

No opinion	60
Sightseeing	24
Be a Cowboy	16

Go to school	16
Travel	16
Work	15
Be a Business man	11
Hunt or Fish	10
Be a Mechanic	9
Play Ball	5
Farm	5
Visit	4
Swim	3
Go to Moving Picture Shows	2
Join Navy	2
No record	48

One boy in each instance named his activity as follows: Be a Druggist; be a Doctor; be a Carpenter; be a Miner; be a Movie Star; be an Aviator; see Moving Picture Making; go in Motion Picture Business; Help Starving Children; Read; Help Mother; see Brother; Strike Oil; do Clerical Work; Study Music; Quit School; be a Banker.

What Would He Buy?

In answer to the third question, "If money [was] no object, what three things would he first buy," the reaction was stronger, 202 boys naming one choice only; 160 boys first and second choices, and 122 boys naming three choices, as follows:

	1	2	3	Totals
Home	83	26	5	114
Auto	29	39	44	112
Clothing	18	17	11	46
Bicycle	11	12	4	27
Savings or Investments	5	5	8	18
Store	4	8	6	18
Buy farm or ranch	12	3	2	17
Food	4	5	8	17
Furniture	0	12	4	16
Gun	5	8	1	14

Motorcycle	8	5	1	14
Charity	3	2	4	9
Airplane	2	2	3	7
Books	2	1	4	7
Horse	2	2	3	7
Toys or Athletic Goods	6	1	0	7
Yacht or Motor Boat	0	2	3	5
Moving Picture Show	1	1	2	4
Hunting and Fish[ing] Outfit	0	2	2	4
Factory	1	2	0	3
Graphophone	1	0	2	3
Tickets to Moving Picture S[hows]	1	1	1	3
Tools	1	1	1	3
Bank	0	1	0	1
Building Lot	1	0	0	1
Give to Mother	0	0	1	1

Is it any wonder that, with 81 per cent living in rented houses or rooms, and with the indication of migrations from place to place, the purchase of a home is the first choice? While the auto, bicycle, motorcycle and airplane have their natural appeal, it is significant that there appears in forty-one choices the desire for investment, 10 would buy books and tools and 9 would give to a charity.

AMBITIONS

Aside from the boys['] ideas of what they would do under free choice, information was sought as to their ambitions under present economic and other handicaps. One hundred seventy-seven of them named them as follows:

To be a Mechanic	39
Business Man	37
Engineer	20
Lawyer	11
To be a Druggist or Doctor	10
Carpenter or Cabinet Maker	9
To be a Banker	8
Farmer	5

Artist or Cartoonist	4
Cowboy	4
Architect	2
Baseball Star	2
Building Contractor	2
Electrician	2
Lumber Business	2
Musician	2
To go to College	2

One boy in each instance chose the following: Adventurer; Banker; Conductor; Cotton Buyer; Dairyman; Detective; Inventor; Navy; News Agent; Oil Man; Plumber; Preacher; Prize Fighter; Sailor; Teacher; Wireless Operator.

NOTE

1. From *The Newsboys of Dallas: A Friendly Study of the Boys, Their Work and Thrift, Home Life and Schooling and of Their General Character, Associations, Ambitions, and Promise of Fitness, as Future Responsible Citizens of Dallas* (Dallas: Civic Federation of Dallas, 1921).

Anxious to Do More

Universal attendance of high school was far in the future—the first era in which a majority of Americans would graduate from high school would not come until after the Second World War—but by 1900, especially in urban areas, an increasing number of teenagers attended high school, at least for a year or two, and at least among the middle and upper classes. Although their activities were, of course, closely supervised, high schools also provided youngsters with a chance to socialize and to develop a youth culture separate from their parents' generation. The following selections from high school newspapers and yearbooks in Milwaukee, Wisconsin, capture glimpses of the point of view of girls and boys exploring what their lives might mean—both in the present and in the future. Some reflect Progressive-Era attitudes about service and gender, others reveals expectations for future jobs and careers, while the final piece shows the way in which the First World War, the event generally thought to have ended the Progressive Era, brought a sobering but satisfying meaning to these teenagers' lives.

"Girls' Athletics"[1]

Girls play a more conspicuous part in our school and in the framing of the history and destiny of athletics than any one might imagine. Although they do not take an active part in the athletic contests where brute strength is required and the chances for personal injury are many, they form a reserve power which in the hour of need on the athletic field makes its influence felt.

If girls only realized what a responsibility rested on them in the establishing and maintaining of the athletic teams of their school they would no doubt execute a greater endeavor along these lines. Girls form the incentive which gives the contestants the nerve and courage to battle against uneven odds until the goal post is passed.

When a large group of enthusiastic rooters fill the bleachers or grand stand of any athletic field the athletes upholding the name of the school these girls represent feel a grave responsibility to carry the hope that is placed in them by the crowd of spectators that line both sides of the field.

Even after the contest has been started and luck is against the athlete, one ray of hope remains and that is the fair cheerer in the bleachers: With her colors flying and her pennant gayly floating in the breeze she cheers over the rail that bars her from the field. When conditions are critical and defeat seems certain, she gives a yell that starts the red blood coursing through the veins of those athletes for whom the yell was meant, like flames fanned by an angry wind.

What is the result? Why, victory of course, for both the team and the "Girls in the bleachers."

Editor's Note.—Three cheers for the girls. Let us hope we see more of them in the fall.

"The Real Value of Athletics" [2]

Now is just about the time that an athlete is called upon to show his metal, the stuff he is really made of. Strange to say though this does not apply to the man who is going to participate in the various meets, it does apply to the man that has to stay home on the Saturdays that the team is out of town. The little test is simple, but it allows demonstration remarkably well. The whole thing is based upon the fact as to whether a man quits track athletics as soon as he finds out that he is not going on the trip with the rest of the team. When a man quits in mid-season without any reason, it shows the coach and others several things regarding that person. First of all, it shows he's a quitter; secondly it shows he is not an athlete, and does not love athletics or he would have stayed out, the entire season. Last of all, it shows the man hasn't any school spirit, but that he is one of the kind who would make a stab at athletics in the fond hopes of making a name for himself.

Fellows, athletics is not a game you can bluff at and be successful: it's nothing but long, hard and conscientious training that bring one to the front. It would be foolish for one to train all spring and summer if there were no meets to enter or if a fellow didn't receive some benefit from athletics, and if that were the case, athletics in our high schools would have been stopped long ago. This is not the case, though, for the man that goes into athletics and trains faithfully, receives just as much out of it in the long run as the person who is a big point winner. There's one thing sure about it, and that is, you don't have to be a point winner in order to be healthy or to build your body up and know how good it feels to be free from all injurious habits.

These are just some of the reasons why athletics are encouraged and why you yourself ought to stay out for any kind of athletics you start. Remember, it's the fellow who can go into athletics with or without taking any places in a meet and from his athletics is inspired to leave all smoking and so on alone, who receives the greatest award for his work.

West Division Social Service Fund[3]

There are now more than half of West Division's pupils to whom the words, West Division Social Service Fund, probably mean little or nothing. To the rest of the school, and to many alumni, they bring back gratifying recollections of West Division's charitable helpfulness toward an unfortunate fellow student. But even to these latter the actual work and results of the fund which they created are not known.

In the fall of 1910 it became necessary to send away from our school, for the general good, a poor little fellow suffering from the dread disease, tuberculosis. His family were financially unable to do anything for him. Mr. McLenegan, then principal, immediately conceived a plan for raising money to care for this boy. He laid his plans before teachers and pupils, and all pledged their support and aid in the undertaking. With such energy, enthusiasm and success did all take hold of the work, that the vaudeville performance, "Footlight Feats," inaugurated to raise the necessary funds, had to be given twice, and realized more than anyone had hoped for or dared to expect.

The net receipts from the two performances of Footlight Feats, December 2 and 3, 1910, and from the sale of candy, amounted to $420.85. This fund was given the name, The West Division Social Service Fund, and the following board of trustees was appointed by the teachers and the different classes

Faculty
    Charles E. McLenegan, Honorary President.
    Albert C. Shong.

Marie Merchant.
Roland W. Zinns, Treasurer.
Seniors
James Dawson, President, 1911.
Helen Kellogg.
Juniors
Gordon Anderson, President, 1912.
Marie Whiffen, Secretary.
Sophomores
Frederick O'Neill.
Gladys Buchner.
Freshmen
Milton Hagensick.
Emma Damkoehler.

On Wednesday, December 28, 1920, Gordon Anderson took the beneficiary of our fund to the Wisconsin State Tuberculosis Sanatorium at Wales. Satisfactory arrangements for accommodations and maintenance at the sanatorium had been previously made by Mr. McLenegan with Dr. J. W. Coon, superintendent of the institution. Since that time our charge has been at the sanatorium, and frequent reports from Dr. Coon have given us encouragement and hope that our work may not have been in vain.

In March of the present year the funds raised were nearly exhausted, and it became necessary for the board of trustees to consider the future of this boy. It would not do to have him return to his former city life, and so efforts were made to find him some out-door work. Dr. Coon, however, advised that the boy remain at the sanatorium at least another year to allow a full recovery, and so application was made to judge Karel to have the county take care of him. The application was granted, and the transfer on the books of the institution was made to date from March 20, 1912.

Of the fund there is now left on deposit in the First National Bank $38.18, bearing interest since July 30, 1912, when it was changed from an open account to an interest bearing deposit. This sum we earnestly hope may be the nucleus for some future charitable work.

-Net ticket receipts from two performances of Footlight
  Feats, held December 2 and 3, 1910: $385.75
-Receipts from sale of candy at two performances: $35.10
-Total net receipts: $420.85
-Interest on certificates of deposit: $5.18
-Total fund: $428.08
-Total expenditures: $387.85
-Amount of fund remaining: $38.18
  Roland Zinn, Treas.

"February Class Prophecy" [4]

It was the night of February 4, 1935. Without, the wind whistled loudly and the air was cold and biting. It was just twenty years ago since I graduated in the first February class—that of 1915. As I sat gazing into the fireplace, my classmates appeared in procession before me.

Alma Burull was first—the famous suffragette leader, swaying the multitude by her impetuous words, in her zealous attempt to further the noble cause. Then came the enthusiastic Adolph Mandelker, who is now traveling in Chautauqua, issuing forth fiery speeches. As I listened, the echo of those old familiar words, "As I said before, I talk too much," convinced me that talking is still a pleasure to him. Then followed the great platform speakers—Joseph Adamkiewicz, Harry Mandelker, Elmer Fox, Emil Reitman and Henry Kassner.

Yonder, in a merry group, I saw Betty Wegner, Melina Kessel and Anna Hausmann. They informed me that they were stenographers for Swenson Bros., manufacturers of pushmobiles. Helen Hansen had deserted the ranks to marry her employer, Reuben Swenson. The ceremony was performed by the Rev. Mr. Ellicott Stillman, whose name truly does not disguise him.

A year or more seemed to pass, when I found myself entering a large harbor. On each side great buildings stretched heavenward. Then throngs of people rushed by me, for there I stood in the heart of New York.

Presently I was affected with a throbbing tooth-ache and decided to visit a dentist. Stepping into an office building, I found the name Harold

Schiffer, dentist. The name sounded familiar, whereupon I stepped in and found it to be truly he. The directory showed Harvey Steinhoff and Clarence Siegman, lawyers. Their latest case was "Tubbie" Schroeder's breach of promise suit.

Next I met Eddie Hornbach; life insurance salesman, who introduced me to—whom do you think? To my old friend Flora Nelson, now a famous journalist. Later in the day, I visited the beauty parlors of Helen Dougherty and Kathryn Shaw. Here I met Elizabath Wait and Raymond Schroeder the well-known tango dancers. They had an engagement at the Majestic that week (the theater is managed by Strassburger and Rumpel); I was further gratified to learn that Maurice Kassner, the comedian, would also appear.

When I returned to my hotel, the mailman, Mr. Heinrich, gave me two letters. One was from Inez Redel, who has been traveling in Europe, where she met Viola Momsen, prima donna. Mildred Buege, Helen Geil, and Edith Kurth are Red Cross nurses. But Edith Kurth met Count Soergel in Germany and is living in great happiness.

Crash! Down fell a huge lump of coal. I sprang to my feet to find myself in utter darkness. The fire had died out, and slowly the truth came upon me—it was a dream!

"Before the War and Now" [5]

> He was a gay and jolly lad,
> The year before the war.
> His books, his cash he got from Dad,
> And often asked for more, more, more,
> And often asked for more.
> He never studied very hard;
> He said, "What is the use?
> I'll work just hard enough to pass,
> So I won't be a goose, goose, goose,
> So I won't be a goose."
>
> She was a gay and jolly lass,
> A year or so ago.

She danced, she sang, she played, and off
To parties she did go, go, go,
To parties she did go.
She studied, too, a little bit,
Because "the others" did;
But she cared more for parties and proms,
She always had a bid, bid, bid,
She always had a bid.

But now the times are different
The war has done it all;
These young Americans do work,
At their country's beck and call, call, call,
Their country's beck and call.

The lad, he bought a Liberty Bond,
He's buying Thrift Stamps, too;
He gave "his bit" to the Y.M.C.A.,
And worked for Hoover, too, too, too,
And worked for Hoover, too.

And the lass, she, too, is enlisted
For her country's service here;
She sews, and sews, but not for herself
For orphans "over there, there, there,"
For orphans "over there."
And then you'll see her knitting, too,
When not doing other work,
Like studying, canning, or making bread;
Oh, no! she'll never shirk, shirk, shirk.
Oh, no! she'll never shirk.

Yes, boys and girls are happy now,
In these stirring times of war,
But it's all in service for Uncle Sam,
And they're anxious to do more, more, more,
And they're anxious to do more.

NOTES

1. George Pendergrast, "Girls Athletics," *Comet*, West Division High School, October 1912.
2. "Rob" Lewis, "The Real Value of Athletics," *Comet*, West Division High School, May 1917.
3. "Ze Footlight Feats Do Ye Remember?" *Comet*, West Division High School, June 1912.
4. Inez Combs, "February Class Prophecy," *Cardinal Yearbook*, 1915, South Division High School.
5. Mildred Rahr, "Before the War and Now," *Scroll*, Washington High School, April 1918.

QUESTIONS FOR CONSIDERATION

1. What forces came to act on children and youth during the Gilded Age and Progressive Era that had not affected them in the past (or had not affected them as deeply)?
2. What expectations did the adults who appear in this book have for children and youth in terms of behavior, work, and schooling?
3. In the contexts of the lives of children and youth, how was the Progressive Era "Progressive"?
4. Robert Wiebe argued that politicians and reformers were engaged in a "search for order" during this period. What did that mean in the lives of children and youth?
5. The primary documents and a number of the essays featured the voices of young Americans. What concerns and interests can you detect in their words? How did they see the world differently than the adults who were trying to shape their lives?
6. How were the experiences of girls and boys different and/or the same during this period? Did reformers believe that young people had separate needs and possibilities?
7. Historians and social scientists often use the word "agency" to describe situations when normally powerless people exert some kind of control over their own lives. How did children and youth during the Gilded Age and Progressive Era exert "agency"?
8. What would it have meant for the twentieth century to have truly been the "Century of the Child?" What would have been different?
9. In what ways and in what places are the issues and conditions that appear in the book—child labor, infant mortality, and family disruption, to name just a few—still reflected in the discussions among politicians and policy makers in the United States?
10. Is there a "Right to Childhood" in the twenty-first century? What factors encourage or inhibit Americans' efforts to protect that right?

REFERENCES

Alexander, Ruth M. *The Girl Problem: Female Sexual Delinquency in New York, 1900–1930*. Ithaca, NY: Cornell University Press, 1995.
Alonso, Harriet Hyman. *Peace as a Women's Issue: A History of the U.S. Movement for World Peace and Women's Rights*. Syracuse, NY: Syracuse University Press, 1993.
Ashby, LeRoy. *Endangered Children: Dependency, Neglect, and Abuse in American History*. New York: Twayne, 1997.
Baldwin, Peter C. *Domesticating the Street: The Reform of Public Space in Hartford, 1850–1930*. Columbus: Ohio State University Press, 1999.
Bardaglio, Peter W. *Reconstructing the Household: Families, Sex, and the Law in the Nineteenth-Century South*. Chapel Hill: University of North Carolina Press, 1995.
Beatty, Barbara. *Preschool Education in America : The Culture of Young Children from the Colonial Era to the Present*. New Haven, CT: Yale University Press, 1995.
Beatty, Jack. *Age of Betrayal: The Triumph of Money in America, 1865–1900*. New York: Knopf, 2007.
Berrol, Selma Cantor. *Growing Up American: Immigrant Children in America, Then and Now*. New York: Twayne, 1995.
Blair, Cynthia. *I've Got to Make My Livin': Black Women's Sex Work in Turn-of-the-Century Chicago*. Chicago: University of Chicago Press, 2010.
Blight, David W. *Beyond the Battlefield: Race, Memory, and the American Civil War*. Amherst: University of Massachusetts Press, 2002.
Bordin, Ruth. *Alice Freeman Palmer: The Evolution of a New Woman*. Ann Arbor: University of Michigan Press, 1993.
Boyer, Paul S. *Urban Masses and Moral Order in America, 1820–1920*. Cambridge, MA: Harvard University Press, 1992.
Brewer, Holly. *By Birth or Consent: Children, Law, and the Anglo-American Revolution in Authority*. Chapel Hill: University of North Carolina Press, 2005.
Brown, Victoria Bissell. *The Education of Jane Addams*. Philadelphia: University of Pennsylvania Press, 2004.
Brumberg, Stephan. *Going to America, Going to School: The Jewish Immigrant Public School Encounter in Turn-of-the-Century New York City*. New York: Praeger, 1986.
Calhoun, Charles W. *From Bloody Shirt to Full Dinner Pail: The Transformation of Politics and Governance in the Gilded Age*. New York: Hill and Wang, 2010.
Carpan, Carolyn. *Sisters, Schoolgirls, and Sleuths: Girls' Series Books in America*. Lanham, MD: Scarecrow, 2009.

Cavallo, Dominick. *Muscles and Morals: Organized Playgrounds and Urban Reform, 1880–1920*. Philadelphia: University of Pennsylvania Press, 1981.

Censer, Jane Turner. *The Reconstruction of Southern White Womanhood, 1865–1895*. Baton Rouge: Louisiana State University Press, 2003.

Chudacoff, Howard P. *Children at Play: An American History*. New York: New York University Press, 2007.

———. *How Old Are You? Age Consciousness in American Culture*. Princeton, NJ: Princeton University Press, 1989.

Clapp, Elizabeth J. *Mothers of All Children: Women Reformers and the Rise of Juvenile Courts in Progressive-Era America*. University Park: Pennsylvania State University Press, 1998.

Clement, Priscilla Ferguson. *Growing Pains: Children of the Industrial Age, 1850–1890*. New York: Twayne, 1997.

Conrad, Susan Phinney. *Perish the Thought: Intellectual Women in Romantic America, 1830–1860*. New York: Oxford University Press, 1976.

Coontz, Stephanie. *Marriage, a History: From Obedience to Intimacy; or, How Love Conquered Marriage*. New York: Viking, 2005.

Crantz, Galen. *The Politics of Park Design: A History of Urban Parks in America*. Cambridge, MA: MIT Press, 1989.

Davis, Allen F. *Spearheads for Reform: The Social Settlements and the Progressive Movement, 1890–1914*. New York: Oxford University Press, 1967.

De Luzio, Crista. *Female Adolescence in American Scientific Thought, 1830–1930*. Baltimore, MD: Johns Hopkins University Press, 2007.

Diner, Steven J. *A Very Different Age: Americans of the Progressive Era*. New York: Hill and Wang, 1998.

DuRocher, Kristina. *Raising Racists: The Socialization of White Children in the Jim Crow South*. Lexington: University Press of Kentucky, 2011.

Edwards, Rebecca. *New Spirits: Americans in the "Gilded Age," 1865–1905*. New York: Oxford University Press, 2011.

Faderman, Lillian. *Odd Girls and Twilight Lovers: A History of Lesbian Life in Twentieth-Century America*. New York: Penguin, 1991.

Fitzpatrick, Ellen. *Endless Crusade: Women Social Scientists and Progressive Reform*. New York: Oxford University Press, 1990.

Flanagan, Maureen A. *Seeing with Their Hearts: Chicago Women and the Vision of the Good City, 1871–1933*. Princeton, NJ: Princeton University Press, 2002.

Frankel, Noralee, and Nancy S. Dye, eds. *Gender, Class, Race, and Reform in the Progressive Era*. Lexington: University Press of Kentucky, 1991.

Frankfort, Roberta. *College Women: Domesticity and Career in Turn-of-the-Century America*. New York: New York University Press, 1977.

Friedman, Lawrence M. *Private Lives, Families, Individuals, and the Law*. Cambridge, MA: Harvard University Press, 2004.

Fuller, Raymond G. *Child Labor and the Constitution*. New York: Crowell, 1923.

Glenn, Myra C. *Campaigns against Corporal Punishment: Prisoners, Sailors, Women, and Children in Antebellum America*. Albany: State University of New York Press, 1984.

Goan, Melanie Beals. *Mary Breckinridge: The Frontier Nursing Service and Rural Health in Appalachia*. Chapel Hill: University of North Carolina Press, 1998.

Gould, Lewis L. *America in the Progressive Era, 1890–1914*. London: Pearson Education, 2001.

Graff, Harvey J. *Conflicting Paths: Growing Up in America*. Cambridge, MA: Harvard University Press, 1995.

Grant, Julia. *Raising Baby by the Book: The Education of American Mothers*. New Haven, CT: Yale University Press, 1998.

Grossberg, Michael. *Governing the Hearth: Law and the Family in Nineteenth-Century America*. Chapel Hill: University of North Carolina Press, 1985.

Hall, Jacquelyn Dowd, et al. *Like a Family: The Making of a Southern Cotton Mill World*. New York: Norton, 1987.

Hardy, Stephen. *How Boston Played: Sport, Recreation, and Community, 1865–1915*. Knoxville: University of Tennessee Press, 1982.

Harrison, Robert. *Congress, Progressive Reform, and the New American State*. New York: Cambridge University Press, 2004.

Hawes, Joseph. *Children in Urban Society: Juvenile Delinquency in Nineteenth-Century America*. New York: Oxford University Press, 1971.

Hay, Melba Porter. *Madeline McDowell Breckinridge and the Battle for a New South*. Lexington: University Press of Kentucky, 2009.

Hindman, Hugh D. *Child Labor: An American History*. Armonk, NY: Sharpe, 2002.

Hofstadter, Richard. *Age of Reform: From Bryan to F.D.R.* New York: Knopf, 1955.

Holoran, Peter C. *Boston's Wayward Children: Social Services for Homeless Children, 1830–1930*. Rutherford, NJ: Fairleigh Dickinson University Press, 1989.

Holt, Marilyn Irvin. *The Orphan Trains: Placing Out in America*. Lincoln: University of Nebraska Press, 1992.

Horowitz, Helen Lefkowitz. *Alma Mater: Design and Experience in the Women's Colleges from Their Nineteenth-Century Beginnings to the 1930s*. New York: Knopf, 1984.

———. *The Passion and Power of M. Carey Thomas*. New York: Knopf, 1994.

———. *Rereading Sex: Battles over Sexual Knowledge and Suppression in Nineteenth-Century America*. New York: Knopf, 2002.

Hoy, Suellen. *Good Hearts: Catholic Sisters in Chicago's Past*. Urbana: University of Illinois Press, 2006.

Hunter, Jane H. *How Young Ladies Became Girls: The Victorian Origins of American Girlhood*. New Haven, CT: Yale University Press, 2002.

Illick, Joseph E. *American Childhoods*. Philadelphia: University of Pennsylvania Press, 2002.

Inness, Sherrie A., ed. *Nancy Drew and Company: Culture, Gender, and Girls' Series*. Bowling Green, OH: Bowling Green State University Popular Press, 1997.

Jabour, Anya. *Scarlett's Sisters: Young Women in the Old South*. Chapel Hill: University of North Carolina Press, 2007.

———. *Topsy-Turvy: How the Civil War Turned the World Upside Down for Southern Children*. Chicago: Dee, 2010.

Jacobs, Margaret. *White Mother to a Dark Race: Settler Colonialism, Maternalism, and the Removal of Indigenous Children in the American West and Australia*. Lincoln: University of Nebraska Press, 2009.

Johnson, Joan Marie. *Southern Women at the Seven Sister Colleges: Feminist Values and Social Activism, 1875–1915*. Athens: University of Georgia Press, 2008.

Kaestle, Carl F. *Pillars of the Republic: Common Schools and American Society, 1780–1860*. New York: Hill and Wang, 1983.

Katz, Michael B. *In the Shadow of the Poorhouse: A Social History of Welfare in America*. New York: Basic Books, 1986.

Kett, Joseph. *Rites of Passage: Adolescence in America, 1790 to the Present*. New York: Basic, 1977.

Knupfer, Anna Meis. *Reform and Resistance: Gender, Delinquency, and America's First Juvenile Court*. New York: Routledge, 2001.

———. *Towards a Tenderer Humanity and a Nobler Womanhood: African American Women's Clubs in Turn-of-the-Century Chicago*. New York: New York University Press, 1996.

Kunzel, Regina G. *Fallen Women, Problem Girls: Unmarried Mothers and the Professionalization of Social Work, 1890–1940*. New Haven, CT: Yale University Press, 1993.

Lasch-Quinn, Elisabeth. *Black Neighbors: Race and the Limits of Reform in the American Settlement House Movement, 1890–1945*. Chapel Hill: University of North Carolina Press, 1993.

Lassonde, Stephen. *Learning to Forget: Schooling and Family Life in New Haven's Working Class, 1870–1940*. New Haven, CT: Yale University Press, 2005.

Lindenmeyer, Kriste. *A Right to Childhood: The U.S. Children's Bureau and Child Welfare, 1912–46*. Urbana: University of Illinois Press, 1997.

Macleod, David I. *The Age of the Child: Children in America, 1890–1912*. New York: Twayne, 1999.

———. *Building Character in the American Boy: The Boy Scouts, YMCA, and Their Forerunners, 1870–1920*. Madison: University of Wisconsin Press, 1983.

Marshall, Anne E. *Creating a Confederate Kentucky: The Lost Cause and Civil War Memory in a Border State*. Chapel Hill: University of North Carolina Press, 2010.

McGerr, Michael. *A Fierce Discontent: The Rise and Fall of the Progressive Movement in America, 1870–1920*. New York: Free Press, 2003.

Meckel, Richard A. *Save the Babies: American Public Health Reform and the Prevention of Infant Mortality, 1850–1929*. Baltimore, MD: Johns Hopkins University Press, 1990.

Mennel, Robert. *Thorns and Thistles: Juvenile Delinquents in the United States*. Hanover, NH: University Press of New England, 1973.

Milkis, Sidney M., and Jerome M. Mileur, eds. *Progressivism and the New Democracy.* Amherst: University of Massachusetts Press, 1999.
Mink, Gwendolyn. *Wages of Motherhood: Inequality in the Welfare State.* Ithaca, NY: Cornell University Press, 1993.
Mintz, Steven. *Huck's Raft: A History of American Childhood.* Cambridge, MA: Belknap Press of Harvard University Press, 2004.
Mohl, Raymond A. *The New City: Urban America in the Industrial Age, 1860–1920.* Arlington Heights, IL: Harlan Davidson, 1985.
Muncy, Robyn. *Creating a Female Dominion in American Reform, 1890–1935.* New York: Oxford University Press, 1991.
Nasaw, David. *Children of the City: At Work and at Play.* New York: Oxford University Press, 1985.
Odem, Mary E. *Delinquent Daughters: Protecting and Policing Adolescent Female Sexuality in the United States, 1885–1920.* Chapel Hill: University of North Carolina Press, 1995.
Palmieri, Patricia Ann. *In Adamless Eden: The Community of Women Faculty at Wellesley.* New Haven, CT: Yale University Press, 1995.
Peiss, Kathy. *Cheap Amusements: Working Women and Leisure in Turn-of-the-Century New York.* Philadelphia: Temple University Press, 1986.
Perlman, Joel. *Ethnic Differences: Schooling and Social Structure among the Irish, Italians, Jews, and Blacks in an American City, 1880–1935.* Cambridge: Cambridge University Press, 1988.
Pickerell, Michael J. *Constitutional Deliberation in Congress: The Impact of Judicial Review in a Separated System.* Durham, NC: Duke University Press, 2004.
Piott, Steven L. *American Reformers, 1870–1920: Progressives in Word and Deed.* Lanham, MD: Rowman and Littlefield, 2006.
Reagan, Leslie. *When Abortion Was a Crime: Women, Medicine, and Law in the United States, 1867–1973.* Berkeley: University of California Press, 1998.
Reese, William J. *The Origins of the American High School.* New Haven, CT: Yale University Press, 1995.
Ritterhouse, Jennifer. *Growing Up Jim Crow: How Black and White Southern Children Learned Race.* Chapel Hill: University of North Carolina Press, 2006.
Robertson, Stephen. *Crimes against Children: Sexual Violence and Legal Culture in New York City, 1880–1960.* Chapel Hill: University of North Carolina Press, 2005.
Rosenzweig, Roy. *Eight Hours for What We Will: Workers and Leisure in an Industrial City, 1870–1920.* Cambridge: Cambridge University Press, 1983.
Rupp, Leila. *A Desired Past: A Short History of Same-Sex Love in America.* Chicago: University of Chicago Press, 1999.
Sanders, Elizabeth. *Roots of Reform: Farmers, Workers, and the American State.* Chicago: University of Chicago Press, 1999.
Sanders, Joe Sutliff. *Disciplining Girls: Understanding the Origins of the Classic Orphan Girl Story.* Baltimore, MD: Johns Hopkins University Press, 2011.

Schmidt, James D. *Industrial Violence and the Legal Origins of Child Labor*. New York: Cambridge University Press, 2010.

Schrum, Kelly. *Some Wore Bobby Sox: The Emergence of Teenage Girls' Culture, 1920–1945*. New York: Palgrave Macmillan, 2004.

Sklar, Kathryn Kish. *Florence Kelley and the Nation's Work: The Rise of Women's Political Culture, 1830-1900*. New Haven, CT: Yale University Press, 1998.

Sundue, Sharon Baslaw. *Industrious in Their Stations: Young People at Work in Urban America, 1720–1810*. Charlottesville: University Press of Virginia, 2009.

Tatum, Beverly Daniel. *Why Are All the Black Kids Sitting Together in the Cafeteria? A Psychologist Explains the Development of Racial Identity*. New York: Basic Books, 2003.

Tiffin, Susan. *In Whose Best Interest? Child Welfare Reform in the Progressive Era*. Westport, CT: Greenwood, 1982.

Trattner, Walter. *Crusade for the Children: A History of the National Child Labor Committee and Child Labor Reform in America*. Chicago: Quadrangle Books, 1970.

Welter, Barbara. *Dimity Convictions: The American Woman in the Nineteenth Century*. Athens: Ohio University Press, 1976.

Werner, Emmy E. *Passages to America: Oral Histories of Child Immigrants from Ellis Island and Angel Island*. Washington, DC: Potomac Books, 2009.

White, Barbara A. *Growing Up Female: Adolescent Girlhood in American Fiction*. Westport, CT: Greenwood, 1985.

Wiebe, Robert. *The Search for Order, 1877–1920*. New York: Hill and Wang, 1966.

Willrich, Michael. *City of Courts: Socializing Justice in Progressive-Era Chicago*. New York: Cambridge University Press, 2003.

Wright, Gavin. *Old South, New South: Revolutions in the Southern Economy since the Civil War*. Baton Rouge: Louisiana State University Press, 1988.

Zelizer, Viviana A. *Pricing the Priceless Child: The Changing Social Value of Children*. New York: Basic Books, 1985.

ABOUT THE CONTRIBUTORS

Gwendoline Alphonso is Assistant Professor of Politics at Fairfield University, where she teaches courses in American politics, Congress, family values, American political development, and the presidency. She has published articles in *Studies in American Political Development*, the *Journal of Law and Medicine*, the *Central India Law Quarterly*, and *Lawyer's Collective*. Her dissertation, "Hearth and Soul: Political Parties, Family Ideologies, and the Development of Social Policy in the 20th Century" (2011), won the American Political Science Association's 2012 Walter Dean Burnham Award for the Best Dissertation in Politics and History.

Sarah E. Clere received her PhD in English from the University of North Carolina and is currently a Visiting Assistant Professor at the Citadel in Charleston, South Carolina. She has presented more than a dozen papers and invited lectures and has published articles and chapters in the *Mississippi Quarterly* and three collections of original essays.

Paula S. Fass was Margaret Byrne Professor of History, University of California–Berkeley, and is currently a Distinguished Scholar in Residence and Lecturer in the Department of History at Rutgers University–New Brunswick. She was president of the Society for the History of Children and Youth from 2007 to 2009. She is the author or editor of many books, including *Inheriting the Holocaust: A Second-Generation Memoir* (2009); *Children of a New World: Essays in Society, Culture, and the World* (New York University Press, 2007); *Childhood in America*, edited with Mary Ann Mason (New York University Press, 2000); *Kidnapped: Child Abduction in American History* (1997); *Outside In: Minorities and the Transformation of American Education* (1989); and *The Damned and the Beautiful: American Youth in the 1920s* (1977).

Claire B. Gallagher is Professor of Education at Georgian Court University. She has consulted on curricular issues with charter schools, the

Republic of Ireland, and Queensland University in Australia, and created the "Architecture for Children" program at the Carnegie Museum of Art. She has published and spoken widely on educational philanthropy, the school at Ellis Island, and architectural history, delivering papers and invited lectures in Finland, Great Britain, Scotland, France, Sweden, and Belgium.

Anya Jabour is Professor of History at the University of Montana. Her books include *Topsy-Turvy: How the Civil War Turned the World Upside Down for Southern Children* (2010); *Scarlett's Sisters: Young Women in the Old South* (2007); and *Marriage in the Early Republic: Elizabeth and William Wirt and the Companionate Ideal* (1998). She is also coeditor of *Family Values in the Old South*, with Craig Thompson Friend (2010) and editor of *Major Problems in the History of American Families and Children* (2005). She is currently working on a biography of Sophonisba Breckinridge.

Erika K. Jackson is an Assistant Professor of American History at Colorado Mesa University. She specializes in the history of gender and sexuality, as well as immigration and ethnic history. Her research focuses on ethnic and gendered identities within the Scandinavian communities of Chicago during the late nineteenth and early twentieth centuries. She is currently revising her dissertation into a book manuscript, tentatively entitled "'Vikings and Dumb Blondes': The Creation and Negotiation of a Nordic Ethnic Identity in Turn-of-the-Century Chicago."

John James teaches in the English Department at Bellarmine University in Louisville, Kentucky. His poems, essays, and reviews have appeared in the *Boston Review*, the *Los Angeles Review*, *DIAGRAM*, *Washington Square*, and elsewhere. His honors include an Academy of American Poets Prize, the Elizabeth Norton Hagan Literature Award, and a scholarship from the English-Speaking Union to study at Exeter College, Oxford.

Mary Linehan is an Assistant Professor of History at the University of Texas–Tyler. She has published articles and chapters in *The American President: Politics, Power, and Personality*, the *Filson Historical Quarterly*, and the *U.S. Catholic Historian* and presented papers at the Oral

History Association, the Midwest Regional Conference of the Organization of American Historians, the Popular Culture Association, and the Great Lakes History Conference. She has completed a book manuscript entitled "Abandoned Women: Prostitution and Gender Politics in Chicago."

James Marten is currently Professor and Chair of the History Department at Marquette University. He is founding secretary-treasurer and current president of the Society for the History of Children and Youth. In addition to forty journal articles, essays, and chapters in books, he has written or edited a dozen books, including *Children and Youth in a New Nation* (New York University Press, 2009); *Children in Colonial America* (New York University Press, 2006); and *The Children's Civil War* (1998). *The Children's Civil War* won the Alpha Sigma Nu Jesuit National Book Award for History in 1999 and was named an Outstanding Academic Book by *Choice Magazine.*

Fawn-Amber Montoya is currently an Associate Professor of History and Coordinator of Chicano Studies at Colorado State University–Pueblo and cochair of the National Association for Chicano and Chicana Studies (NACCS), Chicana caucus. Her research focuses on the U.S. Southwest with an emphasis on ethnicity and gender. She was the Bessemer Historical Society's 2012 scholar in residence and is currently working on an edited collection focused on the Colorado Fuel and Iron Company and the Ludlow Massacre.

James D. Schmidt is Professor of History at Northern Illinois University. He is author of *Free to Work: Labor Law, Emancipation, and Reconstruction, 1815–1880* (1998) and of *Industrial Violence and the Legal Origins of Modern Childhood* (2010). The latter was winner of the 2011 Phillip Taft Book Prize for best book in labor and working-class history He is currently working on a book about corporal punishment and the legalities of school authority in the nineteenth- and twentieth-century United States.

Nicholas L. Syrett is an Associate Professor of History at the University of Northern Colorado. He is the author of *The Company He Keeps:*

A History of White College Fraternities (2009) and articles in *American Studies*, *Genders*, the *Journal of the History of Childhood and Youth*, the *Journal of the History of Sexuality*, and the *Pacific Historical Review*. He is currently writing a book about the history of minors and marriage in the United States.

Tom Ue is Social Sciences and Humanities Research Council of Canada Doctoral Fellow and Canadian Centennial Scholar in the Department of English Language and Literature at University College London, where he researches Shakespeare's influence on the writing of Henry James, George Gissing, and Oscar Wilde. He was a Visiting Scholar in the Department of English at Yale University, the 2011 Cameron Hollyer Memorial Lecturer at the Toronto Public Library, and an Everett Helm Visiting Fellow at Indiana University. He is editor of a *World Film Locations: Cities of the Imagination* collection on Toronto (2014), published to coincide with the city's 180th anniversary, and he has published widely on Sherlock Holmes. He is concurrently at work on a piece on photography and phonography and their impact on the forms of late-Victorian and Edwardian writing and is beginning a monograph on legal theory and the British novel in the nineteenth century.

Deborah Valentine received her PhD in Childhood Studies from Rutgers University–Camden and is currently a Visiting Assistant Professor of Early Childhood Education at St. Joseph's University. In addition to making a contribution to the *Encyclopedia of Play in Today's Society* (2009), she published "'Little Children Are Constructed of Malleable Material': Conceptions of Children and Childhood in Anna Chapin Ray's Playground Books" in the online journal *Childhoods Today* in December 2011.

INDEX

Ableman v. Booth, 135
Abortion, 174–79
Addams, Jane, 166, 212, 245, 247
Adolescence, 5–6, 104–6, 146, 147, 148, 155, 156, 161, 163
African Americans, 13; discrimination toward, 35, 103, 105, 108, 117–18, 237–39; education, 239–41; in Philadelphia, 20–37; and prostitution, 179; and underage marriage, 149
American Association for Organizing Charity, 161
American Library Association, 87
American Missionary Association, 90
American Playground Movement, 19, 20
American Tract Society, 95
American Woman Suffrage Association, 234
Americanization, 34, 42–56, 82–83, 110–11, 212–14, 216, 224–25
Anderson, Sherwood, 187, 198–205
Angel Island, 96
Anthony, Susan B., 234, 242
Atlantic School Reform Movement, 127
Avondale Mills, 122

Bacon, Albion Fellows, 116
Barton, Clara, 110
Baseball, 54–56
Beattie, W. E., 75
Beveridge, Rep. Albert J., 65
Boarding schools, 113, 253–54
Booty, Bertha M., 86
Boy problem, 6, 33
Boy Scouts of America, 70
Bradford, Mary, 53
Breckinridge, Curry, 242
Breckinridge, Desha, 243
Breckinridge, Ella, 231, 232, 237, 243
Breckinridge, Issa, 231, 232, 234, 237, 243

Breckinridge, Robert Jefferson, 236
Breckinridge, Robert, 243
Breckinridge, Sophonisba: and African Americans, 238–41; autobiography, 236, 237, 240, 245; in Chicago, 247; education of, 231–33; pacifism, 236–37; and public service, 235–36, 241–42; relationship with parents, 231, 244; sense of duty, 231, 233, 242, 244, 247; and sexuality, 245; and women's rights, 234
Breckinridge, W.C.P., 230, 245, 247; in congress, 237, 242; scandal, 243–244
Bureau of Immigrant Work, 82, 95
Bushee, E. K., 70, 73

Camp and Plant, 45, 47, 48
Chicago: Great Fire, 166, 168; the Levee, 179–80, 182; Scandinavian immigration to, 209, 212, 214, 219, 224
Chicago Urban League, 241
Child labor, 7–8, 12, 121–22, 219–22; advocates of, 65–67, 70; campaign against, 59–80; children's point of view on, 255–62; Congressional debates, 64–65
Child-rearing, 7, 72–76, 145, 157–61, 195–96, 231–33
Children's Aid Society, 131
Children's Bureau, United States, 17, 64, 71
Children's rights, 1–2, 13–14, 65, 146, 158, 169. *See also* Law, and children and youth
Child-savers, 1, 10, 12, 64
Church of the Crucifixion, 24
Civil War, memory of, 103–4, 108–10, 187–88, 236–37
Cole, Justice Orasmus, 135, 136
College Settlements Association, 83

>> 293

Colorado Fuel and Iron Company (CF&I), 42, 44; and Americanization, 43, 48–49, 50, 51, 53, 54, 56; *Industrial Bulletin*, 51–52, 53, 54; Industrial Representation Plan, 51; kindergartens, 45–48; Sociological Department, 43–45, 49, 50; Sopris Plan, 53
Colored Mission Sabbath School, 21, 25
Committee on Labor, United States House of Representatives, 76
Commonwealth versus Patrick Coad, 128
Comstock Laws, 174
Conant, Frances Weld, 89
Congress (U.S.), 60, 73, 74–75
Cook County Hospital, 173
Copley, Rep. Ira, 65
Coppin, Fanny Jackson, 32
Corporal punishment, 125–44
Corwin, Dr. Richard, 45–48, 49
Courts, juvenile, 10–12, 142, 263–66
Crapps v. Smith, 151
Cronk, E. C., 33, 209, 221, 226

Dan River Cotton Mill, 74
Darling, Grace, 83
Davis, J. M., 70
Declaration of the Rights of the Child, 13
Delinquency, juvenile, 6, 10–11, 64, 130–31, 184, 263–66
Discipline, 7; in schools, 125–44
Douglass, Frederick, 240
Du Bois, W. E. B., 36

Earll, Charles, 174, 176–77, 231–33
Education, 7; African American, 28–29, 239–41; corporate, 42–58; and discipline, 125–44; of immigrants, 81–101, 208–29
Ehrhorn, Oscar W., 86
Ellis Island, 81–82, 86, 224–25
Erring Women's Refuge, 170, 173, 174

Families, as economic units, 60–63, 72–75; size of, 6, 7, 189, 195–96
First World War, 110–12, 279–81
Fitzgerald, H. R., 74
Freeman, Alice, 239
Froebel, Frederick, 26, 27, 88, 89, 98

Gardiner, Elizabeth, 85
Gender, 6, 32, 49, 102–18, 167–73, 192–93, 231–34, 246–47, 274–75
General Committee of Immigrant Aid, 96, 99
Georgia Supreme Court, 139, 150
Gilded Age and Progressive Era, defined, 2–3, 6
Gilman, Charlotte Perkins, 72
Girlhood, 6, 32, 153–57, 166–85
Girls. *See* Girlhood
Great Coalfield War, 50
Gulick, Dr. Luther Halsey, 71
Gypsies, 107

Hall, G. Stanley, 105, 106
Hallowell, Anna, 20, 26, 28
Hammer vs. Dagenhart, 65
Health, 8–9, 17–18, 23, 64, 174–79, 218–19, 234–35
Health care. *See* Health
Hearst, Phoebe Apperson, 88
Hebrew Sheltering and Immigrant Aid Society, 94
Hegborn, Pauline, 213–14
Henry Street Settlement, 76
Herrman v. Herrman, 152
Hine, Lewis, 121
Historic American Building Survey, 85, 90, 92
Historic Resource Study of the Statue of Liberty/Ellis Island, 86
Homosexuality. *See* Sexuality: same sex
House of the Good Shepherd, 170, 183
Housing, 23, 35, 61, 69–70, 94
Hubbard, Elbert, 73
Hull House (Chicago), 34, 212, 214, 246
Huxley, Florence, 87

Illinois General Assembly, 169
Illinois Supreme Court, 169
Immigrants, vii, 1, 4, 8, 19, 21, 24, 31, 34, 39, 105, 108, 117, 242; education of, 42–56, 81–101, 208–29, 254; and prostitution, 179, 181
Institute for Colored Youth, 32
International Child Welfare League, 69

International Congress of Women (1915), 236
International Order of the Kings Daughters and Sons, 112
Iowa Supreme Court, 138
Italian-Americans, 42–43, 54–56

Jewish-Americans, 31
Jim Crow. *See* Segregation
Johnson, Brigadier Thomas, 96
Johnston, Annie Fellows, 102, 103, 104–5, 108, 110, 111, 117
Juvenile Protection Association, 70

Keating, Rep. Edward, 73
Kelley, Florence, 66, 73
Kentucky Agricultural and Mechanical College, 233
Kentucky Court of Appeals, 139
Kentucky Equal Rights Association, 234
Kenyon, Rep. William S., 65
Kindergartens, 26–29, 34–35, 45–48, 85–86, 88–90, 98.
Kitchin, Governor William, 73

Labor, child. *See* Child labor
Lancasterian system, 128
Lathrop, Julia, 17, 246
Law, and children and youth, 4, 8, 125–44, 145–62, 169
Lawton, General Henry Ware, 109
Libraries, 29–34
Lindgren, J. O., 215, 216
Literature, children's, 29–30, 102–20
Little Colonel, The (book), 105, 107
Little Colonel, The (film), 103
Little Colonel in Arizona, The, 113
Little Colonel, Maid of Honor, 117
Little Colonel series, 102, 103, 109. See also *Mary Ware's Promised Land*
Little Colonel's Christmas Vacation, The, 108, 117
Little Colonel's Hero, The, 110, 111, 116
Little Colonel's Holidays, The, 109, 114, 115
Little Colonel's House Party, The, 105, 106, 117
Little Colonel's Knight Comes Riding, The, 105, 107

Lloyd, Sherman, 102, 103
Lloydsboro Valley, 102, 104, 107
Lopez, Aladino, 48
Lost Cause, 103, 109, 236, 237. *See also* Civil War, memory of
Lowe, Martin E., 61
Ludlow Massacre, 50–51
Lutomski, Josephine, 84–85

Mackenzie-Durham, Constance, 27
Marriage, underage, 145–65, 173–74; statistics for, 148–49
Mary Ware's Promised Land, 103, 116–117
Massachusetts State Board of Education, 129
Mayes, Justice Robert Burns, 135–136
Mayflower Band, 97–98
Mayflower Program Book, 97
McKelway, A. J., 67, 72
Mexican-Americans, 48
Middle class, 7, 23, 103, 104, 105, 106–8, 113–14, 175, 196; as cultural "ideal," 52, 62, 64, 189; as reformers, viii, 9, 102, 130–31, 174
Miller, N. Du Bois, 25
Milton Bradley Company, 90, 97, 98
Mississippi Supreme Court, 135
Missouri Supreme Court, 136, 137
Moody Bible Institute, 210
Moore, Frank L., 90–94
Morgan, Julia, 88
Morrow v. Wood, 134, 135
Mother Bethel African Methodist Church, 24
Mother Herrick's Place, 182

Napton, Justice William Barclay, 137
National Association for the Advancement of Colored People, 241
National Child Labor Committee, 67, 69, 71, 72, 121
National Congress of Mothers and Parent-Teacher Associations, 106
National Consumers League, 66
Native Americans, 13, 113, 253–54
Nelson, Pauline, 220–21

New Jersey State Industrial Home for Girls, 140
New York Bible Society, 95
New York City, 87, 94; and child marriage, 152, 155; and corporal punishment, 131; Public Schools Athletic League, 139
Newberry Cotton Mills, 70, 74
Nolan, Congressman John I., 76
North Park College and Theological Seminary, 208, 216, 217, 218, 221

Osgood, John, 44
Owen, Senator Robert, 65

Palmer, General William Jackson, 44
Palmer, Rep. Mitchell, 64
Parker, Lewis, 66, 75
Patterson, S. F., 74, 75
Pewee Valley, 104, 112
Philadelphia: Board of Education, 27; Centennial Exposition, 90; Fifth Ward, 23
Philadelphia College Settlement, 21, 31, 34, 35
Philanthropy, youth, 112–18, 235–37, 241–42, 276
Phillips, Reverend Henry, 20, 24, 25, 36
Phoenix Indian School, 113
Piedmont Manufacturing Company, 75
Play and pastimes, 10, 19–41, 54–56, 71–72, 84–87, 130, 139–40, 157, 267–73
Playgrounds, 10–11, 19–41; at Ellis Island, 84–87
Playgrounds Association of America, 21, 71
Pletzer, Marie, 95
Poe Mill, 61
Poindexter, Rep. Miles, 65
Progressive Era. *See* Gilded Age and Progressive Era, defined
Progressive Workingmen's Club, 24, 25
Progressives. *See* Progressivism, defined
Progressivism, defined, vii–ix, 9–13
Prostitution, 173, 179–84
Public Schools Athletic League (New York City), 139

Race, 13, 20–37, 48, 103, 116–17, 232–41
Red Cross, American, 87, 110–11, 113
Religion, 24–26, 29, 94–99, 126–27, 203–26
Republicanism, 88, 127–28, 130–31
Rescue of Princess Winsome, The (play), 111
Richmond, Mary, 148, 149
Rights, children's. *See* Children's rights
Riverside Cotton Mill, 74
Roanoke Mills, 74
Rockefeller, John D., 44, 50
Rockefeller, John D., Jr., 44, 50–51
Romjue, Rep. Milton, 70
Roosevelt, President Theodore, 76

Saint Raphael's Society for German Catholic Immigrants, 94
Salvation Army, 96
Scandinavian-Americans, 208–26
Sectional differences, in attitudes toward children, 59–80, 102–18
Seevers, Justice William H., 138–39
Segregation, 28, 103
Settlement houses, 9–10, 21, 22, 34–35, 82, 212, 265
Sexuality, 150–54, 166–86, 192–93; same sex, 171–73; Victorian attitudes toward, 167–70
Sinclair, Eunice, 69–70
Sports, 42–43, 49–50, 55–56, 139–40, 208, 218–19
St. Mary Street, 22, 23
Starr, Theodore, 20, 22, 24, 25, 28
Starr Centre Association, 19, 30, 36
Starr Garden, 19, 22, 35
Stuart, George, 21
Suffrage, women's, 234, 242
Swedish Evangelical Mission Covenant, 208, 210, 215, 218, 224
Swedish University Land Association, 216

Temperance, 115

United Daughters of the Confederacy, 237
Urbanization, 2, 4–5, 9, 29, 199–200

Veterans, Civil War, 102, 187, 235–36
Violence: against children and youth, 125–27, 133, 134, 136, 138, 140; committed by children and youth, 132–33

Wald, Lillian, 76
Watson, Constance, 84–85
Watson, Elizabeth, 69
Wharton, Susan, 31
White supremacy, 237–41
Williams, William, 86
Willson, Justice Samuel P., 136
Wilson, Mary B., 96
Wilson, President Woodrow, 65
Wingate, George F., 139
Wisconsin Supreme Court, 135

Woman's Home Missionary Society, 82, 94, 95, 97
Women's Christian Temperance Union, 89, 95–96, 97
Women's Peace Party, 236
Women's Trade Union League, 245
Work Among Foreign Speaking People Bureau, 96
World War One. *See* First World War

Young Men's Christian Association (YMCA), 51
Young Women's Christian Association (YWCA), 88, 97
Youth culture, 7, 130–31, 209–10, 224, 267–73, 274–76, 278–79